FIFE CULTURAL TRUST

D0248467

★★ ⋯ own'

★★★★★ 'F⋯ a must-read'

★★★★★ 'Compelling, raw and brave'

Plea ★★★★★ 'Heartbreaking… a thought-provoking read'

★★★★★ 'Engaging, amusing and entertaining'

★★★ 'Well written, very sad, and very honest… I loved this book'

★★★★★ 'Deeply moving. Read it'

★★★★★ 'Funny, open and honest…
He will have you laughing one second, crying the next'

Praise for the author

unny, from the heart and utterly wonderful from start
finish" **Jennifer Selway, *Daily Express***

witty, revealing, heart-warming and honest account of his
umphs and travails" **Andy Cooper, *Devon Life***

's a ten from Len!" **Len Goodman**

nchanting" ***Daily Mail***

nspirational" ***The Sun***

treasure-trove"
Adam Henson, BBC One's *Countryfile*

Rene Wonderful book"
by in **Michael Caines, MBE, two-star Michelin chef**

in pe An amazing story of love, laughter and the challenges of living off
by p he land. Simon's self-sufficient rural life is an inspiration to us all"
Ben Fogle

the Boy without Love

SIMON DAWSON

MIRROR BOOKS

First published in hardback by Mirror Books in 2019

This paperback edition published in 2019

Mirror Books is part of Reach plc
10 Lower Thames Street
London EC3R 6EN
England
www.mirrorbooks.co.uk

© Simon Dawson

The rights of Simon Dawson to be identified as the author
of this book have been asserted, in accordance with the
Copyright, Designs and Patents Act 1988.

All rights reserved. No part of this publication may be reproduced, stored in a
retrieval system, or transmitted, in any form or by any means without the prior
written permission of the publisher, nor be otherwise circulated in any form of
binding or cover other than that in which it is published and without a similar
condition being imposed on the subsequent purchaser.

ISBN 978-1-912624-13-3

Typeset by Danny Lyle
DanJLyle@gmail.com

Printed and bound in Great Britain by
CPI Group (UK) Ltd, Croydon, CR0 4YY

A CIP catalogue record for this book is available from the British Library.

Every effort has been made to fulfil requirements with regard to
reproducing copyright material. The author and publisher will be
glad to rectify any omissions at the earliest opportunity.

1 3 5 7 9 10 8 6 4 2

Cover image: Arcangel

WARNING: CONTAINS STRONG LANGUAGE

For Debbie, as always
and in memory of The General
2004-2018

The hallway is dark. It's probably a money saving thing. Shame they didn't reroute the saving into smellies. The place could do with it.

At the end of the hallway is a door that has the look and feel of a school. Ironic, really, everything goes in a circle. I push it open. Inside is a dayroom. Lots of high-backed chairs and easy-to-clean Formica tables. And that smell. Fusty clothes, tea and old person's skin.

Over in the corner a television with the volume turned all the way up shows a TV shock-jock pointing at a girl with tattoos and calling her a slag for sleeping with her boyfriend's best friend. He is whipping up a storm, but in the dayroom nobody cares.

I scan the blue rinses, the grey perms, the washed, the unwashed. There. She isn't facing me, but it's unmistakably her. She is sitting at a table, her blonde hair shorter than I remember. Making my way over, I sit down opposite and smile.

'Oh,' she giggles. 'Hello.'

'Hiya.'

Someone screams, 'Don't fucking touch me you black bitch!'

Nurse and an… inmate? Guest? *Friend?* The nurse places her hands on her wide hips and cocks her head to one side, looking amused. She says, 'Now Ann, that's not very nice.'

'Fucking arsehole.'

'Okay, that's enough. You can go outside until you learn some manners.' Two more nurses appear and together they manhandle the lady out into the dark hallway and plonk her down on a chair. As the door closes on her I hear her scream, 'Fucking fuck, fuck bastards!'

I settle back. Opposite, she is still looking at me and smiling. She hasn't even noticed the commotion. 'So,' I say, 'how've you been, Mum?'

'Good. You know, everything got sorted in the end – well, it always does, doesn't it. It was difficult for a while, but it all got sorted out.'

'What was difficult? What happened?'

'Oh, you know. But it all got sorted. We did it together. A few of us. It was quite nice actually.'

I nod. She's rambling, spouting stock phrases she uses to fill dead air. 'This place is okay,' I say, looking around. 'Landed on your feet here, it's like a country house hotel,' if you like your mini breaks in hell.

'I know.'

She's clean and washed and well fed. Her hair's done and her nails are filed and painted. She leans forward, 'I'm desperate for the toilet,' she whispers.

'Do you want me to take you?' Oh God, please say no. But she nods. We both get up. 'Where is it?'

She looks panicked. 'I don't know.'

A nurse comes over, the same one who was spoken to so horribly. Her name badge reads: ESSIE.

'Rose, are you going to show your son your room?'

'I think she needs the bathroom,' I say, thinking, Nurse Essie I want to hug you and tell you I'm so sorry for what that lady called you. You shouldn't have to put up with it. Nobody should. But God forgive me, I'm so glad you do.

'Toilet's on the way. Down there,' nurse Essie points. 'Just after is her room.'

We head off and find the loo. When she's done we carry on down. The doors don't have numbers; they have black and white printed photographs pinned to the outside. Find your own face, that's your room. We find hers and I say, 'It's you!' and point.

'Oh don't!' She holds a hand up to cover the picture. 'It's awful.'

Laughing, I say, 'Not your best side?'

She strikes a pose and flicks her hair, 'Darling.' This, more than anything, makes me wonder if there's more of her in there than we think.

Inside the room she gets busy. 'They keep moving my bloody things,' she says, irritated, picking up a wicker waste bin from the floor and placing it on a side table. The re-arranging goes on for a while. I could stand back and watch, but I don't.

'Where's this go?' I hold up a chair.

'There,' she points without missing a beat. 'On the bed.'

I put it on the bed and laugh. 'Looks good.'

She doesn't turn around. She's busy.

A bell rings. 'What's that?'

She shakes her head. 'I don't know.'

'Let's go and find out.'

I take her arm and lead her back outside. Others are coming out of their rooms too and everyone seems to be heading for the dayroom, where tables have been set for lunch. I step back from her, let her do her thing. She sits next to a blue rinse.

I go over to nurse Essie and ask if there's anything I can do to help.

'Thank you, m'love. Do you want to do the teas? Half cups, milky, like you was doing it for a child.'

I start. I can hear Mum and Blue Rinse talking.

'Who's he?' Blue Rinse asks.

'I don't know,' Mum says.

'Do you love him?'

She glances over. For the briefest moment our eyes lock before she twists away again.

'No. I don't think I do.'

Chapter 1

There's an old farmers' trick I was taught in my first year of lambing. If you have a sheep who doesn't accept her newborn lamb, you tie mum with a short length of string to a wall so she can't move away when the little one wants to suckle. You keep her there for a minimum of two days. Two days, it has to be two days. No less. After which she'll accept her baby. Job done.

The farmer who told me this looked as though he'd stuck his face in a dehydrator every day for the last hundred years, and the strict routine had meant he hadn't had time to change his clothes. In other words, he looked authentic. Very authentic, and you don't mess with authenticity.

Of course I tried it. I tried it because I was freaked and desperate. In the early spring of 2017, one of my sheep had given birth to a lamb and decided on infanticide as the next best step in her role of motherhood, duffing up her baby and refusing to let it feed. So I was planning to tie her to a wall and force her to bond. But first, I had to catch her.

'What I don't get is why you let her go wandering off in the first place,' Ziggy said to me, adding, 'God I feel rough. I take it you are aware the rest of civilisation has progressed beyond chasing after animals in fields?'

'You don't spend enough time in the countryside.'

'*Au contraire*, I visit you loads! Besides, the countryside doesn't class as civilised. In polite society, anywhere more than a hundred paces from a decent double espresso is automatically out of bounds. Why did you let her go?'

'I didn't know she'd rejected her lamb.'

Ziggy. Picture your best friend at school's annoying little brother, and then imagine that child having grown-up in years, but remaining exactly the same emotionally. Got it? Yeah, *that* bad. Somehow he ended up my oldest and closest friend, but it's a work in progress.

'There she is,' I said. We were in a field surrounded by tall ash and beech trees, the new spring leaves from which shimmered in the afternoon breeze. Over in the far corner a dozen sheep cropped the grass while their lambs played a mix of chase, bundle and let's-see-if-we-can-kill-ourselves. A lamb's instinct for suicide is laser sharp.

'There's loads of them. Which one?'

'Watch.'

Although it looked chaotic, truth was the little lambs kept a close eye on their own mother and tended not to wander too far from her, every now and then gambling back to nuzzle and check-in in a 'Hey Mum, it's me. We okay? Please can I have a drink? Can I go back and play now?' kind of way. All looked happy families until one lamb made an unsteady path towards a ewe who greeted him with a flying head-butt and a mad stamp.

'That's our girl,' I said, making a mental note of where she stood.

'Jesus. You weren't kidding. What's the plan?'

'We need to grab her and the lamb.'

'Yeah, I kind of figured that much. Please tell me you've at least thought this through and you're not just winging it. Tell me there's a method. A technique we should adopt.'

'Of course! Run fast, if you dive try not to land in poo and if you get a hand on her, don't let go.'

2

'Masterful.'

'Thank you. It's all in the detail. Ready?'

'Not at all.'

We set off at a jog which soon increased into a full out sprint, or as close as you can get to sprinting in wellies, which isn't very close. Flapping wellies really screws with your aerodynamics.

'There, grab her!' I yelled, when at one point Ziggy got close. He put a hand out like he was flagging down a taxi. It was more a wave than a grab. The sheep didn't even notice.

'What was that?'

'I *lunged*.'

I started laughing.

'I'm a solicitor, not some straw-up-my-arse farmer!' he said, sinking to the ground in a heap. 'You know, it's got to the point where I hate it when you invite me down.'

I stood over him trying not to show how out of breath I was. 'I don't invite you. You just turn up.'

'And that's another thing we need to discuss.' He lay flat out staring up at the sky. 'I need a drink. One with a twist of something over crushed ice.'

Ten feet away the sheep was back eating like nothing had happened. Although we'd been chasing her around for the best part of, oh… three and a half minutes, the key word in that sentence was 'around', and we were back in exactly the same spot where we'd started. Which was good from the lamb's point of view, as he didn't have the energy to run after mum while we hurtled after her, and had just lain there watching. Now we were back, he decided to try mum one more time, and raised himself onto shaky legs. Without mum letting him take her milk, he was getting weaker by the moment. Wobbling towards her, he baa'd long and loud, *Hey Mum, I'm really, really hungry. Please can I have some milk?*

She let him draw close, then spun around to shoo him away. Momentarily distracted, I took my chance. In the blink of an eye I was flying though the air like I'd been shot from a cannon, landing with my knees scuffing the grass and two handfuls of very pissed off sheep clutched in iron grips. She in turn did what sheep do; kicked out and tried to leg it.

'Aaaahhhhhheelllpp!'

I held on. And on. And on. It was like holding onto a woolly rodeo horse. But soon my vastly superior intellect and human instinct completely outwitted her tiny animal brain. Plus I had fourteen stone on her – quite literally, when she slipped and I hauled myself over her like a duvet. Pinned to the ground, she had nowhere to go. Coincidentally, neither did I.

'Ziggy. I could do with a hand here.'

'I'm on my way.'

I looked up. He wasn't, he was still in exactly the same position on his back staring up at the sky.

'Like, *now!*'

'Okay, okay, okay,' he said, rolling over onto his front and getting up. 'I'm here, I'm here, I'm here.' It must be his legal training: everything in triplicate.

He held the ewe while I fashioned a halty, which is agriculture's equivalent of a child harness and reins, from some bailer twine, slipping it over the sheep's head and nose. When she was secure, we let her up. At first she pulled and twisted, but a halty also acts as a pacifier and after a minute or two she just stood next to me.

'Could you grab the lamb?' I asked Ziggy. The little mite was zonked out on the ground and didn't even make an effort to move when Ziggy approached to pick him up.

Together we carried and walked our woolly cargos back to the barn, the little lamb lolling in Ziggy's arms like a dog's toy with the stuffing pulled out of it, and the sheep strutting next to me.

4

Chapter 1

'I thought you said the halty pacifies them?' Ziggy said, the sheep finding her oomph and beginning to ping up and down as we left the field and made towards the building. 'She doesn't look much pacified to me.'

Me neither. She was going nuts. Part of me tried to ignore her; ignore bad behaviour, that's rule 101 of The Animal Parenting Guide, but another part of me, a part I've never heard speak up around animals before, thought, *yeah, just carry on playing up a little bit longer and I swear to God I'll kick you in the head so hard you'll have brain damage and never move unaided again.*

'Are you okay?' Ziggy asked beside me. I'd kind of shambled to a stop. I've never kicked an animal in my life, but in that instant the urge to lash out was almost overwhelming. I could feel my heart yammering in my chest, my face flushed. I could taste the hate in my mouth. Then in the next instant, it was all gone. All the hate… gone. I was back being me.

Chapter 2

Weird is a word that's overused. These days anything can be weird: a pair of shoes, a look, even a song. So when a feeling you've never felt before takes over your body so completely and makes you feel something you've never experienced, the first word you reach for shouldn't be the same. But it is. It felt weird.

Would I really have kicked an animal? No, of course I wouldn't! Not in a million years. But I could still taste the hate right in the centre of my tongue like a tiny, tiny hotspot. It tasted bitter, and claggy, and when I concentrated on it I could feel the anger bubbling up again.

Anger towards a sheep? What was wrong with me?

No. Like a bad joke that takes a while to land, I got it. It had nothing to do with the fact that she was a sheep, and everything to do with the fact that she was a mum rejecting her baby. Even that simple realisation brought on a storm of confusing emotions. Not even confusing, though, they were more... distant. Like I knew them, knew they existed inside me; I even recognised them, but only in the way someone living in a block of apartments might recognise a downstairs neighbour: they were there, but irrelevant.

'You're starting to worry me now,' Ziggy said, his voice edging towards panic. I was standing there staring at nothing, at a spot in the middle distance.

I looked at him. 'It's okay. I just made a connection.'

Not always the dope he portrays, he said, 'Care to share?'

'Nope. Come on, I need to get this sheep inside and get the lamb fed.'

We bustled about for a while laying a straw bed in the barn and securing the ewe to a fixing on the wall. I tied her so she had enough room to more around, but not enough to get away. Then I got Ziggy to push her flanks so she couldn't move left, right, backwards or forwards. Shifting a hunk of wool, I took the lamb's mouth, gently inserted my finger to open it up and slipped it over mum's teat, nipping my finger out at the last moment so his mouth clamped down on the nipple.

At first, nothing happened and I worried we might be too late. But little by little, he began to suckle.

Smiling, I looked up. 'We're in business.'

'Phew,' Ziggy puffed. 'Walking him back, the way he just sagged in my arms, I thought he was a goner.'

'Me too.'

Even in the time it took to exchange those words, he was rallying. Not quite standing on his own, but almost, he was sucking and slurping like a pig with a hosepipe.

Ziggy was down by her head. 'How's mum?' I asked.

'I'd say she was defeated.'

The words of the old farmer came back to me, *Two days, it has to be two days. No less. After which she'll accept her baby. Job done.*

'There's a bit of a way to go before she's fully defeated. Couple of days.'

'Really?' Ziggy shrugged. 'She looks completely –'

With that one of her back hooves lashed out and caught the lamb in his tummy. The ewe screeched and the lamb twisted and slammed bleating to the floor.

'Grab her head,' I yelled. 'Grab it tight so she feels trapped.'

Thank God that fear for the lamb trumped my anger towards the ewe. Scared she was going to stamp on him while he was on the ground, I bent down and whipped the little one up into my arms. He was still bleating, screaming. I wasn't sure if it was shock, pain or just oh-for-fuck's-sake-ing. 'All right boy,' I shushed, and he started to quieten. There were still some beads of milk around his mouth that I wiped away with my thumb. I touched his tummy and it felt full; he was probably close to finishing his first ever tea anyway.

'Am I still supposed to be doing this?' Ziggy called.

I looked over. He had the sheep's head incarcerated in his arms. She was panting and rolling her eyes. So many jokes, but I wasn't in the mood, so I said, 'Let her go.'

He did, backing away and brushing himself down. He looked a mess, dirt and wool smudged all over his trendy top and jeans. 'If I'd known how this weekend was going to pan out, I'd have stayed in London with Jem and the children.'

The ewe, free from unwanted attention, twitched a few times in feeble attempts at escape before settling for a lie down. When she was still and calm, I nestled the lamb in some straw close by. I checked him all over and nothing seemed sore or tender.

'Are Jem and the kids really back in London?' I said, getting up.

'No. She's away with some girlfriends. They've taken the children to some Mother and Baby Pamper Paradise, no partners allowed. I didn't want to spend the weekend alone getting drunk on the sofa, so I came down here. However, in hindsight...'

We were both watching the ewe, who in turn was watching the lamb.

'What happened back there?' he asked.

'Can't really describe it. I just wanted to lash out at that ewe for rejecting her baby. Not that she was making an actual choice, of course she wasn't. What was going on in her brain for her to turn against her lamb? How does that happen? How is it even okay?'

Chapter 2

A few minutes later Ziggy nailed it. I knew what it was all about, of course I did.

'She reminds you of your mum, doesn't she? Your mum and you.'

I ignored him and carried on:

'So I'm thinking, what if it's not the mother's fault at all? What if there's nothing wrong with her whatsoever. She's fine. Hunky dory. What if it's the baby? The fault, the imbalance, the whatever you want to call it… the bad, it's all in the baby, and that's why Mum's rejecting it.'

Hate and anger bubble up inside me like milk left on the heat too long. Only, this hate is different from the lash-out variety, and actually feels really good. God, it feels good. I welcome it, welcome it all. Let it flood though me. So familiar, so comforting. Bliss. Every corner, get into every nook and cranny. You know junkies that have been clean for thirty years and go back on the blow? I get it. Whatever you need to fill you up. I feel like a child again; I feel exactly like a child again because this is how I spent my entire youth, with a concoction of self-hatred and self-loathing pulsing through my veins that just felt so right, like it was meant to be that way. It's all in the baby: the fault, the bad, the unlovableness, it's not in the mother at all, it's all in the baby. It's all in me.

Chapter 3

Coming back to planet Earth, I realised Ziggy was staring at me and he looked worried. Forcing myself to smile I said, 'You're such a knob,' to ease the tension.

His worry didn't lift. All he said was, 'True though, isn't it?'

'Mm. I don't know. Kind of.' I couldn't remember how much I'd told Ziggy about my mum and my life growing up. I must have mentioned bits and pieces, but I couldn't have said much.

'Is that longhand for yes?'

One thing Ziggy is good at is speaking frankly about how he feels. There's none of this be a man and carry on Mr Strong-And-Silent-Type malarkey. So I said yes, and he nodded, and there followed a respectful period of silence in case I wanted to unburden some more, but as much as I would have liked to, I couldn't. It all felt too new, and intimate, and secret.

In the end I finished the silence with, 'Drink?'

Clapping his hands together he said, 'Desperately,' and we left the ewe and lamb and headed home.

The distance back was short, just two fields. On a bad day with rush hour traffic – chickens, goats and hooligan geese congested as far as a short-sighted man can see – it can take five minutes. In wellies, slightly longer. I tried to walk quickly, keen to get home, but Ziggy was having none of it. Although opening up holds no fear for Ziggy – quite the reverse, he seems to revel in it and enjoy singling out each individual feeling that

10

exists within him and worrying it down to the nub – there is a sense that listening to someone else unburden themselves slightly appals him. Sometimes that can be really annoying, but today, right now, it's fine. I just wish he'd do it at a jog.

Slowing down to kick a boot in the grass he said, 'I spoke to my dad a few days ago.'

Much as I wanted to tune him out and spend the time trying to make sense of what happened back in the lambing shed, that statement was not something I could ignore. 'Huh?'

'Yeah. Was a bit of a one way conversation as you might imagine'. Ziggy's dad has been dead for seven years.

'I bet.' Ziggy has always been a bit like that. He's the only forty-something male I know who reads his horoscope in the newspaper, talks to a clairvoyant and even has a dream-catcher above his bed. But chatting to his dead father, that's a first. 'What made you do that?'

'I found his old mobile phone in a drawer, and got it into my head that I could communicate with him through it. Oh, I knew he wouldn't talk back, but I felt that he would be able to hear me, you know? Anyway, I went through this big build-up, charging the phone, finding somewhere away from people where I could be on my own, and switching the thing on. Then I sat there, staring at it for ages, trying to think of what to say. It's not easy, I hadn't spoken to him for so long.'

'So what did you say?'

He shrugged. 'I told him about my haemorrhoids.'

'What?'

He was still looking at the ground. 'Piles. I gave him an update.'

I started laughing. I couldn't help it. 'I'm sorry,' I said, 'but you phoned your dead dad to tell him about a medical complaint up your bum?'

He was laughing and nodding. 'Yeah.'

'Is this true or a joke?'

'True. Oh man.' His laughing petered down to a smile. 'I'm so stupid. Not just what I told him, but the whole thing. I panicked. Got nervous, and in the moment tried to make him laugh. Now I just feel bad for doing it. I keep waking up in the middle of the night wondering what he thinks of me. Annoyed at myself for not saying what I wanted to say, what I should have said. Anyway, look, I just wanted you to know you're not alone. We've all got parent issues, okay?'

He's a complete and utter idiot, but you can't help but love him. Reaching out I put my hand on his shoulder and said, 'You're crazy, but thanks.'

'Yeah, well.'

We carried on walking, the lights from home and the smoke billowing from the chimney looking so inviting. 'So, how are the piles now?' I said.

'Absolute *agony*.'

I am still elsewhere though, with that lamb and the raw sense of injustice. My mother didn't love me, didn't bond with me, didn't want me. I know how powerful those admissions are. I've been on this downward spiral before – not for a long time, but I've been here – and I know the feelings are more destructive than cocaine, more addictive than cigarettes and will eat me up and take me over like crack. I've been clean for more years than I can remember, not from narcotics, but from this deep sense of self-loathing. I haven't thought about my mum not wanting me for decades, haven't allowed myself to think about it because it's just too big, too massive and I don't understand any of it, and the downward spiral is as fast as a water-slide, and as tempting as it is to leap in, I'm frightened because I have no idea what's at the end of it. But a hit is a hit is a hit, and I feel like I'm back. I don't know why this self-hatred makes me feel this right, this complete, but it does. But I also know how dangerous it is.

Chapter 4

Of course, Debbie knew something was up the second she saw me. Woman's intuition coupled with 27 years of marriage gives her unfettered access to my thoughts and feelings.

'What's up?' she said, as Ziggy and I pulled off our muddy boots.

I waved a hand in Ziggy's direction. 'He's got issues again.'

It's okay, I wasn't betraying a confidence. If Ziggy doesn't want me to share, he makes it clear, otherwise he can get quite antsy if I don't pick up on a problem he wants to work through, and I guessed this recent faux pas with his dad was the real reason he was here.

She put her hands on her hips and said, 'What have you done?'

Grinning ear to ear he said, 'Phoned my dad. Only it went a bit wrong and now I've got the night shudders over it.' Bustling past her he made his way into the lounge where Solomon, our Great Dane, was sprawled in front of the fire.

With Ziggy out of earshot, she whispered, 'That's not it. Are *you* okay?' Heavy emphasis on the *you*.

Honestly, it's like living with a white witch. Not so long ago they'd have dunked her in a lake, or built a bonfire under her feet. 'I'm fine. Can we talk about it later?'

She looked worried. 'Sure.'

Dinner was homemade pizza because I needed something to do rather than sit there watching Debbie cook and listen to Ziggy, who had circled away from the phone call with his dead dad for the moment and was currently mulling over such intricacies as whether his true happiness wasn't being thwarted by the fact that he didn't love himself enough (ha!), which, I admit, I would normally have found highly entertaining. But not tonight. So I took a bowl, added flour, yeast, salt and water and began kneading it into dough for the pizza base. The action felt good and kind of took me out of the room, and I thought, I wonder what I would say if I could hold a telephone conversation with my mum? I know she's not dead, but the Alzheimer's has really taken hold and there's very little of the person I knew left inside anymore, certainly not enough to converse with. But a conversation with the old her, a chance to talk once again, what would I say? Let's be honest, it probably wouldn't involve my bum. Actually I did have her old mobile phone someplace. But I didn't feel like it would work for me. Maybe the recipient had to have passed on for that.

When the dough was finished and left to prove, I said, 'I'm just going to check on that lamb and do a final walk around before it gets too dark.'

Ziggy jumped up. 'I'll come,' he said.

I was about to put up a halt hand and mumble some excuse when Debbie stepped in and said, 'Stay with me, Ziggy. Let him go on his own. Meanwhile you can tell me more about this fascinating topic of not loving yourself enough.'

While Debbie and I smiled at one another, he pantomimed preparing for some great soliloquies that I half expected to begin with *To be, or not to be.* I wouldn't have put it past him. I pulled on boots, baseball cap, shoved a torch in my back pocket and stepped outside. The light was dimming towards dusk. It's this point in the day, along with the corresponding one in the morning, that is the best. That sense of peace and ease. High up above the trees

Chapter 4

I could hear a murder of crows searching for a place to sleep, and off to one side a barn owl made his first tentative call of the night. On the ground I could see my four ducks padding towards their house, their day's work done. Off to the side a white chicken had perched on top of her coop rather than in it and was just beginning to nod off.

I took a different route to the lambing shed, one that circled past the goats, and called, 'Hey guys, how we all doing?' to a couple of pens of pigs, and, 'Have a nice night, everybody,' until I reached the General, where I hung over the gate. 'Big man, you in?'

Inside, the straw shifted as a huge black mass rose up. The General, our boar, the pig daddy, fifty-five stone of utter gorgeousness and my best friend on the farm came over and I made a fuss of his head. 'We need to talk, mate,' I said. If I'm Ziggy's confidant, the General is mine. 'Something happened to me today, and I'm…' the next word came out in a whisper, 'scared.' General shook his head, his enormous ears slapping side to side. Then he nudged me, turned and made his way back to his straw bed.

'No, but thanks,' I said. Quite often I'd slip in beside him, cuddle up and talk through whatever was on my mind, but I was worried about the lamb. 'It can wait until tomorrow. Sleep well and I'll see you at breakfast.'

A minute later I approached the lambing shed as quietly as I could, inched the door open and peered inside. I could see the ewe and lamb in exactly the same positions Ziggy and I had left them; well, obviously the sheep couldn't move about too much, but the lamb could, and I'd expected him to have explored a little, or at the very least shifted and rolled over in his sleep. But nothing. No movement. It was all as still as a grave.

Oh shit, *shit!*

Chapter 5

Flinging the door back on its rusty hinges I barged my way in, groping for the torch in my back pocket.

The ewe stood up and made an indignant 'Baaahhhh.' Ignoring her completely I made for the lamb, who raised his head and blinked at me.

My heart kabooming in my chest, I said, 'Jesus, I thought you were dead!'

Clearly not, but so weak I set about plugging him onto mum, who after a token effort at argy-bargy allowed him to feed. While he did, I kept a close eye on those pistoning hooves of hers, but maybe she was tired, or bored of the fight, because she let him drink until, full up, he pulled away.

'There you go, little one,' I said, lifting him up into my arms and moving across where I slithered my back down the wall until I was sitting on the floor, the lamb nestled in my lap.

It was almost completely dark now. I could hear the ewe snuffling a few feet in front of me and that barn owl outside, now much more confident, calling for a mate.

There are some benefits to age. Not many, but some. One of the bigger ones is a greater understanding of which internal battles are worth fighting, and which are best left alone. Throughout the entirety of my twenties, my thirties, even into my forties, I thought it best to avoid introspection completely. I was Ziggy's opposite, refusing to explore any emotion that wasn't one of the top ten, which, especially after today, I was starting to realise leaves a septic tank of unresolved issues that fester, waiting for a chance to *ta-dah*! you.

Looking through the blackness in the direction of the sheep, I wondered again: would I really have kicked her? Same answer, no, because it wasn't the sheep I was angry at, it's what she stood for. So does that mean that if the hate and anger wasn't focused on her as a sheep, but on her as a young mother rejecting her baby, was I therefore in some messed up way seeing my own mother in her? And if I was, did I want to kick my mum?

No, she's a little old lady in a nursing home, 'course I didn't.

Okay, not now, but back then? Back when she rejected me? Back when she tried so hard to give me away?

No, not even then. Not kick. But scream, shout and yell, oh yes.

Maybe I did need to have a conversation with her, maybe Ziggy's idea of a mobile phone chat wasn't so nuts after all. But the tiny matter of her being very much alive still meant it didn't feel as though it would work, not when I could pick up the phone and *actually* speak to her. The conversation may turn out to be gobbledygook, but she would at least be on the other end of the line.

What to do? Do my usual trick of forcing confusing emotions down into the septic tank and tossing a carpet over the top of it so they can't be seen, and hope they won't reappear? To be honest, it didn't feel as though there was a carpet big enough in the world, even the imaginary world, to cover it. That hate, the taste, the feeling, the delicious sense of comfort in self-loathing was just too huge. Talk about an elephant in the upstairs room.

I know I don't want to go back to that feeling. If I let it continue it wouldn't be long until it came back bigger and stronger and I wouldn't be able to stop it. It would take me over. The person I am now would revert to the person I was as a teenager. I can still remember all that young anger, the fear, the confusion and that familiar sense of self-disgust and self-destruction. When I met Debbie I was 21 years old, and fell more deeply in love with her than I could ever have imagined possible. It was *horrible!* and at the same time utterly, utterly, beautifully, incredibly amazing. But I had a problem. I knew she could never love me in return because I was unlovable. You see, up until now it had all been about me, but now the stakes were much, much higher. Now there was a possible 'us' to consider. So I decided to take action the only way I knew how. I decided to sever all contact with the person I hated so much: me. I killed him. Killed him and started again. During the course of the next few months I became someone else, someone less angry, less destructive, less hateful. Sure there's a residue inside me of the person I was, echoes, and it doesn't take much to go back there – but to all intents and purposes, I was born at twenty-one years old. I made myself forget the rest: the person I was and the childhood I had.

I hugged the lamb and thought, it had worked so well for so long, and now my downfall is a bloody sheep.

What was the alternative? To fight? To do battle? Sounds odd to think that you need to send in the troops to defeat your own emotions, but that's how it felt. Let them take me over, or prepare to skirmish.

So as I sat there cradling the lamb whose mother I had forced to care for it, I started to think back over my own lost childhood, that faraway little boy who found himself with a mum who simply didn't love him, however hard he tried. I felt that treacherous pit of self-loathing beckoning me and I realised I had a choice. Sink back into it, or fight it. I was an adult now, I had a partner who loved me, good friends, and a warm and comfortable home. And although I had no children of my own, I had a farm full of animals who depended on me. It was time to face my demons.

Chapter 6

'Jesus, fuck, fuck, fuckfuckfuck, *aaahhhhhhhhh!*'

By all accounts I came out head first, which is traditional, coughed a bit and started crying, possibly because of her language.

So far, so good.

Then something goes a bit haywire.

You see, what's supposed to happen next is the baby gets swaddled tight in fluffy white towels and handed to the mother, who, despite her complete exhaustion and pain from her lady-bits getting tailored with needle and thread back into something resembling a vagina, looks down at the little mite and swoons with overwhelming love. Mother, meet baby. Bond established. Only, that doesn't always happen.

'It's a boy! Oh Rose, it's a boy!' That's my dad, Pete, speaking. And Rose, that's my mum. Did you know they used to secure a woman's feet in stirrups when she gave birth? Honest, back in the 1960s they really did. I know this because Dad said Mum was strapped into a metal contraption with her legs high up and wide open on a table facing an open door so the doctors could wander by and peer in, see if anything's happening. Modesty being way below the needs of a doctor to perform a stroll-past consultation. It might also have had something to do with the fact that this was Dartford Hospital, which, if they'd had a mind back then, could have been twinned with Bedlam Royal.

But I'm out and screaming and healthy. Quick snip of the umbilical cord and I'm ready for my inaugural hug. I'm handed to my mother who looks down at me and goes… 'Oh.'

Or it might have been… 'Hhhuummm.' Either way, that zing of overwhelming love and affection and good stuff between mother and baby, it didn't happen to us.

When a woman holds out her hands to receive her newborn child for the very first time, the expectation must be enormous. Relief it's healthy, of course, that's her first thought, but it's probably followed by something like, what will he/she look like? Will I see myself in him/her, will he/she have my nose, my mouth, my eyes? Are my genes more dominant than the father's, or will I just see him mirrored back at me and have to spend the rest of my life saying, 'You're just like your Dad.' What if he/she doesn't love me? And then, fleeting or lingering, the other question, the one nobody likes to talk about. What if I don't love it?

When my mother looked down at me she said she felt nothing. Zilcho. Absolutely nothing at all. *Can I exchange him for one I might like? No, sorry madam, it doesn't work that way.*

If I'd have known how things would pan out, I'd have made a concerted effort to stop crying and give her a smile. Hi Mum, good to finally meet you. I should have pulled a funny face. Blown her a raspberry or made a comical noise. But I didn't, I just yelled and yelled and probably pooed.

I know she didn't enjoy her pregnancy, my dad told me that she hated it, often refusing to leave the house. She thought her bump made her unattractive. That feeling spilled over into her relationship with my dad, and was probably the beginning of the end. I wasn't planned and I'm not sure if she blamed me, him or both of us. Probably both of us. Maybe that had a bigger impact on her rejecting me than even she realised at the time, and certainly put an irreparable strain on their marriage. One pregnancy, two people pushed away.

Of course, these days women are told not to worry if they don't bond instantly, that it might gradually happen over a few days, or weeks. I don't know if that was the case back then, she never said. If it was, she wasn't party to that chat, or she took no notice. Either's possible.

· These days we'd identify this pretty quickly as postnatal depression. But is that what she had? In this story, the one I've grown up with, it seems quite instant, doesn't it? More like a switch, 'one last push Rose, there you go… yes, yes, here it comes…' and *bang!* instant apathy. Is that really how it works? You'd have thought there might be a moment or two where she went '*Aahhhh*'. But no, she told me later there wasn't even a smidge.

So there we were, the three of us sitting up in the hospital bed, Mum, dad and me. I know a lot of what happened next because she was quite open about it. But I don't know everything. I don't know the small things. For instance, I don't know how or when she told my dad. Was it straight away, or did she ponder it for a while before taking him to one side.

'Um, I think I might have a bit of a problem here…'

Equally, I have no idea how he reacted.

'You don't feel *anything* for him? Not *anything?*'

So I guess. I fill in the blank spaces, because that's how the mind works.

'No, nothing. Is that bad?'

'Well, yeah.'

There are alternatives to this imaginary conversation. Depending how I feel she'll either be in floods of tears or wandering down the isle of a supermarket slightly distracted by the special offers. On the whole, I plump for tears. Rivers of them, because although I'm a sweetie, I'm ego-centric with it.

Hospital bed. The three of us. After a couple of days' recuperation, we were pronounced fit to go, and I was taken home where she set about looking after me. I was fed, burped, had my nappy changed, my bum powdered and my sick wiped away. She was functional and attentive, but distant. Sure, she did what needed doing, but there was no cuddling with it; at least, that's what she used to tell me, saying things like, 'I didn't cuddle you because I just didn't want to, but you were fine.' As a social experiment, you have to admit it's quite interesting. How would a baby grow up devoid of a mother's affection? Would it grow up feral with a guttural fear of touching another human being? Or worse? A mass murderer screaming all the way to the cells that it was lack of a mother's love that drove him to the heinous crime? The answer – in my case – is neither: I quite like touching and being touched, and to the best of my knowledge I haven't slit anyone's throat, though there's a few I'd quite like to.

That's not to say I was *unaffected*. I just haven't topped anyone because of it.

Home was a two up, two down in a terrace of identical houses just outside Dartford in Kent, with homemade curtains and a put-together kitchen of my dad's design – he was pretty handy like that. And here's irony for you: when I came home in July of 1967, the number one record was The Beatles, *All You Need Is Love*. Yeah, the universe is one hell of a comedian. I imagine it coming on the radio quite a bit in those first few weeks, though I can't exactly picture Mum bopping about to it. I bet she turned it off. I would have.

My room was blue for boys, with toys and snazzy child's outfits. People drop by to inspect and coo over the new arrival, and I was a hot topic for a while the way a newborn is. It must have been so weird for her, wondering what had gone wrong, why she didn't feel anything for her new baby. The constant flow of visitors wouldn't have helped. Did she think, '*How come they all seem to love him, yet I'm his mother and I don't?*' I wonder if she confided in anyone? I hope she did, I hope she had a friend with whom she could talk things through, although she was never really like that so somehow I doubt it.

Then a handful of weeks into my life, something happened, something that shook her so profoundly she reacted in a way that was almost unheard of back then. She picked up the telephone and booked an appointment to see a psychiatrist.

I don't know what the catalyst was — she would never tell me even though I pressed her on it. I have imagined all sorts of things: I can't imagine she felt suicidal, but it's possible; perhaps I kept crying and she didn't know how to stop me. More likely she was afraid of what she might do to me. All I know is something happened, and she thought, 'okay, that's enough, I need to go and get this checked out.'

With me looked after, she dressed in her smartest clothes and caught a train to Harley Street, which was where all the shrinks hung out. I imagine her sitting petrified by the window, watching the backs of all the houses skid by as the train rumbles closer and closer. It was 1967, and psychiatry, although not exactly in its infancy, was still very unpredictable. These days you can take a lunch hour to nip out to see a therapist dressed in funky jeans and slouchy t-shirt who will chat about anything you want over a cup of coffee, but back then psychiatry was a serious business performed by overly serious men in overly serious brown suits. She lasted three sessions, and never went back.

Whether she felt she'd achieved all she could from the meetings, or whether they started to unearth issues she wasn't prepared to look at, I couldn't tell you. The morning she opened up and told me about it, I was too busy trying to be good; which was of course back in the early days before I realised being bad got me a whole lot more attention.

'Hand me the mirror, Simon,' she said. I was 11 years old, two weeks before I'd turn 12; two years before I'd burn the house to the ground and two more until I'd lose my virginity. Life was about to become more confusing than I could ever imagine. But for now, I'm 11. I liked football, the film *Grease* and watching my mum get ready for work.

With father hoofed out a few years earlier, mornings had a routine, a ritual before school. Both of us in PJs, sitting cross-legged on the floor eating toast with marmite and drinking coffee, the radio playing in the background and mum putting on her makeup. We sat by the French windows at the back of the lounge because you have to put makeup on in natural light; apparently artificial light makes a woman look like she's been made-up by Edvard Munch.

I passed her the small mirror and grabbed a triangle of toast. 'Crumbs!'

'Sorry Mum,' hovering over the shared plate so the bits wouldn't go on the floor, I took a bite.

She was in a chatty mood. I didn't understand much of what she was saying, but it was nice to have this moment with her before school. '…so I went to see the psychiatrist. He was a horrible man. Smelled of cigarettes and sweat.' She paused to dab on her foundation, the dots of cream always landing on the exact same spots each morning with ninja precision. Then she gently smoothed them over her face. 'I only went three times, and that was enough.'

I've always liked mornings, and I liked listening to Mum talk and watching her do her makeup. Leaning forward I took another mouthful, one with too much marmite on and nearly choked.

'DON'T COUGH! You'll blow crumbs on the floor!'

Keeping over the plate until I was confident I could keep the cough in, I finally sat back.

Next layer of makeup on top of the foundation is a powder that gets brushed on. It's quite a bland colour, not much different from the foundation, but that's only because the layer above that is the highlighter for her cheek bones, and that's a kind of reddy colour, but you have to be really careful putting it on because too much and you'll ruin everything.

'He didn't say much, just sat there smoking in his big leather chair. I told him I didn't love you and hadn't bonded with you, and you know what he said? He said, what's *your* relationship like with *your* mother? Like that's got anything to do with it! This was about me, not nanny.'

It seems odd now to think that she would chat so calmly and so openly with 11-year-old me about not loving or bonding with me, but I think to her it was no big deal. It was just normal. Probably in her eyes *everyone* felt like it.

'What's a 'schatrist?' I asked.

No answer. That was common if I asked a question she didn't want to answer, so I asked something else. 'Did you smoke, Mum?'

'Sometimes, but not often. Everybody did back then.' Pause. Eyeliner next, black, makes your eyes look bigger. Then the eyes themselves, which are surprisingly tricky to pull off. There's two different colours above, and one below that needs to get smudged in just the right way, and of course both eyes have to look identical. 'Waste of money, if you ask me.'

I took this to be the cigarettes, not the psychiatrist, although it might have been both.

'How do I look?' she asked, moving the mirror out of the way. She was done making-up, all bar her pillar-box red lipstick, which went on after toast in case the bits got stuck to her lips.

This was the only part when I felt uncomfortable, because I didn't understand the question. She looked like Mum,

25

stunningly beautiful in a girl-next-door kind of way, she was slim with blond tousled hair that fell in soft curls down to her shoulders and a beauty spot on one cheek. As far as I was concerned, the version unmade-up was the stranger. So I said with a big smile, 'you look like you.'

'Thanks,' her voice edgy. I hated myself for making her cross, and decided to work on something different to say next time. For a while we sat quietly, munching breakfast.

When the toast was done, she dropped the bombshell, 'Your aunt paid for the psychiatrist. She was worried about me, and about you. That was back when I was still hopeful she might take you away and be your new mummy.' I went cold, but she was continuing, 'I asked her if she would, and she thought about it, but in the end she said no. Such a shame, I really thought she might want you, but she didn't. It would have been good for both of us. Even after she said no, I still kept asking but she was adamant.'

So there it was, and the silence sat between us like a toad. The confession that I'd look back on many, many times in the future as the moment that everything changed. I knew she didn't love me, she'd told me that loads of times before, but this was the first time she'd said she didn't want me to the point she tried to give me away. She had tried again and again, and my aunt, her sister, didn't want me either. Why did she tell me this? I don't know why it came out, what she thought she was doing. Was she out to hurt me, punish me? It's possible, though unlikely. I think it's more likely she thought that by telling me, I'd understand how much unhappiness I'd caused her, and how much I should be grateful to her. I owed her, big time – that's a theme that would come up *a lot*. She was mum, she brought me into the world, therefore I owed her everything. Which I guess is true.

She gave a disappointed face.

'I'm sorry,' I said, looking down.

'Yes, well… Go and get ready for school.'

I got up and made to leave.

'Kiss,' she said.

I'd always found kissing a horrendous, complicated business that involved timing and coordination, neither of which, at ten years old, I had in abundance. I couldn't understand why anyone would want to do it, not willingly. I wondered if I could leg it up the stairs claiming I'd be late if I didn't rush, but it would only antagonise her, and she was being so friendly and nice this morning. So I moved forward and forced myself to concentrate. Sitting dead still, she held out her cheek, lifted a finger, and pointed to it, the light bouncing off the ruby-red nail varnish. I took a deep breath and moved closer, all the while looking down to prevent my feet knocking over any of the makeup pots and bottles and brushes pooled around her. Spying a gap in which I thought my foot would fit, I stepped in.

Rule number one was no touching. No hands, no cheeks, no contact of any kind. Just an air kiss, landed with all the precision of a clever engineer, which is really difficult when you're a kid and your body keeps growing and changing and the distance that worked yesterday might not work today. This close I could smell her perfume and shampoo so strongly, and it smelt really nice.

With all the care a boy can muster, I positioned my cheek close to hers and made a kissing noise. She didn't make one back, she never did. But it was nice to be so close, and I didn't want to move away. I could hear her breathing, feel the tickling of stray strands of her hair on me, and that smell, that smell of mum was just so comforting and warming, even though I wasn't cold.

'Move!'

I jumped and moved quickly. Upstairs I sat on the bed, thinking. It felt like there was a lot to take in, to try and understand, but you know what? On the whole I thought the morning had gone rather well. She seemed friendly, chatty and she'd spoken to me like she wanted me to be there. Sure, what she said would take a while to sink in and process, but right then, life felt as though it was all right. I got dressed, grabbed my school bag and ran down before she needed to call me.

At the bottom of the stairs I turned towards the kitchen and came face to face with a man I'd never seen before. He was short and stocky, like a rugby player, with shaggy blond hair and rough, shaved face. I stopped dead. He was dressed in a shirt and tie that looked crumpled, as though he'd slept in it, and he had a jacket slung awkwardly over one shoulder and a pair of shiny black shoes dangling from his fingertips. Dropping my bag I moved forward, holding out my hand for him to shake just the way I'd been shown. 'I'm Simon,' I said.

Chapter 7

He dropped the shiny black shoes and they thumped to the floor, not in an awkward fumbling manner, but in a confident 'so what' way that made me nervous. 'Hello Simon, I'm a friend of your mother's. She's told me all about you.' His voice was rich and deep and hinted towards a posh schooling, and when he gripped my hand he did so much tighter than necessary, but I didn't flinch. He also stank of cigarettes.

'She asked me to drop by this morning and pick her up. Her car's, you know… So, you're a football fan, I understand! Good lad, who do you support?'

'Same team as my dad.'

He nodded. 'Best way.'

I don't know what made me say it, maybe it was the stink of cigarettes. 'Are you Mum's 's'ch'atrist?' I asked.

Suddenly Mum was there, yelling. 'Don't you ever speak like that again! Do you hear me? Ever!' She was apoplectic. Grabbing me, she shoved me out the front door.

'I'm so sorry. I'm so sorry, Mum.'

'Go to school!' she screamed and slammed the door in my face.

I walked down the path, turned left and headed along the pavement towards the train station. I felt *amazing*. I couldn't stop grinning. I kept thinking, I'm adult now. Grown up. The way she yelled at me, and pushed me, she's never done it quite like that before. That's what she used to do with Dad. And some of her boyfriends. She'd do it and then she'd sit with me and tell me that she had to do it because it made them come back. Treat them mean and they'd always come back for more, that's what she said. She said it probably looked nasty, but she only did it because she liked them. So that means she must like me. She likes me, she likes me, she likes me, and she wants me to come back. You couldn't have wiped the smile off my face with a smack.

The pavement was full of people. Dark suits, unhappy faces, briefcases bumping against quick walking legs.

I wonder what a 's'ch'atrist is? Must be something bad. Or good. But important. Definitely important. And a good word to use, one I must remember.

'Are you okay, love?'

I looked up. It was a lady. She's stopped and was blocking the pavement in front of me. She knelt down, reached out and stroked my hair.

It felt weird and I flinched.

'You're crying, what's the matter?' she said.

Crying? No, I'm smiling. I'm happy. I put my hand to my face and touched the tears. How odd, how really, really odd.

School was a run of big old Victorian terraced houses that had been converted into classrooms and stood on a main road just this side of central London. My aunt had offered to pay for my schooling and my mum jumped at the chance. A budget had been set and a school chosen. The train I needed was the 8:14 from Barnhurst to Blackfriars: yeah, that one. The one that famously never, ever ran, to the point some wag wrote a song about it, '*Isn't it a shame, there's never a train, from Barnhurst to Blackfriars,*' that was a hit for a while, and people on the platform would hum it when the inevitable announcement came over the tannoy that the train was yet again cancelled. So I got the one after and had to run-walk the other end to avoid the humiliation of getting to class late.

'Dawson?'

Puff, pant. Desk, seat, sit, bag down. 'Here!' just.

Sigh... school. I didn't hate it, but I did have problems.

***

'We need to talk about Simon,' the head teacher said, motioning the three of us, Mum, Dad and me to take a seat. He had called a meeting some months earlier to discuss my future.

'Is everything okay?' Mum asked, nervously. She was done up to the nines in a brown pencil skirt, ivory blouse and some killer red shoes. Her blonde hair was teased and sprayed. She looked beautiful, like a model. I'd purposely walked as slow as I could to the head's office in the hope that some of the other kids would see her, and as a result my standing in the playground hierarchy would improve several notches.

'Yes. And no. He's a bright lad,' the head smiled at me, 'but there are issues. Are you aware of just how much he struggles with spelling?'

While I stared at the ground I could feel Mum and Dad look at each other over the top of my head.

'Can I ask,' he continued, 'Does he read much at home?'

Mum said, 'Well, no. Not really.'

'I see. Are there books around, does he see you reading? Children often imitate their parents.'

'Um, no. I don't have time.'

He nodded. 'Do you read to him? Bedtime stories, that type of thing?'

'No.' I could feel her bristle. She was getting annoyed.

'I see. Well I have looked at his English class work, and I'm pretty sure he has a condition called Dyslexia. Research is new at the moment, and it seems there are many different types, but early indications show it has something to do with the mind's inability to see, recall and construct words on the page.'

'Oh my God,' my mum's hand flew to her face. 'We just thought he was a bit simple.'

Oh great, thanks Mum.

My dad, who'd been quiet until now, said, 'Is there anything we can do?'

'Probably not.'

Oh Jesus.

'Although,' he continued, 'there are signs that repetition and reading can help. The boy should read a book a week for the rest of his life. That way he might stand a chance. A slim chance, but a chance.'

'What about exams? We were hoping he might go on to university.'

'Not a hope.'

'But if he's diagnosed with the illness, isn't there some sort of dispensation because of it?'

'It isn't an illness, Mr Dawson.'

Thank God for that.

'It's just the mind's inability to work correctly.'

Oh God.

'And no, there are no dispensations.' He smiled at me. 'The lad will just have to work hard and hope for the best.'

He got up. So did my parents. I didn't. I couldn't move. 'So I'm going to fail my exams,' I said. 'Exams that I won't even take for another five years. I'm going to fail them.'

'Not all of them,' he said. 'I hear you're very good at art.'

That was the point that we all, including me, wrote me off. The thing is, the fact that I could have gone to uni and become a success was something Mum was very keen on. It was one of the few things she *liked* about me. Now that was taken away.

love = zero
future = zero
by Simon Dawson, age 11
Really there was only one direction to go from here.
Rebellion, baby. Rebellion.

Chapter 8

Outside the barn I could hear whispers, the little lamb and I both could. He snuggled deeper into my lap.

Ziggy: 'You're absolutely sure dinner won't be ruined?'

Debbie: 'Ziggy!'

Ziggy: 'Sorry. You're right, it hardly matters. Did smell good though, didn't it?'

'I'm in here,' I called, more than a bit miffed at the interruption. Look, I know it was nice of them to worry, and of course I'm grateful they want to make sure I'm okay, but sometimes good people can be very annoying.

Shining a torchlight straight into my face, Ziggy said, 'Ah, and the winner of today's disappearing person saga is... sitting on the floor hugging a lamb. Of course you are. It isn't dead is it?'

He came in and Debbie followed.

'No, he's fine.'

Nodding, he sat one side of me, Debbie on the other, so we were in a line, backs against the wall, bums on straw, legs outstretched. They both had their torches trained on the ewe in front of us.

'She doesn't look bothered,' Debbie said. 'How's he doing?'

Giving him a little squeeze, I said, 'He's doing okay.'

'Better than you?'

'I wouldn't say that.'

'By the way, I told her everything,' Ziggy said with a large helping of pride. 'I left nothing out. Memory like a computer. Nuances, facial expressions, the works. Fully up to speed.'

'Mm.' I knew he would.

Continuing, he said, 'You have no idea how much it pained me to eat into time I could have been talking about myself, but it's what friends are for. Apparently.' He lifted a wine glass and took a sip.

'You brought a drink?

'Mm, oh sorry. I was going to be like a St. Bernard, you know, rush in and pour alcohol down your throat. But it's quite a good Chablis and you don't seem like you need it.'

'Thanks.'

'Welcome.' He offered me the glass anyway.

'You know we can't stay out here with the lamb all night, don't you?' Debbie said.

I nodded. Of course I knew, but I hugged him closer all the same.

Debbie was the first to get up. 'Come on,' she said. 'Let's go and eat.'

Ziggy was up and out of there like a goat caught in a feed store. I took a little more time, settling the lamb down for the night, then followed, hand gripped in Debbie's as we made our way across the dark field. We didn't really need torches; we could have just followed the scent of freshly cooked Italian dinner.

Inside I bagged the table with the computer, while Ziggy threw some logs on the fire and wittered on and Debbie handed out slices of pizza with gooey melted cheese still bubbling on top. I twisted the screen so nobody else could see what I was doing. I wasn't sure it was what my mother had, but it had to be a starting point. Two words typed into Google: 'postnatal depression'.

More than two million hits. Popular topic.

Scrolling down there were lots of official-looking sites; medical, psychological, counselling and broad-sheet newspaper articles with headlines that I guessed were written to scare and shock you into clicking. I was scared and shocked, but avoided the urge to click. Instead I hit the *In the News* link, and several pieces pinged up about the singer Adele. Apparently she'd battled postnatal depression following the birth of her son. I'd been aware of her talking about it in the press, but it hadn't resonated at the time, probably because that was all before.

Skimming a couple of the articles, I thought, I don't know but it seems like Adele had it quite bad. Words stood out like 'Death Sentence', 'Heartbreaking', 'Destroy' and 'Suffering'. Is that how my mum felt?

All these years later, it's hard for me to imagine what it must have been like for my mother, but in my memory that's not how it came across. Was it like that for her in my early years? By the time my memories kick in, around the age of 4, things had settled down. Our relationship, dysfunctional though it probably was with frequent fights, tears, anger and horrible dramas, felt normal. There was never any sense that she was struggling; if she felt something, if she thought something, she'd just say it. She could be Queen Bitch Number One, but she was utterly open and honest with it. Maybe she was just selfish?

Not at all convinced that's what she had, I moved the cursor back up to the search bar and typed, 'What is postnatal depression?'

It seemed it was a lot of things, depending what site you went on. Some talked about symptoms such as sadness, isolation and feelings of inadequacy, while others went Full Monty with urges to kill: kill the baby's father, themselves or even their baby.

I don't even want to go there. Seriously, I don't want to go there. Red X-ing the screen, I slammed the laptop shut. But that hotspot, that tiny hotspot of anger right in the centre of my tongue was back, all claggy and bitter. I tried to ignore it but it *burned*.

Anger at what? Why the hell am I getting so angry?

It's later and I'm in bed with Debbie and the dog, while Ziggy's zonked out in the other room. The bed's a normal double, nothing special. The dog, on the other hand, is everything the bed isn't: abnormal, king-size and very special, and he's currently alternating between running in his sleep, wagging his tail and blasting methane ozone-breakers out into the bedroom. But a farting, galloping, happy Great Dane isn't the only reason I can't sleep, though let's be honest, even with everything else that's gone on today, it's quite a big part of it.

Making myself blissfully uncomfortable by folding myself up on the pillow and taking tiny shallow breaths through my mouth, I wonder what farmers count to nod off. Insider knowledge precludes sheep, that's a given; do doctors count arteries, mechanics sparkplugs or bankers wads of cash? 'Course not. That's just business. So I settle on people at a train station but soon get bored, and not in the sleepy way.

I reckon the body does things for a reason. It's got something to do with the subconscious being 'all knowing' about what's good for you, although for some unknown reason it draws the line at coming right out with it, favouring more subtle approaches. Right now my body's under the impression that wakefulness is just the ticket and is communicating that by making my brain do the equivalent of a mental zumba class. Bloody do-gooder.

Nestling a little deeper into the pillow I stare up at the dark ceiling, and accept that sleep won't come.

Chapter 9

School. I'm late from the cancelled train and take my seat in class as close to the back as possible, and doing that thing kids do – wishing they were invisible while at the same time feeling frustrated nobody's looking at them.

The class was tiny. Fourteen including the teacher.

'Morning spelling test,' Mrs Parkside announces with a crocodile's smile.

Oh my God, I'd forgotten about the spelling tests. Teacher calls out ten words, you write them down and hand them to the person next to you to check.

'First word, *mystery*,' she says.

I look down at the page in front of me and realise I'm seeing it though the eyes of the 11-year-old me, and I can't for the life of me remember how to spell it. I can't, I really, really can't. I feel sweat blossom under my arms.

'Everyone done?'

No, I'm not. In the future they'll have spell-check. You don't need this to get on in life anymore. In the 21st century, millions of people can't spell and they'll all be billionaires.

'Okay, next one…'

I write *mysrty*. It looks kind of right.

'…*alleged*.'

alladgede

'*Anxiety*.'

Chapter 9

Yep, okay, thanks subconscious, I get it. Much appreciated. Now, moving on, and fast forward the memory…

…to lunchtime.

The bell rings. 180 children in twelve classes swipe the contents of their desk into waiting bags with zero panache and hurry off to the canteen, while the teachers dodge that culinary bullet and bolt for the safety of the staff room.

The school canteen. *You will never find a more wretched hive of scum and villainy anywhere in the universe* – clearly Obi Wan Kenobi hadn't had lunch with us. I don't remember a sign above the entrance reading 'May the force be with you', but it would have been fitting, and not just because *Star Wars* was big at the time. As lawless as the Wild West, and as for diversity… there were punks, skinheads, mods and rockers, and that was just the girls. And *loud!* A room full of children all yelling to be heard would have had the members of AC/DC, at the time reckoned to be the loudest rock band in the world, asking for a bit of 'Goddamn shush.'

The tables were crammed in so tight you had wiggle your hips like a belly dancer to negotiate the room, and the overly bright strip lights gave everyone a stark, slightly shocked look, but at least it topped up your vitamin D.

My table was over to the left. It's not where the cool cats hung, but we did have girls sitting with us so it wasn't completely dorky. With no money to buy anything I'm the first to sit, and wait for my dining companions to shuffle their way along the queue to the cash register.

'Hey,' the first to arrive says, taking the chair opposite. 'You not eating?'

'Not really hungry,' I lied. His plate is stacked with chips and beans and a fresh bread roll.

He nods. 'You want half my roll?' Without waiting for an answer he flips off the top and passes it across.

'Thanks.'

He counts off half a dozen chips and separates them on one side of his plate before tucking into the rest. I reach over and one by one place the six chips side by side in the roll. He knows I have no money, but he doesn't mention it. Instead he says, 'How'd you do in the spelling test?'

I take a bite. Around the mouthful I tell him, 'Rubbish. Nought. You?'

He shrugs, 'Ten.'

I nod.

'I don't understand how you can't get any right.'

'Me neither,' I admit. And it's true, I don't understand. Since the head teacher spoke to my parents, nobody has mentioned it. All I know is I could look at a word and recite the letters in order 100 times over and over again. Five minutes later, I couldn't get it right if my life depended on it. I know this for a fact because I've tried it. It's VERY annoying!

'Why were you late this morning?'

'Train cancelled.'

'Happens to you a lot.'

Happens to a lot of us a lot. For a while there's silence while we both munch. Food is like a spacer in the conversation that picks up a few moments later on a different topic, that of TV. *Wonder Woman, Mork and Mindy* and *The A Team* are discussed to the point of exhaustion.

It's funny: the memory of mum screaming at me and shoving me out of the house didn't really make a dent, but this, remembering my younger self in the school canteen with his desire to fit in and have friends makes me want to reach out and hug the boy, tell him it'll be okay.

I don't bother trying to remember the rest of the day and fast-forward the memory to home time. The bell rings and as I stand the door to the classroom opens. The school secretary pops her head in and says, 'Simon, your mum phoned. You're to go to your dad's tonight, okay?'

Nodding, I think, oh. I hadn't thought about home all day. I'd planned on doing that on the journey back. So, she didn't want me tonight. Didn't want to see me. Didn't want to be with me.

I pack my books and writing pad. The news has slowed me, and I'm still doing it when everyone else has left, so I'm the only one there.

She must have phoned my dad. They still spoke occasionally, though when they did it mostly degenerated into my mum screaming at him, and him slumped so his shoulders almost hit his knees. As the last of my stuff goes into my bag, I picture her telling him he has to have me tonight as she couldn't stand to be near me. I bet he had plans. I bet he had to change them. I feel bad, but I don't know what to do. I have to go somewhere.

Making a path between the desks I head for the door. Outside the corridor is a tumble of children shouting, singing and swearing along with good and bad natured micky-taking. It's nothing personal, it's just kids being kids: finding boundaries, discovering hierarchy and exposing the weak. If half of them didn't sob themselves to sleep that night it would have been a good day.

'Dawson! Oi, Dawson, coming for a fag?' Metal, short for Heavy Metal on account of his musical taste struts against the tide of children, and does so effortlessly without a single bump or knock.

'I can't, my dad's picking me up.'

'So?'

'So he'll smell it.'

Metal's got his jacket on inside out, his tie pulled down and the top two buttons of his shirt undone. Behind him, also walking against the tide, is the head teacher. We can both hear him chastising every other kid for some infringement of the school dress code. Metal's not just infringing, he's obliterating.

'Watch out,' I tell him, even though I know what he'll do. It's what he always does. He pulls his tie lower so it exaggerates his scruffiness, before turning to face the head.

'Afternoon sir,' he states, grinning broadly. 'Hope you're not working late and making Mrs Head wait at home for you.'

The head stops, looks Metal up and down, shakes his head and smiles. 'No, I'm off as soon as this place empties. Can you please try and tidy yourself up a bit?'

Metal makes a point of moving his tie back up to where it was before the interaction began. 'Of course. Wouldn't want to give the school a bad name.'

He actually reaches out his hand to the Head, who takes it with an adult's grip. 'You drive me insane, Metal,' he says, using his nickname.

Metal laughs, 'You wouldn't have it any other way, sir.'

He doesn't reply, just wanders off berating immaculate school kids for their apparently disorderly dress that only he can see.

Metal turns to me and I say, 'How'd you get away with it?'

He doesn't answer, just puts his hand on my shoulder and says, 'Doesn't your dad smoke?'

'Yeah.'

'Then he'll never smell it on you. Come on.'

Two minutes later and we're in the Technical Drawing department, also known as the smoking zone on account of the fact that the teacher smokes like a chimney in there between classes, so a couple more ciggies won't make a difference. Metal sits on one desk, his scuffed shoes on a chair, and I do the same opposite. He lights up, puffs and blows a perfect smoke ring before handing the stick to me. I take a drag, my lungs burning like I'm breathing in fire. I quite like the pain.

'How's things with your mum?' he says, taking the fag back.

I try and do a smoke ring, but it's rubbish. I shrug. 'I don't know,' which is the truest thing I can say. 'How's your nan?'

I'm not sure why he lives half his life with his nan. It's something to do with ease of access to school, or something like that. Both of our home lives are details that never seem important to talk about.

'Yeah, good.' He jumps off the desk, and puffing as he walks, goes to the teacher's desk, pulls open the bottom drawer, rifles down to the very bottom and pulls out a magazine. The cover is bright and shiny and features a topless woman in her pants. The magazine is called *Mayfair*. He hands me the cigarette and starts flicking through the pages. I can see pictures of beautiful naked women. The magazine's been there for weeks and we've studied every page, but it's still a thrill to see it. Without making any reference to the magazine, he continues, 'I'm going there tonight, via the pie 'n' mash shop. How comes you're going to your dad's?'

Making mention of pie 'n' mash, the Old Kent Road and all things London is his thing, like location is how he self-identifies.

'My mum's idea.'

Outside the classroom things are starting to quieten as everyone drifts off home. He's still flicking through the pages. I've stopped looking.

Although we're both 11, he always seems so much older. Almost adult, which I know is his aim. Actually it's both of our aims. To be an adult would mean the end to all our problems.

He offers me the smoke and I take a large hit before he knocks off the end – it's only half gone and would be a shame not to keep it for later. With a flourish he slams the magazine shut and stuffs it roughly back where it was in the teacher's drawer. 'We should go.'

I nod in agreement, and moments later we're out the front of the school. The air is cold and I breathe it in quick, deep breaths, hoping to extinguish the smell of cigarette smoke. A combination of after-school clubs, detentions and loiterers means we're not the last out. I can see my dad's car parked. A red MG Midget sports car with the hood down. Good, now he'll never smell anything on me.

'Your dad?' Metal nods in his direction.

'Yeah.' For the longest moment we both just stand there. I know he wants me to ask him to come back to ours, the same as he's asked me to go back to his many times, but I can't. Not tonight.

He speaks first, saying, 'See you tomorrow then,' and walks off in the other direction, and I walk over to my dad.

'Hello son,' he says, not spotting me until I crack the door. There's a smile and it's warm. I throw my bag in the tiny space behind the front seat and climb in. The seats are black leather and cool. There are seatbelts, but nobody uses them. Instead, my fingers move automatically to a frayed bit of leather down the side of the seat and start worrying it.

Starting the car, slipping it into gear and moving out into the flow of traffic he continues, 'Good day at school?'

'I guess.'

'Was that your friend I saw you with? He looks a lot older than you.'

'No,' I assure him, 'he's in the same class.'

I can feel him glance across at me. I don't glance back.

Metal does look older than me, I know he does, and it's not fair. God, if you're up there and you can hear me, pleased, please, please make me older. 15 would do, though 18 would be better.

Chapter 9

Stopping at a red light he says, 'Mum phoned.'

I make a face and he laughs. 'Do you want to talk about what happened?'

Yes I do, but I don't know how to, so I say no. He reaches out and puts a friendly hand on my leg. 'It's okay.'

I know he's being nice but I cringe at his touch, and lie to myself that it's because the images of the naked women are still fresh in my mind, but deep down I know that's not it and it's something else, something more fundamental. Besides, I do want to talk about mum, I really do. But I don't want to upset him, and I certainly don't want to cause a problem between them. Also I don't know what to say. And I'm frightened I'll cry, and I don't want to be a child. I want to be an adult. I desperately want to be an adult.

As dads go, he was pretty cool. In his day he was a mod, wore a parka and drove a Vespa scooter that he'd souped up to double the speed, and would zoom down to Brighton at the weekends to hang out. He met my mum when they were teenagers and married the year before I was born, then divorced a couple of years after, citing Irreconcilable Differences as the cause, which, if anything, was an understatement. I asked him once what he thought of mum and with tears in his eyes he said he still loved her, and probably always would. Which struck me as confusing even at the time because he was also scared of her. We all were.

He would often ask me if I was okay at home, and at the start I would try and talk to him, but when I did it was like he'd switch off, stare out the window or at the TV. He wasn't being nasty, it's just… it's just I don't think he knew what to say. So in the end, when he asked, I'd shrug, and he'd laugh and we'd carry on.

In the car we take an unexpected turn.

'Where are we going?' I ask.

'I've got some work to finish off,' he says.

Smiling we both look over at one another. 'That's bad,' I tell him.

He gets it, but says anyway, 'Bad. As in, bad? Not good?'

'No, bad, as in good.' Every generation has their own slang. Sometimes it's clever, sometimes it's quick-witted. For us, we simply swapped the meanings of good and bad around, which, looking back, was really lazy.

'So it's good?'

I roll my eyes. God he's so old! Okay, I want to be older, but I don't ever want to get as old as he is. We speed on.

Work for him is a recording studio that he owns with a friend. They're both record producers, and together they bought a ground floor Victorian flat in a residential street, soundproofing it by bricking up all the windows and fixing thick black rubber to all the inside walls and ceilings that killed any noise or natural light and leant the place a dense, heavy feel. The drums had a little room all to themselves with a window out into the main studio through which you could see microphones, guitars and any number of musical instruments.

The mixing desk is in a separate room, again with a window into the main studio. The desk itself is huge, must be six feet long with hundreds of twisting knobs and sliders, each designed to tweak a tiny, tiny bit of a song into a hit record.

But when you first shoulder the big heavy front door and go in, it's the smell that hits you. It's a sickly-sweet smell that's part tobacco, part sweat and part something unidentifiable you just don't want to dwell on.

Danno was the studio's session drummer and seemed to live in the place, which struck me even then as unhealthy. He was a big guy with long wavy hair and a lazy face. He wore skin-tight jeans and a vest top that showed off his muscly tattooed arms. And he was my mate.

As soon as dad barged the door open I zipped inside looking for Danno. I found him in the mixing room puffing on a roll-up.

'Hey kid!' he said as I barged in. In my memory I've put an exclamation point at the end as I want to think he was pleased to see me, though I've no way of knowing as the thump, thump, thump of the music was so loud all you could do was lip-read. The room was full, probably a band mixing their latest hope for world domination. I have no idea what groups passed through there, though I understand some of them would later go on, if not to world domination, at least to be household names.

Ignoring everyone else I yelled, 'Hi Danno. Can we have a lesson please?' though he would never have heard me over the din.

He laughed, gave up with words and nodded. I grabbed his hand, the one without the smoke, yanked him up into a stand and pulled him out and into the studio, the mixing room door closing behind us. Suddenly there was silence.

'Wow, that was loud,' I said. 'Why does it have to be that loud?'

'So you can get the sound right, man.'

Nodding like I understood exactly what that meant, we made our way into the drum booth. With the door closed behind us and my dad safely out of sight in the mixing room, he offered me his cigarette, which I took, while he gathered up his sticks and sat down at the kit. As I took a puff, be began tapping out a ride on the high-hat.

After a while he said, 'Here. You try.'

I pulled off my school tie and undid the top button, hating the fact that this stupid uniform marked me out as a child, placed the smoke in the overflowing ashtray down on the floor and sat on the stool. Holding the sticks as Danno taught me, I tried to copy his ride.

'Don't try so hard,' he said, standing behind me and taking hold of my hands and working the sticks. Little by little, like a father letting go of a bike when the child first tries riding without stabilisers, he moved his hands away. 'Keep going, keep going,' he yelled, and I did, but it fell apart pretty quickly.

'Awesome dude,' he said, ruffling my hair. 'Keep practising. You cool if I go back in?'

I said I was.

'You want me to leave you this?' he motioned towards the cigarette.

'No thanks, I'm good.'

Nodding he said, 'Okay. Bad for you anyway, especially at your age.'

I shrugged, not at all understanding what age had to do with it. Besides, I'd be turning 12 soon.

The door to the booth opening and closing behind him dragged some of the smoke out, but not all of it. There were clouds still in there, thick like dry ice at a rock concert. The prospect of stinking of cigarettes at school the next day didn't even cross my mind. This was the 1970s, and everyone stank of cigarettes, young or old, smoker or not.

Settling down I began tapping out a rolling beat I'd been working on. There were mistakes in it and it wasn't very fluid, but it wasn't too bad. Through the window of the booth I could see a huge round clock on the opposite wall in the main studio, presumably so bands paying by the hour could see how much time and money they were clocking up.

It was 4.55. An hour and a half after school finished, and the time I'd normally be arriving home. The house would be empty. Mum finished work at seven and got back just after. Between now and then there was a lot of TV to fit in.

I wonder if she'll want me back tomorrow. I wonder if she'll want me back at all. If she doesn't, I've decided I'm going to be a drummer and spend the rest of my life on the road. That way I won't need a house. Or a mum. Or anyone.

Chapter 9

Suddenly the door slams open and Danno and my dad both pile into the booth. They're both yelling at the top of their lungs, yelling for me to stop. It's only then I realise I've stopped tapping out a beat and have just been smashing the sticks down as hard as I can onto the skins. No rhythm, just smash, smash, smash as hard as I can.

Chapter 10

'Spelling test. Don't groan, you're first years, not kindergarten!'
Mrs Parkside shouts to the class.

Dad dropped me off this morning so I wasn't late. It also gave
me a chance to bag a seat at the back of the room.

'Pads and pens at the ready…'

The memory is deeper now. There's colour and texture, and,
at the thought of another spelling test, actual fear.

Pen and paper are in front of me. Top of the page, in neat
handwriting, I write the date. Next to it, my name. Then I
number one to ten down the left-hand column.

'…okay. First word is *skeleton*.'

I've no idea. I should have a best guess, scrawl some letters
that could conceivably make up the word, but why? What would it
achieve? It would be wrong, I know it would. So what's the point?

'Everyone done? Next word is *unsatisfactory*, which is
something I hope not to find in your work today, ladies and
gentlemen.'

Again, I don't know. So I don't put anything.

At the end of the test I haven't written a single word down. We
swap pages with the person beside us. He looks down at the almost
empty sheet, just a column of numbers one to ten down one side
with vacant gaps beside them, then looks up at me. I shrug.

As the teacher calls out the correct sequence of letters to
form the words and I check his off, I feel scared that he's going to

say something and I'll be caught out, but I also feel elated. God this feels great. I don't feel thick or stupid, I don't even want to die. It's wild.

'Going around the class, call out the name of the person on the sheet in front of you that you've just marked, and the number of correct answers. Start at the front here...'

They do. There are lots of eights, nines and tens. When it's his turn, he simply says, 'Simon Dawson. Zero.'

Mrs Parkside nods. Without even looking up she says, 'I've no idea why you find that so amusing, Mr Dawson!'

No, I'm sure you don't.

End of school comes around way too slowly, but is finally signalled by the bell.

'Where's home tonight?' Metal asks.

'My mum's. You?'

'Nan's again. Cigarette before you go?'

'Of course.'

I feel bad that I never have any of my own and always have to bum his, but he doesn't seem to mind, and besides, I only have a couple of puffs. While I pack books away in my holdall, Metal switches his jacket inside out and undoes his tie and top shirt button. I want to do the same but know from experience it has the opposite effect on me and actually makes me look younger, whereas the slouched-down look makes Metal look 14, maybe even 15.

A few minutes later and we're alone in the TD department, girly magazine open on the desk, fag alight.

'Oh, the damage I could do to that,' Metal says, skipping through the pages to his favourite girl.

'Yeah, me too,' I agree.

He looks up and asks, 'What would you do?'

Blimey! This is uncharted territory. We've only ever had it there as a kind of prop before. It's what men do, have magazines with beautiful girls to look at. All of mum's boyfriends have them. They are under her bed. She showed them to me them once, told me it's what adult men look at and I shouldn't be upset if I found them. But neither should I look at them, which of course I do.

But this 'what would you do?' isn't anything that had ever occurred to me. I don't know. To be honest, the stories next to the pictures are so confusing and make no sense, and are nothing that I ever want to be involved in. Looking at pictures of girls is what men are supposed to do, clearly, but to actually be in the same room as a girl without her clothes on is horrifying!

Metal's staring at me, and I can feel myself blush red. I can't think of anything to say.

'Aah, I'm just messing with you,' he says, punching me in the arm.

I wonder why he's decided to make it a point now? I don't want to look at him, and I certainly don't want to look at the pictures. I wish I hadn't come here tonight. I wish I'd gone straight home. But now I am here I don't know how to get away without looking like a scared child. I should just say I want to go, but I can't. I never do.

On the train journey home I know I should be worrying about seeing mum, and I am, but I also can't get the question Metal asked out of my head. What should a man do? I don't mean the mechanics, I know that. But that's, like, the middle bit. Sex doesn't even feel that scary. It's the rest of it. The bit before you get to it. And after. None of mum's boyfriend's magazines say anything about that. What do you talk about? How do you even get undressed without dying of embarrassment? And there's something else. I don't even want to form it into a thought because I know it's childish and it's not what I should be thinking, not as a man. But it's too big to ignore. I can't concentrate on it too much because it feels like I'm going to cry whenever I do, and that would be catastrophic in a busy trail carriage, but it's… I just want someone to put their arms around me; more than anything in the whole wide world I want to be held and cuddled. But nowhere in any of the magazines does it mention that people can do that. That's all I dream about, and I'm frightened that when you get older all you're allowed to do is have sex, and cuddling is laughed at because that's what children do. I feel like I'm missing out and when I grow up I'll never be able to return to it and I'll never experience it, not for the whole of my life.

But as the train pulls into my station and I disembark, all thoughts on that subject blink off and mum fills my mind. Last time she saw me she was fuming. I haven't spoken to her since.

I walk slowly along the pavement, school bag banging against my leg. The walk has to be slow so I can avoid the cracks. If I make it all the way back without treading on a single crack, then everything will be okay. I even know all the danger points are where there's sneaky hairline cracks in the tarmac, and it's those suckers that can catch an unsuspecting person out. But I'm wise to them and make it all the way back without putting a foot wrong.

I walk up the path to the front door. There are no lights on and the place looks deserted. I put my bag on the ground and reach inside it, beginning the search for the key. Tonight I find it in the first few seconds, which confirms what I already know, that my feet haven't hit any cracks. Good.

Good, good, good.

Kind of elated, I let myself in.

I've missed some children's TV, but they always put the good stuff on later so kids who have to travel by train or bus back from school, or have detention, can still watch. That's kind of nice, don't you think, that the person who decides what time the shows go out has thought about kids like me? The heating is on and the house is warm as toast. I lie on the floor with my sock-covered feet up on the sofa and my body in a line facing the television so I'm watching the screen upside down. I'm not allowed to do this when mum's home, but it's the best way to watch. I just have to listen out for her car so she doesn't peek through the window before she knocks and catches me.

The trick is to keep an eye on the time. She leaves her office at seven and gets back about ten past. As long as I'm sitting up nicely by then it should all be good.

Seven o'clock comes and I sit up. Any minute now she'll be back.

Ten past…

7.30. Still no sign of her. I keep going to the window and looking. Nothing.

It's 7.45. Still nothing.

Maybe she's left me and gone. Maybe she's finally had enough. But that can't be right, I know I didn't hit any cracks, I've been so, so careful.

Finally I hear her car pull into the drive. My heart's pounding so much I can feel it in my neck and hear it in my ears. I run to the door and stand behind it. I'm not allowed to open it until she knocks because it will let the cold in. I can't stand still. I'm frightened and excited at the thought of seeing her. I feel sick. I don't know whether to smile or not and realise that I am, so I leave it there.

On the other side of the door I can hear talking. Mum and someone else. A man. The man who was here the other morning?

Fast as I can I bound upstairs, making it to the top just in time before the front door opens. The landing light is off so I know they can't see me. I look around the banister, see them come in, kick off their shoes. She's got a red skirt on with a cream blouse and a jazzy silk scarf around her neck. She looks as beautiful as an air stewardess.

'Simon?' she calls. There's no tone to the word, no good, no bad. It's simply a name spoken aloud.

I don't answer, hoping she'll call again but He distracts her by reaching over and trying to kiss her.

She takes a step back, pushing him off. With venom in her voice says, 'don't you dare touch me in front of my son!'

'He's not here.'

'Yes he is,' she says. She knows. She always knows.

He waves an arm, but takes the hint anyway, shrugs off his jacket and slings it on the bottom banister before walking ahead of her into the kitchen.

'Simon, are you upstairs?'

With Him out of the picture I run down.

'Don't run!' she screams, and I stop altogether.

'What were you doing up there?' she says.

'Nothing.'

'Yes you were.'

'No I wasn't mum, honest.'

She looks at me for the longest second. I'm five steps from the bottom and feel like I'm on a stage with a million people staring at me.

'I don't believe you. What were you doing up there?'

'Mum I wasn't doing anything, I promise.'

'If I find out you're lying…'

'I'm not.'

She nods, turns and follows Him into the kitchen. I moved slowly to the bottom step but don't go any further. I can hear them opening wine and the glug of the liquid as they fill glasses. They're talking, but there's no intimacy in the conversation. It's just office-related stuff, and by listening carefully I work out that they work for competing companies and that if either of their bosses knew about the friendship they'd both be sacked. It's the only subject they don't laugh about.

Dinner is a take-away that He has to go and collect.

While He's gone, Mum says, 'How was it at your dad's?'

'Okay.'

'What did you talk about?'

Shrugging, I say, 'I don't know.' I don't want to be so monosyllabic, but I'm frightened to say much more in case I say something that upsets her.

After dinner I make an excuse and go to bed. I try and analyse how the evening's gone, but there's not much to work with. Truth is, I don't know if mum and I are okay or not. It's like we've been ghosts to each other tonight.

In bed I feel like there's a lot I want to think about, but I can't stay awake for even one of them and drift off as soon as my head hits the pillow.

It feels like seconds, but might have been minutes or even hours when I wake with a ping. At first I wonder where I am, but with that established, look towards the clock. As my eyes focus on the green digital numbers that show it's almost three in the morning, I hear someone scream. It's long, and loud, and full of terror. And it belongs to my mum.

Chapter 11

I sit up. There's the scream again, this time longer and louder. In movies a woman's scream is pitch perfect. In real life it's uglier, more… grimy.

I don't know what to do. I don't know why she's screaming. It could be nothing, and then I'd get in trouble for being up. But it's not nothing.

There's a thud, kind of similar to the sound my school holdall makes when I chuck it down on the hallway carpet. Then talking, but not talking. I can hear her voice, but not the individual words she's saying. Just the tune, kind of singsongy, tra-la-la-la-la, as though she is nonsense rhyming. Another thud. More words, louder, but fuzzy. Just on the edge of intelligible. Then clear as a bell, 'No! No, don't hit me!'

Tears run down my face. I don't know what to do. I get up then sit back down. Brush my hand over my hair. My heart's beating and I can't stop crying. Quickly I change out of my pyjamas and into my school uniform, which oddly makes me feel more prepared. Socks, tie, shirt buttoned up, tucked in, the lot. Then I steal a look outside my bedroom door.

The landing's dark. There are three other doors, two into bedrooms, one to the bathroom. Under mum's bedroom door I can see her light's on. Slowly, I open my door wider.

While not a nightly feature, this isn't uncommon. She seems to end up fighting with all her boyfriends. I lie awake in bed and listen, crying and praying with all my might for God to make it stop, but if he's up there, and he's heard me, he doesn't do anything about it. The fights come in waves, and after a few nights you kind of get used to it. Boyfriends come, the fights start, then they split up and all goes quiet for a while.

When I was younger I really believed that praying had the power to protect my mum, and that by doing so I was doing something positive. God wouldn't stand by, not once he heard me and realised what was going on. All I had to do was beg him hard enough. So I begged, I begged with every fibre of my being. It's only after a while that you realise praying makes absolutely no difference at all. Which is why this time I didn't bother, and got up instead.

'Go on, go on!' mum's voice, strong and commanding and much clearer now. Then singing, 'You can't do it, you can't hit me.' Scream. '*No!*'

Thud.

Crying. Mum's crying.

For the first time I hear His voice, 'It's your fault. This is all your fault. You made me do this. You've got nobody else to blame but yourself.' He's puffing, out of breath.

Before I have even a moment to process the words, she's saying, 'You're no man! Look at you! You want to hit me, then fucking hit me. Go on! Hit me!' Then that horrible singsong voice that now I'm nearer doesn't even sound like her, 'Cos you can't do it, you can't hit me.' Again, scream. Again, '*No!*'

Thud.

I'm on the landing. Tears wash down my face, but the worst thing is I can't breathe. Every time I try and take in some air it catches. I'm at her door. I can hear breathing on the other side, and crying. I think they're both crying.

I push her door. As it opens I see them. She's scrunched up on the floor and He's standing up, standing over her, his back to me. Neither of them have clothes on. I can see his strong wide back as he's bending forwards, his hands formed into fists. For her part she's not looking away, not trying to hide, but looking up at Him and actually pointing a finger at her own face, saying, 'Go on! Go on! You think you're such a man, do it. DO IT!'

Suddenly he smashes a fist straight into her face. I see her head rock back, and that noise, that horrible, horrible sickening noise. She's crying, she's really crying, and screaming over and over again, 'No, no, please don't hit me. Oh God, please don't hit me.' He doesn't move, doesn't shift. He's breathing heavily, still standing over her.

'Mum? Are you alright?'

As soon as they hear me He turns and she scuttles, scrunching herself up further into a ball. Their faces look like they're shocked at being caught. Neither of them speak.

'Are you hurt, mum?'

She still doesn't say anything. He's now standing facing me. His legs wide apart, hands on hips, His straggly blond hair hanging limp. His naked body makes him look like a giant. There is no body hair, which just seems to enhance his muscles, and his skin is gleaming with sweat. In that instant I realise how far from being an adult I am. Compared with him I'm so puny and young and pathetic. I look into his eyes and they're filled with so much hate I take a step back. And that's when it happens. I blow-off. Just a little one. The fear, the terror, churns my tummy and sends out a pop.

It's as though the spell has broken. He looks down, and when he looks back up his eyes no longer have hate in them. They have laughter. He's laughing. They're both laughing.

I can see blood on her face, and as he moves his hand to cover his bits, I can see blood on his knuckles. Neither of them say anything, they just laugh. So I do the only thing I can, I start laughing too. And suddenly we're all in bits. That real, deep, hysterical I-can't-stop-laughing that takes over your whole body.

Finally, when she's calmed down enough to speak, mum says, 'Go to bed Simon, it's fine now. I'll speak to you in the morning.'

And I do. I go back to my room, get undressed, get into bed and close my eyes. But sleep doesn't come. I think…

Is she hurt?

Should I call her an ambulance?

I hate Him.

Why did He say it was all her fault?

Why was she sing-songing for Him to hit her?

I hate Him, and I hate me. I farted. How could I have done that? The shame.

The shame. The shame. The shame.

I wish I was older. If I was older I'd kill him. I wish I was older, I wish I was older.

At some point I must have slept. I don't remember it, but I must have done.

In the morning, He was gone.

I go down stairs and she's putting on her makeup. We share coffee and marmite on toast, and I watch her dab double spots of foundation on her blotchy face before smoothing it over.

Then she says, 'We need to talk about last night.'

Chapter 12

Normal people wake to the sound of the radio, or a gentle little tune from the alarm app on their mobile. Few people, and by few I mean me, wake because the Great Dane who's asleep on their bed has decided to dream he's running the Olympic 400m final, and doing rather well.

There are paws flying everywhere. It's puppy carnage on the bed.

'Solomon, please!' I yell, one of his legs whizzing millimetres above my face. 'Solly, enough!'

It's the second shout that wakes him. Reigning in his wayward feet until they're once more tucked into him, he opens one eye, looks sleepily up at me, and wags his tail.

'Yeah, morning to you too.'

It's still dark outside and the place is silent. Debbie, it seems, has missed his nocturnal running race and dreamt her own dreams straight through it. I pat his head and tell him, 'Good effort.' Then I get up.

I could wake Ziggy, and know I'd enjoy doing so, but he's proper grumpy in the mornings and I'm not sure I'm up to dealing with that. Instead I duck out the front door and into the cold morning.

You'd be surprised what a tonic zero-degree air is to one's just woken-up face. My brain pings from nought to absolute clarity before the door even clicks shut behind me. Forget meeting mother ayahuasca for revelations into your psyche, warm bed to bitter cold outside will do that no trouble at all.

My revelations? Yesterday was one long, confusing day.

I don't need light to find my way over to the barn. The grass is crisp and fresh underfoot and makes a satisfying noise as I negotiate the path in the dark. Even in the pre-sun you can't miss the barn. Inside, the little lamb greets me with a *bbaaarrrr*, and his mum gives me one I'm-a-right-little-madam stamp of the foot.

In a soft, sing-song voice, I say, 'you're a lamb-er, nothing but a lamb-er.' It's not the words, it's the tune that's stuck in my head. At first I can't place it, then suddenly it hits me. It's her.

'You can't do it, you can't hit me.'

The words come and almost knock me off my feet, they're so harsh. And they're not alone. There are images too. Images of my mum scrunched up naked on the floor while her boyfriend stands over her. But she's not hiding, she's taunting Him. The image is so vivid that for a second I'm not sure what is remembered and what is happening right now. Am I in the bedroom with mum and Him and imagining I'm in a farmer's barn, or is it the other way around?

'Baaaarrrrrrrr!'

No, I'm definitely in a barn.

I run my hand over my head as the images seep away. It's all very weird.

Moving over towards the ewe I force myself to relax. I have a job to do and if I'm stressed and tense she will pick up on it.

'Come on you,' I tell her, gently coercing her body closer to the wall until she is flat up against it. I'm not sure if the lamb is too weak to stand unaided or he hasn't got the hang of food time yet, but either way he's not making much effort to do his part of the mealtime deal. Lifting him up, I aim his mouth and plug him in.

I can feel my head spinning and it would be so easy for it to go off in a million different directions right now, but the reality is I have to take care of the animals. For good or ill, that's my role in this crazy life, and it's not something you can do with only half focus.

This little farm has been part of our lives for almost twenty years, having moved away from South East London and relocated here to Exmoor. I'd love to say it was a cleverly executed plan to escape a world in which I never really felt I fitted, and in a way it was, but the catalyst was booze. Isn't it always. I was horrendously drunk in a bar on New Year's Eve when Debbie asked me if I'd be up for changing our lives, leaving our friends, family, our home, our careers, everything we knew, understood and had worked for and starting again. I was pissed, and did what pissed people do and slurred, 'sure!'

I was 32 at the time: a pup! a kid! a piglet! and the following morning also very hung-over. But we did, we went for it. It seemed like an adventure.

Oh, was it ever an adventure. Overnight I went from being an estate agent to a smallholder, from on-grid to off-grid, from weekly shopping trips to self-sufficiency, I fell in love with pigs (yeah, I do know how that sounds), learnt how to milk a goat, steer clear of killer geese, pluck turkeys for Christmas and discovered just how much I hate killing anything, and even though I'm a meat producer realised I'm never more than a breath away from turning vegan. Which means we have a lot of four-legged and two-winged hangers on, or to put that another way, my crazy mates. I guess that's the therapy bit of this place. When you have mob that include an agoraphobic pig, a cat with Tourette's, a one-eyed collie dog who thinks he's a duck, Senorita micro-pig and her sex addiction, a goat who will only eat stolen food and a horse who acts like a Kray twin, it's hard to feel anything other than completely normal and well adjusted.

Behind me the barn door smashes open.

We all, me, the sheep and the lamb jump. I whizz around to be confronted with Ziggy, or more precisely, Early Morning Ziggy – there is a difference.

'What fucking time do you call this?' he demanded. He was only just dressed with not all his clothes meeting, and those that did didn't necessarily meet the same garment. His boots were unlaced, and his hair looked like a bad impression of Albert Einstein.

Plugging the lamb back in I said, 'Have you really come out here to ask me the time?'

Pause. 'What?'

'It's about 6.30.'

'Yeah, my point exactly, what fucking time do you call that? Do you not do coffee around here? Would it be too much to ask for a bagel, a measly bagel and a slither of smoked salmon? Jesus, I feel like Oliver Fucking Twist.'

Stumbling in he left the door open, dragged his feet noisily on the ground and slumped against the wall like a drunk horse. He's like that, full of drama and very sweary first thing. Over his shoulder, through the open door, I noticed it was getting light.

'Why would you do this to yourself, this… morning? Have you any idea how bad it is for you? There've been studies, you know. Very negative studies.'

Amazingly, the lamb was ignoring him, for which I give him full credit.

'No there haven't,' I said.

Yawning he said, 'You're probably right. But there should be. They should use me as a lab rat.' Then, with all the observational skills of a prairie cat, pointed at the lamb and said, 'I see he's still alive then.'

On cue the lamb pulled his head away from Mum's teat and gave a full body shake.

'Sheep's milk, liquid energy,' I said, releasing the ewe, who seemed to be getting in the swing of motherhood.

'Tempting to take a turn, but I think I'll pass,' he said, as if my comment had been an offer.

The lamb waddled off to retake his spot in the straw and the ewe slumped down where she was, understandably nervous Ziggy might change his mind. I dug out some sheep nuts and some hay and set out a little breakfast for her.

'You didn't need to come out, you know, I'm quite capable of doing this on my own.'

He nodded, shrugged himself off the wall so he was using his own strength to hold himself upright, and said, 'But you're glad I did. Introspection can only get you so far. Sooner or later you're going to want a partner to share it with.'

'*You?*'

'I'm right though.'

'Suppose.'

'When I heard the door close and realised you'd gone out,' he continued, 'I decided it was the perfect time for me to catch up with you and talk about the phone call with my dad. You see, I've had some more thoughts…'

'Really?'

'Really. And we can talk about you, but you're not as open a book as me, so there's always less to discuss and it's less fun.'

'That makes me feel good.'

'Where are you going?'

I'd walked out of the barn and was strolling down towards the pigs. 'Morning rounds,' I shouted over my shoulder. 'Make sure you close the barn door behind you or the lamb will get out.'

I heard closing and scurrying noises behind me, then heavy panting as he struggled to catch up. 'Slow down, I haven't even had a cigarette yet and my lungs won't work properly until I do. WILL YOU PLEASE SLOW DOWN!'

It was well on the way to full daylight now, and there was that gorgeous early spring morning smell in the air: fresh and clean, a little bit herby and a little bit green. I wasn't the only one to notice it either. Robins, dunnocks, blackbirds and song thrushes chorused all around me. In the distance I could hear a chainsaw, or it might have been a cow closer up, it's very difficult to tell.

Then everything shattered as Ziggy caught up, and, having lit his ciggy, blew the smoke into my face. 'Don't get the hump with me,' he said.

I hadn't. I used to think he was high maintenance and hard work, but increasingly began wondering if that wasn't me. 'I haven't,' I told him, adding, 'I thought you were giving the cigarettes up.'

He took a long drag, held it in for way longer than necessary before slowly blowing it out.

'You ever smoked?' he asked.

'Of course. When I was young.'

'And you loved it, right? But you gave up because it was bad for you, which I accept it is. But it's my only vice.'

Coughing, I said, '*What?*'

Through a grin, he said, 'Okay, one of the main ones. But vices are there for a reason, and the reason is, *they're so nice!* Besides, everyone agrees you should have a little of what you fancy, and I consider myself fortunate in that I fancy most things, and indulge whenever, and wherever I can – Oscar Wilde said that, and if it wasn't him it should have been. Where are we going, by the way?'

'Pigs.'

'Oh goody.'

'They need breakfast.'

'So do I, old chap. Guess I'll have to make do with a smoke. Listen, I slept okay last night, first time in… I can't remember. No night shudders. No thinking about my dad.'

I held a gate open for him. On the other side was the feed store for the pigs, which is more secure than some bank vaults.

'That's good,' I said, beginning the arduous task of unlocking the door.

Watching me avidly he said, 'Who, exactly, do you think is going to come and steal your pig food?'

'The pigs, obviously.'

He did the simultaneous down mouth, tip of the head, tiny nod people do that accompanies the words, 'Fair enough.' You see, pigs are Houdinis at getting out of their pens, into anywhere that contains food, and scoffing the lot. I can't count the times I've come down to find one of them fast asleep and groaning in the middle of ten open bags of dinner, most of which has been eaten in one long but immensely happy sitting, leaving only the scrapings for the others. So I stopped it by upping the security. Halfway down the line of knots, chains, padlocks, twisty wooden bars that turn the opposite way to how you'd think and a cleverly positioned rock, I said, 'Your dad?'

'Oh yeah! Hardly thought of him at all last night. Not sure if it was talking about it or being down here that did it. It's very, um, different down here.'

I laughed.

'It is,' he insisted. 'If you've got a problem, this is the place to come and work it out.'

Filling a bucket with pig nuts and turning to leave, I said, 'Unless you already live here. Then it's just home.'

'You haven't told me how your night went. Did you get the night shudders over your mum?'

He followed me out. 'No, not really. It's more reliving the memory of when I was young, but *really* vividly, like I'm there. There was even a moment when I wasn't sure if I was dreaming, awake, asleep, I've no idea.'

'*Inception*, never sure whose dream you're in. It's a thing.'

It was a short trek to Senorita's pen, the first pig on the breakfast list. Part micro-pig, though only a tiny part because she grew into the size of a small vehicle, Senorita is complicated, being both friendly and loving, whilst at the same time aggressive and hateful.

'Good morning my baby girl,' I called.

Leaning over her fence I'm welcomed with an *oof, oof, oof,* which is porcine for 'Where the heck have you been and where's my blinkin' breakfast!' I just avoid her gnashers with a swift tip of the bucket, as she falls into the pile of food open-mouth-first.

'I see a lot of her mother in her,' Ziggy said from behind me. Quite a long way behind me. He's such a coward, and she's so misunderstood.

Not to be left out of the deal, nine one-week-old piglets trot out Indian-file to join their mum. When they get to her they just kind of spill on the ground all around her.

'Oh that's so cute, look at the piglets,' Ziggy gushes. But I'm not. I'm watching mum, because it suddenly dawns on me just how much communication is going on. Sure, I'm always having two-way conversations with my animals, but if I'm honest, I've never looked much at how they chat between themselves. I've never tried to understand how the mums are with their babies.

Of course, I recognise this as the blue car syndrome: you buy a blue car and all you see are blue cars, or, God forbid, someone you love is diagnosed with cancer and suddenly every TV show, every book or social media update you read is about the big C. I get it. The world is a mirror to your thoughts. Either that, or we all have the same thoughts, only it takes something to happen before you step out of your bubble and recognise it. Either way, it's hard not to feel mocked. But if the universe is mocking me, maybe this time I can use it.

During the first week of a piglet's life you can't give them very much straw on account of the fact that they'll get themselves tangled up in it, and if that happens there is a very real danger that a clumsy mum will come along and unwittingly tread on them or lie on them, and Senorita does have a bit of previous on that score. But once they're a few days old and bigger and stronger, mum becomes more aware of them. So I was safe to ask Ziggy to go and get me as big an armful of straw as he could carry. And with that I was alone. Just me, Senorita and her nine babies.

I watched the babies – tentative at first but growing in confidence, moving around under her fat belly and around her eating chops – and thought, they're brave little things, I wouldn't want to risk getting between her and her food even if I was her child. But they zipped back and forth at faster and faster speeds until it was woohooooooo, come on everybody, we can do this at a gazillion miles an hour!

Although it's tough to concentrate on anything other than the tiny zip-zip streaks of piglet dashing about, it's mum I really want to watch.

At first Senorita paid no mind to the antics going on around her and steadfastly worked her breakfast. But as the mound of nuts diminished, she began paying more attention. It's hard to ascertain if her awareness was driven by an instinctual interest and worry over the welfare of the little porky racers, or, knowing Senorita, more of a concern that as the food was running down she needed to have a better sense of what was happening around her in case the kids pinched any. Which they started doing. By the look of it I think they were mimicking mum, and she was also making a noise that I guessed was, 'Come and eat.' It wasn't long before they'd stopped charging around and were all gathered to eat.

It was comical to watch the tiny piglets trying to eat the great big nuts. They'd get one in their teeth and it would look like a big cigar.

Senorita for her part would allow them one or two bites before shooing them away by moving over and eating from their spot, which isn't easy when there's nine of them.

I remember my mum would always have one mouthful of whatever I had. Every time, without fail, whether it was a sandwich or a dinner, and even if she had exactly the same on her plate, she would get up, come over, and take a bite of mine.

Is Senorita doing the same thing?

If so, what is that, dominance? I'm boss and don't you forget it, kind of thing? Or is it something else, something more to do with teaching them to share nicely? I guess it could be either.

Then there's the eye contact. I tried to work out what she was looking at, and why. For example, would Senorita look at one of her babies and feel actual, real, what we recognise as, love? With so many, would she love some more than others? Is there a favourite? Would there be some she loves but doesn't like, and some she likes but doesn't love?

I tried to keep track of which one she was looking at, see if she favoured any, but it was impossible to tell.

Instead I switched to body language, and started taking note of how she reacted physically to each piglet. At a week old it's pretty easy to tell the little ones apart, and as each approached I tried to work out if she was tensing or softening, but if there was a difference it was too slight to spot.

Then I wondered if I wasn't going too deep, too specific? Should I be looking at them more broadly, getting more of an overview? Maybe take a step back.

Clearly she cared for her babies or she would have killed them by now, as some sows are known to do. We call these – and please, do try and keep up – we call these 'bad mothers'.

She was talking to the piglets by making noises and they were responding. She was even, in her way, sharing dinner. Surely in any language that spelled love. Okay, maybe it's the most basic form of love, but it's still love. Isn't it?

A straw bale on legs waddled up. When it reached the pen by bumping into it, it said, 'Where do you want this?'

But I suppose the biggest test of a mother's love towards her baby is how she reacts when threatened. Any mother who protects her child must love it.

'You'll have to climb in and spread it out,' I said.

In many ways it doesn't matter if it's real or perceived – if she feels her babies are in danger and she reacts to eliminate that threat and save them, that's got love written all over it like a stick of seaside rock.

'Will she be alright if I go in?'

Adjusting myself so I was a little more comfortable leaning against the side of the pen, I said, 'Absolutely.'

'So I just go in? Climb over, and kick this around? And she won't mind?'

Come on, it's only Ziggy. And besides, if you can't sacrifice the odd friend in the name of research and study, what can you do?

'Yeah.'

And he did.

Chapter 13

Putting down her own corner of toast Mum looked up at me, wagged a finger and said, 'Toast.'

Funny, maybe all that had happened over the past few days had had an effect on me, because rather than hand it over as I'd always done, I said, 'Why?'

'Now!'

But I was only so brave. So I moved over and offered her my toast from which she took a single bite. Around the mouthful she said, 'Because I'm mum.'

I sat back and she continued doing her makeup. It was taking much longer, and she was using loads more than normal, but the effect was pretty good. One eye was a little more shut than the other, and was bloodshot, but you couldn't see any of the bruises where His punches had landed.

'Were you cut?' I asked. 'There was blood last night.'

'That was my lip, but it was on the inside so that's okay.'

'Did it hurt?'

'Yes, but I wasn't going to let him know that.'

'Why not? If he knew he was hurting you wouldn't he have stopped?'

She didn't answer straightaway. Instead, she worked a particularly tricky bit of eye shadow. When she did answer she said, 'If he knew he was hurting me he would have done it more. That's how they work. I'm not strong enough to fight, so I have to do it other ways.'

'He said it was your fault. Was it?'

'When did he say that?'

'Last night. I heard him when I was standing outside your door.'

Looking away from the mirror towards me she held my eye for the longest minute before saying, 'No it wasn't my fault.' Her voice was sharp without a single warm edge. 'Go and get ready for school. Now!'

Putting down the toast I said, 'Mum I'm sorry. I didn't mean…'

'Why would you think it was my fault?' She was no longer hunched over the mirror but twisted fully towards me, shoulders back, dressing gown open to reveal her baby blue and white striped PJs. But take away the clothes and she didn't look that dissimilar to the way she had last night. All that was missing was Him standing over her, fists clenched, deciding when to smash her in the face. She was nodding now, her face all sneery, 'You would think it was my fault, wouldn't you.'

'But I don't, mum. Honest I don't.'

'Then why did you say it?'

I knew my tears annoyed her, but the sobs that sometimes accompany them went further and made her angry, so I concentrated as hard as I possibly could to keep my breathing even. When I felt I could trust myself, I said, 'I didn't, I promise I didn't.'

'Yes you did, and stop crying, you're not a baby. And stop being so bloody sensitive!'

Control, control, control, deep breaths. 'I'm sorry.'

She was back looking in the mirror. 'What for? What are you sorry for?'

'Me.'

She tutted. 'Stop being so dramatic.'

I sat as still as I could, didn't stare at her, but didn't look away either. The tears had stopped and I was pleased I hadn't sobbed. In the background the radio played quietly and through the French windows I could see both our cats playing in the garden. The weather looked nice out there, which would be handy for the walk to the train station.

After a while mum said, 'It's what men do.'

I guessed she meant last night, but this was not a time to ask questions.

'He blamed me because it made him feel better. But it wasn't my fault. Do you understand?'

I thought, no not really, but emphatically said, 'Oh yes!'

'Good. Men are bastards. Every last one of them, including you.' With her finger she poked me hard in the chest. 'I don't need them, I don't need anyone.'

'So you're not going to see him ever again?'

'No I'm not!'

She would. She always did. I said, 'I didn't like it last night.'

She didn't say anything to that.

'Mum, why didn't you tell him to stop? He might have stopped if you'd asked him too?'

Turning demonic she yelled, *Don't you dare question me! Don't you dare! You don't know what you're talking about, you have no idea what it's like to be a woman!*

Although I've never actually got up and gone in to her room before, I've listened to her fights a hundred times, lying in bed, crying into a pillow so I wouldn't make a noise and willing with all my heart for her to ask them to stop. Just ask them to stop. That's all. But instead all I ever heard was her yelling at them to carry on and hit her if they thought they were man enough.

She was crying herself now. I thought, I don't care if you hate me, I don't care if you never want to speak to me for the rest of my life and you want me dead, I don't care, if it just means that next time you ask them to stop. God, if you're listening, that's my swap, I'll give everything up if next time you make her ask them to stop.

Suddenly she got up, the tears gone, and stood over me. I had one little bit of toast left and carefully put it back on the plate, but otherwise remained where I was, cross-legged on the floor.

She started messing with my hair, pushing me this way then that, slapping the back of my head. 'Tell me to stop,' she said. 'Go on, tell me to stop.'

'Please stop mum.'

'No.'

The slaps were getting harder, moving from playful to spiteful, vicious even.

'Mum you're hurting me, please stop.'

'Or what? What will you do?'

'Mum this isn't fair.'

'Yes it is. I'm mum, I can do what I like.' The blows that followed weren't hard, they were just annoying. I tried to shield my head with my arms but with my eyes closed they were useless. Still the slaps, taps and pokes rained down.

In a much stronger voice that I hardly recognised, I said, 'Mum please stop.'

'No.' And she didn't.

Frustration, hurt, confusion, fear and anger came like a wave of heat up my chest, through my neck and burst like an atom bomb in my head. In that instant I put down my arms and looked up at her with every ounce of hatred I had inside me. The feeling was powerful, really powerful. Recognising the shift, she stopped hitting me. 'Now do you understand?' she said.

Through gritted teeth I said, 'I hate you.'

'Good. But do you understand? Even when there's nothing you can do, even when you're not strong enough to fight back, you can still take their power away. That's what I was doing. It's a game. Yes?'

Yelling at the top of my voice, *'I hate you!'* I ran upstairs.

Chapter 14

'Arseforfuckssakeofshitshitshit,' cursed Ziggy, to which I thought, oh how interesting, it seems Senorita does love her babies after all.

'She's going to kill me!' Ziggy yelled from inside the pig pen.

'It seems so.'

'*What!?*'

She wasn't, but he didn't know that. She was just warning him by pinning him up against the wall and snarling at him. She was clearly protective over the piglets, but she wasn't a nasty pig and would have to be provoked an awful lot more than someone simply refreshing her bed before she'd attack.

There were lots of ways to defuse the situation, one of which was for him to simply walk away. But I had another idea. 'She's stronger than you and she's miffed,' I said. 'If you ask her to stop it's only going to make her madder. The only thing you can do is try and take her power away. Try taunting her, show her you don't care.'

'*But I do care.*'

'Yeah, but she doesn't know that.'

Every day's a school day.

'Are you serious?'

'Never been more so.'

'And that will make her go away?'

'Almost certainly.'

'Okay.' Bending down he pointed a stiff finger at her face and said, 'You don't scare me. You're an overweight, pig-breathed bacon-making machine and you're about as scary as a sumo wrestler in a tutu, and if I – Oh Jesus, she's attacking!'

Wowzers, this time she really was!

'Turn your back and walk away! Quickly!'

The instant he turned she quit and calmed down.

'What the hell was that all about?' Ziggy stammered once he'd climbed out. 'She's dangerous. She was going to kill me.'

'I know. Wasn't it fascinating?'

'Fascinating?'

'She's never done that before. It was when you started taunting her; now obviously she doesn't understand what you were saying, she only picks up on the tone and the volume and the body language. You crouching down and pointing in her face, that could be seen as aggressive. Next time…'

'Next time?'

Putting my hand on his shoulder, I said, 'You need to calm down.'

Feeling safe again, Senorita had gone into her house where she'd stationed her piglets. She brought them all out and flopped down on one side so they could feed. Her head was facing me, her eyes caught in mine. Pigs have very kind, soft, expressive eyes, and I swear hers were laughing – I wouldn't put it past her to have played to the crowd.

I smiled at her and called her a bitch, at which she looked extremely pleased with herself.

Spotting our moment, Ziggy said, 'Wait a second, are you two doing a number on me? Of course! You sods,' he was laughing with his hand on top of his head, spinning in circles. 'I should have guessed! Wow, it felt so real – how did you teach her to do that?'

'She's one of a kind.' She's that alright. Shame, for a moment there I really thought I was onto something. But I guess using your best friend who knows you inside out in an experiment is always going to be compromised, and on top of that, I'd also used Ziggy. In anyone's book that's a double negative.

'I'll be back at dinner,' I called to Senorita, and walked away.

The morning was now fully underway with the sun reaching the top of the trees. Being the bottom of a valley there was little wind. Beside me Ziggy said, 'You're very distracted, is it your mum?'

Nodding I told him it was, adding, 'Sorry.'

Batting the apology away with the back of his hand, he said, 'Don't be. I've been so wrapped up in myself lately…'

'Lately?' I mocked.

He laughed. 'Well, it might make a refreshing change to hear how rubbish you're feeling for once.'

While we fed the rest of the pigs I told him about the memory of mum getting beaten up by her boyfriend, and about her little role-play session the morning after.

He went quiet for a few beats before saying, 'You weren't doing a number on me with Senorita, were you?'

'No,' I admitted, 'but I think she was. She's really smart and she's got a wicked sense of humour. I think she was playing to the crowd.'

'I'm a bit narked you'd sacrifice me to prove or disprove a theory – which is it by the way?'

I shrugged.

'Well, I am. That was properly frightening. I might have to go into therapy just so I can be in the same room as a sausage sandwich.'

He's such a dramatist. 'You were never in any danger,' I told him, and he wasn't. Not, you know, not really. 'She's a sweetie.

I just wanted to see what would happen if you tried to take her power away.'

Okay, so it hadn't worked, and maybe it was flawed from the outset. Too contrived. To use animals you really have to do it on their terms. Observe them expressing their natural behaviour preferably without introducing a galumphing Ziggy into the equation for any worthwhile results. After all, if you wanted to get inside the head of someone and really understand them, you wouldn't monitor them at work, you'd watch them at home. It's *The Truman Show*, and to an extent *Big Brother* and *I'm a Celebrity Get me Out of Here!* Clearly we're not watching any of those programmes for the individuals, we're watching to see how they interact and how they negotiate all the different relationships and tensions around them. What I'm doing with my animals is no different. It's just a little more agricultural.

I felt that if I could understand the relationship I had with my mum, I'd understand everything, because all my other relationships span out from there: me and Debbie, my animals, friends and family, working relationships, online relationships, the whole shebang. Even Ziggy. But it all begins with mum. Crack that one and it feels like I'll understand the lot.

'Penny for them?' Ziggy said. Don't you find it annoying when someone asks you that because it leaves you no wiggle room? If they say, what are you thinking, it's perfectly acceptable to answer, 'Oh, nothing,' or to brush them off, but offering a penny for your thoughts you feel obliged to give them. It must have something to do with turning a profit.

'I was just thinking that done the right way maybe the animals could help me figure some of it out. About my mum and me.'

He did a sideways head wobble the way people do when they're not sure. 'Maybe.'

'Are you still angry with me?'

We were nearly at the goats. I'd recently put a boy, Buster the Billy, in with the girls. They weren't too sure about him, especially when he tried to get sexy for them by urinating on his own beard by aiming the stream at his face, which is ten out of ten for direction, less for hygiene.

'Yes. A bit. My God, what's that smell?'

'That'd be Buster,' I said.

'Oh, my!'

'Mm. I know.'

He waved a hand in front of his face and said, 'oh, that's… he's not ill or anything, is he? He smells like he's decomposing.'

'No, he's a Billy goat. The smell is him trying to entice the girls.'

'In my opinion he's trying too hard. Whooo, the boy desperately needs a crash course in personal hygiene. He smells like a tramp who couldn't be bothered to find a toilet. Call me old fashioned, but doesn't that put the fairer sex off?'

'Yeah, that's what he's finding,' and he was. It'd been two weeks since I'd put them together and he hadn't even had a cuddle. But give him his due, the more they shunned him, the harder he tried. And that was the problem. I couldn't help feeling sorry for him.

In order to take Ziggy's mind off Billy the Whiffy, I said, 'So, tell me, where are you with your dad?' In conversations with Ziggy it's best to forget subtly.

He talked while I arranged the goat's feed. He said, 'Better. I think. Still confused, still want to down a case of Chablis to obliterate the memory of the phone call whenever I think of it, but at least I don't want to kill myself.' He held up a stop hand and insisted, 'Not that I ever would. It just felt appropriate to give the thought a hat-tip, you know?'

No, I don't know. All my killing myself thoughts showed up in neat little packages with all the details woven in, such as when, where and how, and would be front and centre of my mind. It never occurred to me that you could simply observe the thought and let it go like someone trying to meditate. I think about killing myself every day. Every day. It's weirdly comforting. But I don't act on it because of Debbie and the animals.

'Anyway,' he continued, 'I guess I feel more comfortable with what I did, you know, telling him about my piles. Don't get me wrong, I still feel bad, but I'm getting comfortable with it.'

'That's good,' I said.

He didn't miss a beat. 'I know. Time gives one perspective and whilst I'll always regret what I said, I just panicked, and you can't condemn someone for panicking, can you? Heat of the moment and all that. He would understand.'

'Do you still believe he heard you?'

This time he did miss a beat, lots of them. We walked the entire length of a field before he said, 'Yes. I know he did. And I know that because he came and spoke to me.'

Chapter 15

I didn't kiss Mum goodbye, didn't tell her I was leaving, just slammed the front door behind me and headed off to school.

Anger in an 11-year-old is white hot, and the sense of injustice hotter, whatever colour that may be; silver possibly. I marched up to the train station, onto the platform and slammed my school bag on the ground in front of an empty seat, but didn't sit. I was too stirred up for that.

I hated her for hurting me. I hated her for hitting me. I hated her for teasing me. I hated her for everything. The hate was all-engulfing, and didn't just point outwards. It went in. All the emotions I felt for her started twisting back on myself, because that is hate's *modus operandi*.

I was late to class and didn't care. When the spelling test came up I didn't even make an attempt. When it came time to swap papers with the person next to me, mine didn't even have numbers down the side. It was just blank.

When school finished I smoked half a cigarette and wished with all my heart Mum would smell it on me. The instant I got home I went upstairs, tore off my trousers and underpants with such a frenzy I almost ripped them, sat on the edge of the bed and masturbated with such anger and hatred I thought I might actually die. But try as I might I couldn't get relief, and stopped when the tears fell from my face and snot bubbled from my nose. Instead I watched TV until Mum came home.

The closest word to describe how I felt was frazzled, like all the wires inside me that transported thoughts and feelings between my heart and my head had got tangled up and frayed, and were now short-circuiting so nothing seemed linear anymore. But as bad as I felt, I knew I had to somehow get mum back on my side, because all said and done, she was my mum and without her I'd have no one who wanted me.

I heard the car. Quick as a flash I ran to the front door. I had it all planned, how I'd throw open the door just as she reached it and welcome her in like an adult, not a skulking child peering down through the upstairs banisters. No, an adult, happy to see his mother. I'd apologise of course, say how sorry I was for my rude behaviour this morning while I helped her unpack any shopping she might have and start dinner, which we'd make together. I'd even make her laugh with a story or two from school.

Footsteps. She was getting close. I put a smile on my face, and at the optimum moment, opened the door wide.

My smile crumpled like a crisp packet in a fire. She wasn't alone. He was with her.

Mum didn't even look at me as they bustled in, just said my name as she moved past. 'Simon.'

'Mum,' I mumbled back, though what I wanted to say was, 'What the hell are you doing? He tried to kill you last night, and yet you invite him back?' I've never felt so small, or so scared. I thought of running out the door and running and running and running, but I wouldn't last five minutes, and besides, I didn't have my shoes on. So I banged it shut.

They were in the kitchen opening wine and sorting dinner. And talking. And laughing.

I went in the lounge and sat down. Why can't it just be us? Why does she need a man, and why does she need Him? I could feel my heart beating in my chest at a million miles an hour. He came in before she did and the million miles an hour doubled its pace. He sat down at the other end of the sofa and faced the television.

'Good day at school?' He asked.

I nodded.

'What do you say you and me have a kick about in the garden? When I was your age I had a trial for Man U. I could have been professional. Football meant everything to me, still does. We could do ten and in, you'll never beat me.' He was talking not like a man who had used my mother's face as a punching bag last night, but like a kindly uncle, and it made me sick.

In that instant I made a decision, and for an 11-year-old boy it was a biggie. In order to distance myself from this mother puncher, I would no longer like football. Yes, that's right, you heard me correctly. I'd turn my back on the game. I'd renounce West Ham United. Trevor Brooking, you mean nothing to me anymore. From this moment on I am no longer a Hammers fan; I am no longer a fan of any football at all. It was a petty victory, but it was all I had.

So I said, 'No thanks.'

'But I thought you liked football?'

'Not any more,' and that was that.

We sat in silence watching TV until Mum came in with plates of food that I ate as fast as I could. When it was done I said I was going to bed even though it was way before my bedtime. If pressed I'd tell them I had homework, which I probably did.

'Okay, night then,' they said. Then as I passed by I heard Mum say, 'Love you son.'

My feet shambled to a stop without me giving the command. I looked down. She wasn't looking at me, she was looking at Him; looking at Him and smiling, and he was smiling back at her. They looked happy. Regaining momentum, I made it out of the room and up the stairs. I didn't get undressed but slipped under the covers fully clothed. If it was going to kick off again tonight I wanted at least to be prepared. Outside I could hear a dog barking, could see the street lamps through the curtains. And I thought, she said she loved me! She said she loved me? But she doesn't, she's always told me she doesn't. So why did she say she did tonight? She's never said it before. I don't get it, *I don't get it!* Does she or doesn't she? I don't care either way, I just want to know. I hate her. And I love her. Is that how she feels about me too, she hates me but sometimes she loves me? I'm so confused. I'm so fucking confused.

I kicked the covers off. It's really hot going to bed with all your clothes on. I know all of the swearwords, even the really bad ones, and while I don't use them outside of my head they feel strong and powerful when I think them, the way Clarke Kent must feel when he thinks of his iron pecks. I fucking hate her, I fuck, fucking hate her.

She said she loves me. I rolled over onto my side so the tears wouldn't tickle my face and annoy me, and, exhausted, fell asleep.

I slept right the way round to morning. If there were any fights, I didn't hear them, and when I got up and went downstairs to find her in the usual spot doing her makeup there was no sign of any drama.

Reading my mind, she said, 'He didn't stay the night.'

I took a seat opposite her, sinking down onto crossed legs.

It was early in the making-up process and she was still on the foundation, which admittedly had been made trickier with the purple bruises now shining like ripe plumbs. 'He said he offered to play football with you but you said no,' she said.

'No, I don't like football anymore.'

'Yes you do. It's important that you do.'

'Why?'

'Don't argue with me.'

Chapter 15

I didn't say anything to that, but thought, if I did like football, wouldn't that make me like Him? Is that what you want? The answer to that was obvious, yes. She loved him, that much was clear. And she didn't love me because I'm not like Him. If I *was* more like Him, maybe she would. Maybe I should stand over her right now and start punching her in the face and she'd look up at me and say, 'Aw son, I do love you.'

'Why did you tell me you loved me?' I said in a whisper.

'When?'

'Last night. When I went up to bed.'

'They're just words,' she said dismissively. The purple bits on her face was proving difficult to hide, the powders and creams just weren't cutting it. 'Your other mother loves you,' she said.

Sitting up I said, 'My what? My other mother? I didn't know I had another mother.' The news was thrilling. My God, I had another mother, and she loved me!

'Yes. Remember I told you your aunt was going to take you, but then she didn't? Well, she's like your other mother. You have two mums, how does that make you feel?'

Elated, and scared. 'I don't know,' I said truthfully. I knew she liked me, she was always so kind when she came round, giving me time and attention and sitting with me and talking to me and listening when I spoke to her. Of course, it made sense now, she did it because she was my other mum. Oh wow!

'She asks after you all the time.'

'Really?'

She put her makeup down and looked at me. 'Stop crying, I've told you before, stop being so sensitive.'

I tried to stop crying, but I couldn't help it. I *hate* the way I cry, I hate it! I know it winds mum up and I know it makes me a girl. It's wrong, I know that, but I can't stop it. It's not in my control.

'I said stop crying, *now*!' she said, her voice stern.

I tensed all my body, from my teeth to my toes. That did it.

She nodded and continued. 'She can't take you, but she is your other mother and she does love you. Do you understand?'

I didn't understand, but that hardly mattered.

'I'll make you some toast,' she said, and got up. 'And a milky coffee.'

She was smiling at me, and as she walked past she touched her hand on the top of my head where it burned warm, so much that when she moved it I could still feel it exactly, even down to the fingers.

For the rest of that week mum was amazing. She was home on time every night, and she was alone; no scuzzy boyfriend in tow. She cooked shepherd's pie and sausage casserole and we watched TV at night and listened to the radio each morning. It was bliss. At the weekend my aunt and uncle came over and my two mums took me to Sunday lunch, and when they'd gone, I was allowed to sit up and watch television until really late. It was the best day ever.

It was arranged that after school on Monday I'd go to my dad's. He picked me up in his red sports car.

'Hello son,' he said warmly as I tossed my bag in the back and climbed in. Unusually we went straight home to his place, a one-bedroom flat on the top of a four-storey block. While he cooked dinner – spaghetti bolognaise where the bolognaise consisted of a tin of tomatoes and a tin of baked beans mixed together and then tipped over the spaghetti – I asked him about the fight mum had with Him.

'She said it had been a difficult week for you. She didn't say why.'

'He really hurt her,' I said.

'Did you see it?'

I said I did.

Chapter 15

'What happened?'

I told him. When I got to the part of me popping off, I hung my head in shame and my voice turned into a whisper. There are things I have done, and things I will do that will forever make me hate myself with every atom of my being when I think of them. Breaking wind with Him having just punched my mum's lights out is at the top of that list.

He took our empty plates, placed them on the side and gave me a hug. 'Your mum's a very difficult lady,' he said, kissing the top of my head, which, it has to be said, was receiving a lot of attention today. 'There's nothing you could have done. You're a kid and he's a grown man.'

Dad knew some of what went on at home, but only the bits that she told him. I didn't talk about it because I was beginning to realise a lot of it was my fault and if he knew how horrible I was he might not want to know me anymore. If I were him, I wouldn't want to know me. So I kept what I could quiet. The only exceptions were when he brought the subject up, which was rare. Don't get me wrong, he was loving and attentive and interested, and would ask me if everything was okay at home and school, and I'd tell him yeah, everything's fine, and I'd smile. And that was that. Move on, nothing to see here. Yet sometimes… sometimes, as frightened as I was to include him, I had nobody else to turn to.

Looking at him I asked, 'What would you have done?'

He thought for a moment, then said, 'I don't know.' But I didn't believe him. I had the feeling he was trying to protect me, which might make me feel warm just for the fact that he cared, but it didn't give me what I needed, information. More than anything else right now I needed information. For goodness' sake, please, tell me what I should have done!

'I wish you were still together,' I said.

'Like I said, she's a difficult lady.'

But it did give me an idea. A good idea, a really, really good idea. An idea so good I couldn't sleep that night. It was my birthday soon, and I was going to turn 12. The birthday boy could ask for anything he wanted. That was the rule. I'd never exercised the birthday right before, mainly because there had never been anything I wanted. But there was now. I broached the subject to mum over makeup and toast a few days later.

'I know what I want for my birthday,' I told her.

That made her raise an eyebrow. 'Do you now?'

'Mm-hum. I want to go out to dinner with you and dad.'

She didn't answer, not for a long time. But when she did, it was the word I longed to hear. 'Okay,' she said.

'Really?'

'If that's what you want. You know we're not together, don't you? And that we never will be? We like each other, but we can't be together. Not anymore. You know that, don't you?'

I told her I did, but if she had the choice between a horrible man who hit her, and my dad, she would want to be with my dad. Who wouldn't? What was she going to do, say oh no, give me the one with the fists? Never.

'But that will be your only present. I can afford that, but I can't afford anything else. The bills at the moment are crucifying me. If I bought you presents I wouldn't have enough money for the electricity or the gas, and we'd be cut off.'

That was a worry. The thought of living in darkness with no heating was terrifying.

Their divorce when I was four had been typical, with angry words and solicitors and each side moaning they were ripped off and lost everything. Had it not been for their son, me, they would never have spoken again. But they took their collective responsibility seriously, and communicated regularly to discuss which nights I should go to which parent. With the exception of school meetings, I hadn't seen them together for three years or more, which I thought was probably a good thing: plenty of time for the bad past to be forgotten and the good memories to take their place. I was confident over my birthday dinner they'd realise what they were missing and fall in love all over again.

The night before my birthday mum reminded me things were still really tight and not to expect any presents. I said it was fine, which it was if the alternative was to be cut off and live in cold darkness. But she wasn't playing fair, and I was too stupid to get it.

I woke the next morning and wandered down. When Mum heard me come in she looked up from her makeup and smiled a smile that was a mile wide. 'Happy birthday, Simon,' she said, and we both switched our gaze to the massive pile of presents that glowed in that way that beautifully wrapped gifts do.

'Good surprise, yes?' she said, looking excited.

I couldn't speak.

'They're from me and your aunt, your other mother.'

There must have been a dozen of them, from tiny little ones to great big hulking boxes. I should have been thrilled; I should have been beside myself, and I was, but in the wrong way.

Backing towards the door I said, 'I don't want them.'

Her face changed. Darkened. 'What? Why not?'

'Because I don't!' I yelled, turned and ran upstairs. The door to my room opened outwards, which was a shame as it meant I couldn't barricade it. I was in trouble. Big trouble. But how could I take the presents if it meant our home was going to be cut off? I got home from school hours before she did. I'd have to sit in the dark. On my own. And it would be my fault because it was my stupid birthday and we'd *all* have to sit in the dark, because of me. I didn't know what to do, how to act. She'd been really nice to me recently and I'd messed it all up because I had to have a stupid, stupid birthday. Could she take them back, get the money back? Or could I?

I could hear her walking up the stairs. She was walking slowly. When she got to my room, she even knocked.

I didn't answer.

After a minute she pulled the door open. Bracing myself for the onslaught, I held my breath. I expected screaming, and yelling, but instead she spoke in a tiny voice. She said, 'You completely ruined that for me. You have no idea how much effort I put into that, and you just dismiss it like it was nothing. You horrible child. Horrible, horrible, horrible child.'

'Mum, please.'

'Don't please me. And you wonder why I don't love you? I don't even like you. You're a horrible, ungrateful child.'

'But mum.'

'I said don't mum me!'

'But please,' I begged. 'I didn't mean it.'

She took a step back. 'What didn't you mean? You didn't mean to hurt me? You didn't mean to,' she swiped an angry hand through the air, 'chuck all that I did for you right back in my face? You might hate me…'

'I don't!'

'Yes you do, I know you do. Well I've got news for you, I hate you too.'

I'd been holding on, locking back the tears because they always annoyed her. But I couldn't hold them back any longer. I thought I could cry, but this was a whole new level. It was like all the moisture in my body was being diverted to my eyes. Tears literally washed down my face.

'Get ready for school,' she said, turned and walked away.

I don't remember the train journey in, I don't remember the day. I do remember saying no to a cigarette. 'Aw, come on, you're twelve now,' Metal said. 'Come and have a fag with me?'

I told him I couldn't, that I was being picked up by my dad. Possibly. Hopefully. I imagined mum telling dad what I'd done and how horrible I'd been. And of course she was right. She'd spent money on me that we didn't have and would cause us a major problem, and I hadn't even been a good enough son to open the presents. Stands to reason he would hate me too. Why then would he come and pick me up? Why would either of them ever want to see me again?

Never before, and never since had I been the first person out of school. The bell went and I *ran,* out the class, along the hallway – something if any of the teachers had seen me was an instant detention – and out through the school doors. I speed scanned the street for a little red sports car. Nothing doing, so I slowed the scan and did it once more in case I'd missed it. I hadn't. There wasn't one. I felt my insides crumple horribly. For that moment I was more alone than I had ever felt before.

Then I saw it, a dash of red as it made its way up the road. My heart lifted, along with all my other vital organs. He pulled up beside me.

'The birthday boy!' he yelled as I bundled in.

'So how does it feel to be twelve?' He asked, pulling out into the traffic, and I grinned and shook my head. He turned the radio up and Gary Newman's *Cars* blasted out as we sped back to his flat. Once inside he said, 'I spoke to mum. Want to tell me about it?'

Plonking myself down on the sofa my face automatically dropped into my hands. He sat next to me and I told him what had happened. What did he do? He laughed. Honestly, he laughed.

'Oh my God, you think she spent the money for the bills on your presents and now you're going to be cut off?' He was shaking his head. 'No, she only said that so it would be a big surprise. You're not going to be cut off.'

'Really?'

'Really.'

'You're sure?'

'I'm sure.'

'Do you think she'll still come tonight?'

'I don't know, we'll have to see,' he said, aiming to tease the birthday boy. Then he spotted my face. 'Yes, I'm sure she will. Look, why don't you go and have a bath and get ready.'

Honestly, it's exhausting being a child. One minute you're up, the next as low as you can go, and then *bang!* way high up in the stratosphere. At school they were always asking us to write about what you did: 'Tell us what you did over the weekend,' they'd say, as if actions were the main things that happen to a kid, which is so far from the truth it's a joke. If they said, 'Write about a conversation you had with your mother and tell us how you went from normal to hating yourself, then right up to loving life again,' I might even be tempted out of curricular retirement.

Rejuvenated, I ran the bath while dad made a couple of phone calls, one of which I guessed was to her. I tried to listen, but if it was to her he was speaking too quietly for me to hear.

We arrived early at the restaurant and the waiter showed us to our table. Dad ordered a beer for himself and a coke for me, and while we waited for her to arrive we ate the breadsticks. While we sat I tried not to think of anything. I knew I was scared to see her again, but I tried not to think about it. I also knew she hated me, something she'd never confessed before. I tried not to think of that either. Not now. Not yet. There'd be plenty of time for that later, once they were back together.

Chapter 15

'I haven't seen your mother socially in years,' dad said, sipping his beer.

'I know.'

Was it my imagination or was he a little nervous too?

Suddenly the door opened and a pile of presents walked in. That was unexpected. I smiled. I'd been determined to greet her warmly and tell her how much I loved her and how sorry I was. But in my wildest dreams I hadn't expected her to bring some of the presents with her.

I watched the waiter help her, and motion for her to follow him towards us, which she did. I put on my widest, happiest, 'I love you mum' smile. And then the door behind her opened again and the second half of my presents came in. They were stacked high so I couldn't see who was holding them. But I didn't need to. It was Him.

Chapter 16

'Can you remember your 12th birthday?' I asked Ziggy.

'What an odd question. No.'

We'd walked back to the shed with the lamb and ewe. I'd made out there were tests and things I needed to do, but there weren't. Truth is, I just wanted to hang out with the little lamb. I was fond of him. I understood him. I thought of him as a brother, and I wanted to show him some love. Stand shoulder to shoulder, show him he wasn't alone, you know?

Putting on a heavy accent, Ziggy mocked, 'In the psychiatrist's chair this week we have a middle-aged, bald, ugly-as-sin farmer who's going to tell us about his 12th birthday. Are you sitting comfortably?' Then, switching back to his normal voice, said, 'God, can you imagine how dull it must be to be a psychiatrist, listening all day to sad sacks moan that mummy didn't turn up for football practice or a piano recital, and that's the reason they got drunk for thirty years?'

'And you don't struggle with your relationship with your dad…'

'That's…'

'Different? No it's not. You made a phone call to him after he was dead, that's hardly the action of an "in control" man.'

'Sod you!'

'No, sod you!'

He grinned, and I grinned back. He is an idiot, that much is undeniable, but he's not nasty and he's not stupid, and that outburst was just him looking for a reaction. He does that when he feels the need to hit the reset button, in the same way a couple use sex or an argument to clear the air. But with friends, you don't have that option. So you need to find other ways in which to open and close chapters. Ziggy's way is to act like an idiot, and you have to admit, he is good at it.

'You want to tell me about your 12th birthday?' he said amiably.

'No. Not really. You said your dad gave you a sign? Do you want to talk about that?'

Asking Ziggy if he wanted to talk about himself was a like asking a fly if he wanted to headbutt a window: it's in their nature. Resisting the urge to go and pick the lamb up and cuddle him, I sat on some straw. Ziggy did too.

While Ziggy started talking I thought, I wish I knew more about my mum's relationship with her mother. I don't think they were close, though I can't remember what she'd said to make me think that.

'That was when I heard the voice of my father,' Ziggy said.

That brought me back into the conversation. 'He spoke to you?' I said, wondering if I heard him correctly.

'Yep!'

'Your dad? Spoke to you?'

'Yep.'

'What, like an actual voice? And when did you hear it?'

'An actual voice,' he confirmed. 'And last night.'

'While you were here? Oh great, now on top of everything else I've got to worry about the ghost of your father wandering around the place talking to people.'

'Relax, Simon, he was just talking to me.'

'You don't know that. Now he's here and started a conversation he might feel chatty. I know he's your dad and all that, but

97

when people die you don't expect to continue conversing with them. Death normally shuts people up.'

Ziggy's always leant towards the spiritual. To him it's comforting. To me it's just plain creepy, and I wasn't sure I believed in it anyway, but when a friend tells you he's spoken to a dead guy you've got to be decidedly incurious not to ask, 'Well, what did he say?'

'He told me not to worry so much.'

'That's it?'

'That's it.'

The silence that followed filled the barn. Even the lamb felt it and looked up. I couldn't fathom it. If you believe him – and I'm not sure I do – but say you did, okay, here's an entity that has been on the other side and popped back for a last recce in this realm to give his beloved son the benefit of wisdom gathered on a higher plain – and all he said was don't stress it? I don't mean to sound ungrateful, and I'm sure Ziggy must have been flushed with joy, but wouldn't you want more? I don't mean lottery numbers, or horse race winners, but something you could use – it's so rare anyone gives you real, solid advice you can use. Put it this way, if you only had one sentence to pass onto someone you loved after you'd gone, wouldn't you want to make it count?

'Didn't he give you any practical advice?' I said. 'Something you could use, like, "Have two days a week alcohol free and look after your kidneys," or, "Make sure you buy good quality tyres for your car, the ability to stop quickly can *never* be underestimated?"'

'No, he just told me not to worry so much.'

'And you're sure it was him?'

'Of course I'm sure it was him. I know the voice of my own father!'

'Well, it has been a while.'

'It was him, I tell you!'

'Okay, okay. So was it audible? If I was sitting next to you, would I have heard it?'

His face took on an expression I've never seen it use before. It looked hurt.

'You don't believe me,' he said.

'I didn't say that.'

'You didn't need to.'

'No. Sorry. Maybe I'm just not open to all that mystic stuff the way you are. I wish I was, it must be very comforting.'

He didn't answer and I felt bad, not for popping his balloon, because I don't think I did, but for deflating it a little. The lamb had settled back down again. I got up and gave the ewe some food and water, and fluffed up her bed. While she might be warming a little towards her lamb, she wasn't warming towards me, and gave me an evil eye. When I was done, I turned my attention to the lamb and plugged him in so he could feed. Mum's eyes widened in order that she could increase the flow of evil in my direction.

'She doesn't like you very much,' Ziggy said.

'No,' I agreed.

'I need to go home,' he said.

I nodded. He was always going to go home today, but it suddenly felt strained. He was my closest friend and he felt a galaxy away. I also knew it was my fault. I was tetchy and preoccupied. He'd come down here with a crisis and I'd welcomed him with one of my own. Then I'd dismissed the way he'd resolved his.

'Do you have to?' I asked.

To which he answered, 'You're too grounded. You've forgotten to leave space in your life for things that can't be explained. That's where a lot of wonder and beauty can be found, not to mention comfort. Not everything is black and white, you know,' and with that he got up and walked out.

'I know,' I said to his departing footsteps, and thought, he's probably right.

By the time he was ready to leave things were better between us. The strain I'd felt was gone, and whilst we'd both made an effort, it was Debbie who soothed most of the sore.

'Here,' she said, bustling around him at the door as he got ready to leave, 'I've made you a flask of coffee and sandwiches for the journey. There's cold chicken and mushroom pie left over from the other day and some homemade chocolate cookies. And I've baked a cake for the family when you get in, make sure you give everyone our love, won't you?'

He looked up and grinned, assuring her he would.

They said goodbye and when it was our turn we hugged tightly.

'Your dad was right,' I said, 'Don't worry so much.'

Snorting, he looked down, then back up again. He didn't speak, but nodded. I nodded back.

'Why do I always feel like I'm interrupting a moment between you two?' Debbie said.

'I've got to go,' Ziggy said, and left.

There's always this sense of implosion when Ziggy goes, like a star that's gone supernova and disappeared and now there's just this emptiness where matter used to be. Before he was even out of sight I was fighting an impulse to text him.

'How was it between the both of you?' Debbie said, closing the front door and leaning her back against it.

'Good, and not so good. I'm not sure I was a very good friend this time.'

'You're preoccupied. You've got a lot on your mind. He knows that, and so has he. How are you feeling about everything, about your mum?'

'Confused.'

Moving forward, she put her arms around me. 'Well, I'm glad it's finally coming out. To have all that bottled up inside you is corrosive.'

My younger self was wrong you know, adults do cuddle. A lot, and it's wonderful.

Sensing there was affection going on and he wasn't involved, Solomon dashed up and wormed his nose between us. Yelling at him we broke away and he had the chutzpah to stand there as the centre of a puppy sandwich wagging his tail looking pleased with himself.

The moment broken, I said, 'I need to go and do some work.'

'Going to see the lamb? Look, it is good that it's all coming out about your mum, but you shouldn't do it alone. Going insular on this worries me.'

'I'm not,' I assured her.

'I know you. I know how you do things. I also had a chat with Ziggy while you were in the shower.'

'Oh, for God's sake!'

'Don't. He's worried about you. He said you're not yourself. He said you tried to feed him to Senorita, is that true?'

'Um, well…'

'You frightened him, and he doesn't frighten easy.'

'He was never in any danger, it's Senorita,' I said, as though that explained everything, which it does. I'm sorry, I really do have to go, the boy needs a feed,' I said, leaning over the dog to give her a kiss.

'Okay, but you're mine tonight. Tonight we sit down and talk, okay?'

Assuring her we would, I pulled on my boots and walked out. It was late, but there was still plenty of daylight in the sky as I made my way to the barn. With all the to-ing and fro-ing, there were tracks in the grass and I could clearly see two lines, one made by me, one by Ziggy. Had I really frightened him?

Reaching the barn, I went inside. The lamb, now used to the routine, greeted me with a long, loud, *baaarrrrrrrrr!* that roughly translates to, 'Where the hell have you been, I'm *starving!*' That's the problem with taking control, the association the lamb should have between mum and food switches to me and food. I had to find a way to reconnect mum and baby if he had any chance of surviving long-term. And no time like the present to start.

'So here's what we're going to do,' I said, 'Tonight I'm not going to plug you in. This time you've got to do it yourself. You're strong enough, look at you, you're so fit you'll be wrestling foxes by the end of next week.'

I did everything I normally do, got the ewe up on her feet, secured her to the wall so she couldn't lash out, spread her back legs and gently moved her udder until two perfect teats pointed out the back. Everything I normally do, except this time I didn't have the lamb. Tonight, latching on was down to him.

'Come on fella,' I encouraged. 'You said you were starving, well here's dinner.'

At first he looked confused. He was lounging on his bed with an expression of, 'Pardon me, but haven't you forgotten my carry?' After a moment when he realised his lift to dinner wasn't imminent, he got up. The movement was smooth and effortless. Now up, all he had to do was walk over to us. That's it. Even for a lamb that's got to be doable. Walk. One foot, then the other and before you know it, *ta-dar!* you're there. But no, that would be far too easy.

No, the lamb decided the only way he could possibly make it from point A, bed, to point B, mother's milk, would be to *boing*. All four legs straight, prepare for take-off, and *boing* two foot in the air. It was as if he were saying, if you're not going to take me, I'll fly. And direction, well that's subjective. Launching himself up into the air he cleared the bed and landed a bit to one side and a little further away.

Mum yawned.

'Well, you birthed him,' I told her. 'He's got your DNA.'

Take-off number two was straight up and down. Number three crashed on landing. I let go of the ewe's udder and stood up straight so the bones in my back clicked. Four was more successful and you might even argue in the right direction, ish.

Five, six, seven, eight, nine, ten... nineteen... thirty something... bored of counting now... tum-ta-tum-ta-tum-ta-ta... something like sixty. Boing, boing, boing, boing, boing, like a 1970s punk at a Sex Pistols concert, and with just as many brain cells. I wondered if I should give up and go and grab him. The ewe and I both slumped against the wall and continued watching. My fingernails grow at a faster rate than he was getting the hang of forward motion. Eventually he found himself back on his bed and laid down. Great.

To the lamb, I said, 'I want you to know that I love you, and support you, but boy, you weren't first in the queue when they were handing out smarts, were you?'

At some point he'd have to stand on his own four hooves, that much was clear. But when? Now, when he was so tiny and vulnerable? Tomorrow, the day after or the day after that? Next week, next month? Never one to back away from a line of thought while it still had room to travel, I had a sudden image of me with a fully-grown sheep in my arms legging it after mum as she high tailed it across a field, with me desperately yelling, 'Mum, come back, your baby wants a feed!'

Oh God.

So I made a decision. I decided I wasn't going to pick the lamb up and take him to mum. He *had* to learn how to do it himself. And there followed a pleasant hour while I encouraged, begged and teased him, but all he did was *baarrrrrr* at me and show not the slightest inclination to get up off his lazy backside.

'What you are, a stuck-to-the-bed teenager? You need to do this,' I told him.

In the second hour I milked mum into the palm of one hand and wafted it under his nose; pretend walked him so his feet dragged on the floor the short distance, then put him back, figuring at least then he knew the route; did the walk myself over and over again, talking him through it so he could see how it was done; waggled mum's teats while saying, 'Mm-m! that looks SO delicious!'; and yes, even got down on all fours and pretended to suckle. That was my low point, both figuratively and literally. Was it Nietzsche who said, *mankind cannot truly call himself advanced as long as there's some dunce on all fours pretending to drink from the back end of a sheep?* I was that dunce.

Getting up, I brushed straw from my knees, then looked over at the lamb. He was asleep. All my best work and he hadn't even bothered to stay awake. I went over, shook him gently and took him to mum. He'd won. I'd been outwitted by a lamb. Even as I plugged him in I thought, he will never learn to do this on his own and I will be his carer for the rest of our days. In years to come people will say to me, who's your friend? And I'll have to explain why I've got a sheep trotting along beside me, to which they'll say, 'The cinema? You brought him to the cinema?' And I'll say, 'Yeah. You never know when he might get hungry.'

Only, he wasn't sucking. I pulled him off and plugged him back in again, which is the same as turning him off and on again because everyone knows that's the first thing you try. Still nothing. His mouth was slack. Was he too tired? Had he got over-hungry and no longer wanted anything to drink?

'Come on, an hour ago this is all you wanted!'

Nothing doing. Out of options and frankly fed up, I laid the lamb back on his bed. He was past critical so missing one feed wouldn't matter. I hoped.

After I'd made them both comfortable for the night I left the barn. There was barely a scraping of daylight left, Jesus, had I really been that long in there? Bit late, but time to feed the animals. When they were all fed, watered and tucked up for the night I split some logs for the fire and took them in.

'You're late, I was getting worried. How's the lamb?' Debbie said from the kitchen.

'Don't! Stupid thing!' I kick my boots off and carry the logs over to the basket next to the fire. It's not that cold, but a fire definitely gives a sense of home and belonging and we've been known to have one in the middle of summer with all the windows thrown open.

'Dinner in half an hour. Come on, tell me about the lamb.'

'What have we got?'

'Oh yeah, um, lamb casserole. Sorry.'

I started laughing. 'Really?'

'It was defrosted and needed using. I'm sorry. How is the lamb?'

'Better than that one,' I said, not at all sure how I felt about eating lamb tonight. But if it needed using, it needed using. The alternative was to throw it away, and I know that would make me feel a gazillion times worse. So it was to be lamb for dinner while discussing the wellbeing of another lamb. Life down here can feel peculiar at the best of times, but evenings like this were out and out weird.

Loading the fire with logs, I told her about trying to teach the lamb to feed from mum himself.

'You tried…'

'Yep.'

'And…'

'Yep.'

Looking thoughtful, 'Mm, what about…'

'Did that too.' 27 years of marriage means we seldom bother with the second half of sentences, and very often a single word's enough. On the bright side, it does mean you can cover an awful lot of conversational ground quickly. When it slows down, there's a reason for it.

'Difficult one,' she agreed. 'And, how are you doing?'

'Oh, I'm fine.'

She moved over to the other side of the kitchen to grab something. 'I'm a woman, I know what fine means.'

The fire was starting to pick up. 'I know.'

Turning to face me she took a deep breath and said, 'Love him to bits, but I am glad Ziggy's gone. We need some time together. I need to be close to you. And I'm worried. This is going to be really hard on you, and you're not going to come out of this unscathed, you know that, right? Reliving what your mother did to you will screw you up all over again.' The night I took Debbie to meet my mum for the first time was terrifying. Mum had scared off girlfriends before, even reducing one of them to tears. But I'd already asked Debbie to marry me, and she'd said yes and a date had been set for six months' time, and the last thing I wanted was for them to meet on our wedding day. We met at a restaurant, neutral territory, and give her her due mum was well behaved, and in the car afterwards Debbie said, 'Tell me about her.' I told her bits, nothing much, but she nodded and said something like, 'figures.' They never got on. They were polite, most of the time, but they never liked one another. Then over the years I'd occasionally share things that happened which only intensified Debbie's dislike. I can count on one hand the number of times we've sat down and really talked about my childhood, because until now it's been a part of my life that I wanted to forget.

I threw more wood into the fire even though it didn't need it, and, disagreeing, said, 'No it won't.'

Chapter 16

She was back at the business side of the kitchen, working and talking.

'It will. It can't not.'

'It wasn't any worse than anyone else.'

'She emotionally and physically abused you.'

'No she didn't!'

She didn't say anything, just looked at me.

'Look,' I said, 'Everyone has their baggage. We all do. And it's all the same pain. You, me, everyone. The only thing that differs is the source of the pain. For one person it might be that mummy forgot to turn up for a football match, and for someone else it could be they grew up in terror around drink, drugs and violence, but how that manifests years down the line is the same for everyone.'

Spinning round she threw the tea towel she was holding on the floor and grunted in anger. 'That is just, *aaahhhhh, bullshit!*'

Sitting back a little I said, 'Okay.'

It took her a while to control her breathing, and when she did she said, 'This is why we need to talk. Okay, right, first of all pain is never the same. What you went through was abuse. I'm sorry, but you know what I think of your mother. Your mother's horrible, and what she did to you was disgusting. Look at you, you hate yourself – you think I don't hear you call yourself a cunt under your breath? "I'm such a cunt, I'm such a fucking cunt!" You think I don't hear that? You think everything's your fault, you shower three or four times a day, you shave your head as a form of cutting yourself, and I'm never fully certain I'm not going to find you hanging from a tree one day!'

She was sobbing but standing bolt upright, eyes fierce, shoulders back, fists clenched. She looked like she was going to belt me one. I wasn't sure whether to go and hug her or stay well back.

'I'm sorry,' I said.

'What for? Why are you sorry Simon? You don't get it at all, do you?'

'Of course I do.' I was quieter now.

'It's not your fault your mother didn't love you,' she said, reached for the kitchen roll and dabbing her eyes.

My turn to bristle. 'How do you know that?' I said, standing up. As I did, Solomon came over and stood in front of me for a fuss. Bending down I kissed him on the top of his head and gave him a squeeze. 'I don't think it was all my fault, but I do think it was partly my fault. It has to be.'

'You were a baby. How could it possibly be your fault? It's a mother's job to protect and love her baby.'

'Nowhere is love part of the deal. Protect, yes. But not love.'

'You don't think love is part of the deal?'

'There is no deal.'

'But you just said there was. You said, nowhere is love part of the deal.'

'Yeah, but that's not what I meant.'

She came over and put her arms around me. With Solly in the middle we were back to the puppy sandwich. 'It wasn't your fault, okay?'

I didn't pull away even though I wanted to. 'Sorry, but that's wrong. I have to take some responsibility. If it was just a, "Oh, I found it hard at first to bond with him," that's one thing, but she never loved me. Not for decades.'

'You think she loves you now?'

'She's beyond that now. But I do think there was a period where she did. In my 40s maybe. But up until then, no.'

'Because her postnatal depression wasn't treated?'

'That doesn't make any sense either. How can you make someone love you with treatment? If they don't, they don't. You can't give them a love drug. This isn't Harry Potter, it's real life, and in real life it doesn't matter how much swishing you do with a wand, or gulping down a potion, if they don't love you, you've just got to accept it.'

'Where are you getting your information?' Debbie carried on. 'None of this is right. I accept that in the 60s they must have been figuring out what postnatal depression was, whereas now it's understood and there are things they can do.'

'We don't even know that's what she had,' I said.

'No, because it wasn't diagnosed. But it's classic symptoms.'

'You think?'

'Hundred percent.'

That was confusing. Sure, it felt good that there might be an underlying reason, but it was also maddening that it hadn't been recognised. So I said, 'I don't know.' Weirdly, it's more comforting to think it was my fault, but I don't know why.

Ignoring that, she continued, 'What I don't get is why you're so determined to think it's all down to you?'

'I'm not determined, that's not fair. I just don't think I was lovable, or made myself loveable. You can't love something if it's not loveable, can you? Maybe not when I was a baby, but when I grew up a bit I shouldn't have been so difficult.'

She poured some wine and pushed a glass over towards me. 'Difficult how? Your mum is a very tricky person to be around. She's very controlling and manipulative, and her thing is to push people away and see if they come back. She pushed you away constantly, and you kept going back until one day you didn't.'

'Proving her right,' I said, quietly.

'What's that?'

'Nothing. Anyway, that was later.'

'But she couldn't control you.'

'And that's the problem,' I agreed.

'All right, control's the wrong word. She couldn't dominate you.'

'She was my mother. I was her child. I should have been more what she wanted.'

'When you were a baby?' she asked, taking the lamb out of the oven and setting it on the side to rest.

'Sure. And all the way through. Debbie, I understand what you're trying to do, but it's so much more complicated than that. It just doesn't feel like it's something that can be simplified.'

'Have you Googled it? Have you Googled the symptoms?'

Brushing my forehead with my hand I said, 'Kind of.'

'What's kind of?'

'I Googled postnatal depression.'

Eyes rolling. 'No wonder. Here, let me…'

Chapter 17

I have never told anyone this before, but I think the General might be an Arsenal fan. But then again, he is 55 stone, lives in the woods and thinks nothing of spending sunny afternoons lying in a muddy puddle, so maybe Arsenal's not that big a surprise.

His pig pen is on a hill beside our lounge, and he'll often lie peering in. One day Debbie was pottering about with the football on, and when Arsenal scored a goal she whooped and the General stood up and roared.

Spinning to me she said, 'Did he just cheer?'

Refusing to look up from my book in case it might encourage either of them, I murmured, 'Oh God.'

Darting to the window she said, 'He did!'

I set *The Goldfinch* to one side and moved up behind her so I could wrap my arms around her waist and together we looked out at the General. 'And to think I believed Ziggy was my disappointing best friend.'

Debbie was brought up in a Gooner family, which explains a lot. 'We should get the General a scarf,' she said.

'Don't you think life is difficult enough for him as it is?' For which I received a playful elbow in the ribs.

'Do you miss football?'

'No,' I said, and went back to my book, thinking, maybe sometimes.

'We never did get you that scarf, did we, General?' I said, climbing over the gate.

In the end, we'd decided not to research postnatal depression last night and save it for daytime, as opposed to night time when things are naturally at their blackest. But first I had everyone's breakfast to make.

The General is always first on the dining roster. I pour his food out, plus a little more, and tell him he's the only one who gets a bit extra when in truth they all do. I tell Debbie they don't. That I'm strict with the portioning because money's always tight. I don't know if she believes me.

While he eats, I crouch down by his head, reach out and stroke him. It's not unlike touching the bristles of a soft broom.

'You okay fella? Sorry I've not been around much. There seems to be a lot going on.' The skin behind his ear is soft, like shammy leather. I let my fingers play with it. 'What's your earliest memory, General? Do you remember your mum?'

He doesn't answer, which is the downside of having a pig as a best friend. The upside is he's a very good listener, but I don't have time this morning, give him a hug, and climb out.

Moving between the groups of pigs distributing breakfast, I wonder what all their earliest memories are? They must have them, even if it's what they did the day before yesterday, they must have them. And if you have memories, it stands to reason you'd be shaped by them.

I know I anthropomorphise animals – in many ways it's hard not to. And the more time I spend around them, the more human they seem, with their personalities and their ways, their needs and their urges. Get right down to the nub and there's not that many differences between me and a pig. Not at our deep, deep core. What does a pig want from life? Food, water, shelter and love. Well, same here.

Chapter 17

Okay, so maybe the General wouldn't remember his mum on account that he was taken away from her at eight weeks old. But I wonder if he remembers his children? After all, he's had enough of them. I wonder if he thinks about them?

At Senorita's pen I toss in her food plus a little more, and lean over the fence.

'Just pig nuts today girl, no Ziggy to eat.' Moving like a bouncing bomb she boo-boom's out of her house and lands on the food. She's got morning hair with some of the straw from her bed sticking out of it. Her piglets are all gathered around her.

So how far into the psyche of a pig is it safe to go before it starts getting weird? Can we talk about the friendships pigs have with each other? That's not odd, is it? Friendships are good. Okay, how about love between pigs? Is that starting to weird you out, or does that still feel okay? Let's jump to something safer, the love Senorita feels for her babies. Surely that's undeniable. So if we accept that love exists between a mother, even if that mother is a pig, and her babies, surely it stands to reason that from time to time that's going to go wrong.

Somewhere inside me a penny drops and a tiny voice shouts 'Bingo!' Turning I yell at Senorita, 'I've got to go!' and run in the direction of the barn.

Banging open the door, I look across at the ewe. 'You've got postnatal depression. That's why you're not bonding,' I tell her, walking in and closing the door behind me. The lamb is on the opposite side of the barn to her. They are as far away from one another as it is possible to get.

'We've got to fix it or you'll never bond.' Moving to the lamb I picked him up. He felt so light. Taking him over to her I set him down, gently pushing him into her woolly side. For a couple of beats she didn't move, then she scooched as far away as she could get, which admittedly wasn't very far, but the point was made.

Missing something to lie against, the lamb flopped on his side. Compared with last night he seemed to have no energy. Missing dinner will do that.

'I know I want you to be independent,' I said, gathering him up again, 'But you've got to eat and get big and strong first.'

Although mum was still stroppy, a lot of the fight in her had seeped away and it didn't take much for me to hold her steady and plug the lamb in. Not having been emptied last night, her udder was bulging, and I'm sure it must have felt better for her as the little lamb drained it.

When he was done, I made a nest of straw and put him in the centre.

To the ewe I said, 'I've got an idea. Don't go anywhere,' but secured the door behind me as I left just in case she had little faith in my abilities, for which I could hardly blame her.

'I think the ewe's got postnatal depression,' I tell Debbie, stripping off my outer farming gear and hanging it up in the hallway.

'Yeah, I knew that was coming. Come. Sit. I've got some stuff for you to read.'

She was in the lounge, at the table with the laptop open in front of her. Lighting the gas beneath the kettle as I passed the hob, I stood beside her, peering at the screen.

'So,' she moved out of the seat and pointed down at it, 'sit. Now, what you said is right, there's a lot of jargon and technical information out there about postnatal depression, but it's very... impersonal. If you want we can look at it later, when you feel a bit more up to speed. But first you really need to know what PND is, and how it affects women – obviously it's different for each woman, but there are common themes. So I've found some blogs written by women who have documented their experiences.'

'Oh. Right.'

She looked at me. 'Not what you were expecting?'

'I don't know what I was expecting.'

'You know, we don't have to do this. If you want I can do the research and then give you a précis. That might be better.'

'No. I do need to do this.' And I did. I sat and read. Some of the stories were heartbreaking, full of anxiety and confusion and upset over why they were feeling the way they were. A couple of the writers encouraged people to contact them if they were going through something similar, even going as far as to offer support. Okay, I'm not going through it, at least not in the way they had, but I had questions and figured maybe they could help.

I sent out four emails, explaining that I'd seen their blog post and was trying to understand my relationship with my mother whom, I now believed, had suffered from PND, although that was back in the 1960s so it was undiagnosed and untreated. I asked if I could talk to them. Then signed off hoping to hear from them and thanking them for their kind consideration.

Not one of them responded.

I understand it. I'm a man and this is a very personal subject for a woman. However, the excitement I'd felt at being able to speak to someone who could answer some of my questions wouldn't leave me. I felt fevered by it: hot and heady and slightly dizzy. So I tried to find someone else to talk to.

I found a university professor who lectured in depression, including postnatal depression, who responded to my first email by saying he'd be happy to chat, and what type of questions did I have?

I wrote back immediately…

Dear sir,

That's so kind of you, thank you!

The questions I'd love to chat about are…

Do we know what PND is − not the symptoms, but rather what's happened in the brain to bring it on?

Is it a chemical imbalance post partum?

If so, is there something that's supposed to happen to a woman at the point she gives birth that makes her bond and want to protect her baby, that might not happen to some?

Can it be corrected with medication?

If so, what part of the brain are you targeting?

Can it be cured without medication?

If undiagnosed, what is the likely outcome?

My mother's symptoms were that she didn't bond with me and felt nothing for me for all my life, is this a common trait of undiagnosed PND?

Also, my mother had me in 1967, so I'm guessing a lot has changed and much more is now understood. Does anything stand out as a majorly significant breakthrough in the understanding of PND in the last 50 years?

Any information or advice would be fantastic, and I'm so grateful for your help.

He didn't respond.

I emailed my G.P. and asked if she'd be able to refer me to anyone. She said it's not anything she'd ever dealt with before, and there was nobody in the West Country specialising in that. Had I tried the Priory? Or possibly London, Harley Street maybe?

Harley Street. Fifty years on from when my mum went there and that was still the place to go. Have we moved on at all?

But I know of the Priory and emailed them. They didn't respond.

Not knowing where else to turn to now, I switched my attention to animals. Surely I can't be the only person in the world ever to have witnessed rejection in an animal?

Speaking to my vet, she said it wasn't something she dealt with, had I tried the RSPCA? I did, they didn't respond.

I phoned a big safari park and spoke to a lovely lady who said, no problem! Send them an email. I did. They didn't respond.

Emailing every zoo in the country, one said they were too busy, another said she had spoken to their keepers who have never experienced anything like a mother rejecting a baby, and the others didn't respond.

I sent messages to animal behaviourists, agricultural colleges, a university with an agricultural department, two authors and a well-known breeder. The university responded saying PND in animals was a recognised thing and was something they lectured on, and for a while it looked encouraging that we might be able to chat, but when I asked for a meeting they stopped getting back to me. None of the others even bothered replying.

Really, will nobody talk to me?

Why are people so reluctant to talk about it? Is it taboo? Is it the way mental illness and depression used to be before we realised it's okay to voice how we feel? Or is it something different, something more base, more fundamental to being a woman and that whole thing surrounding having a baby that I'm not getting?

Look, I'm a man and as such I'm aware what the eff do I know about being a mother and the emotions surrounding child birth. I don't, I can't. I'm aware and respect that. But please don't punish me for my sex. I'm reaching out asking for help trying to understand it as best I can. You'd think I could find *someone* who'd be willing to talk to me about it, wouldn't you?

I don't know where else to go.

I don't know where else to look.

I don't know who else to ask.

I don't even know if that's what my mother had. For all I know she might just have been a bit dysfunctional in the parenting area. But I do know one thing: I need to find out.

Chapter 18

Changes are ahoof in the sheep and lamb department! I went into the barn and the sheep was lying down in one corner, and where was the lamb? Perched on the sheep's back.

I tried not to make a big thing of it, though the inside of me was turning happy cartwheels. Moving about the barn tidying and being generally busy, I said, 'You two seem to have sorted out your differences. So can I ask if you've had breakfast already?'

The ewe baa'd.

'Yeah, not you, big girl. The jockey on your back.'

Not wanting to disturb them anymore, I backed out of the barn. Well, well, well. Moving a few feet away I sank down onto the grass. There hadn't been any rain for a week and the ground was dry and dusty. Kicking my feet out I leant back on my arms and looked up at the sun, the heat penetrating all the way down to my bones. Behind me the wood and corrugated iron construction of the barn groaned a little as the heat hit that too. From the other field a cockerel crowed.

I'd done it. I'd only bloody well done it. Ha! And it had been two days, two days exactly.

Okay, she'd done it, but I'd helped! I'd facilitated. And now, they'd bonded. Mum and son. I'd give them a day or two and then put them out in the field with the others. It's not often I get to feel good about myself, and thought about taking mental snapshots of the feeling so I could refer back to them the way an actor might, but it's not my style. There's no album in my head marked 'Good'. The shelves are too stuffed with files marked 'Self-Hatred' for that.

I wonder how the lamb feels? I wonder if he has any capacity to analyse his situation? I doubt it, and good on him for that.

I wonder what my mum would say if I told her about the sheep and lamb? Wait, I know exactly what she'd say because she'd recognise it instantly and become defensive, and her form of defence was attack on all fronts; she'd have made a fearless Major in the army. She'd scream at me, get right up in my face, little bits of spit hitting my cheeks as she let her temper rip, tell me how it was, how I might think this and I might think that, and how I had *no idea!* We wouldn't talk for weeks. She'd be hurt and I'd feel awful and confused and it hits me just how warming and comforting those thoughts make me feel.

Back when I sent those four initial emails out to the bloggers who'd written about their experiences of PND, the biggest question I wanted to ask was, does knowing you have PND change anything, and if you didn't know you had it, if PND wasn't a recognised thing and you just thought that how you were feeling was normal... actually, I don't even know where I'm going with that question. Maybe it's a good thing nobody came back to me. I don't even know the questions I want to ask. Sometimes I'll read a book, or be watching TV and a character will be talking about their life and say something like, 'I had *so* many questions!' And I'll think, really? I mean, I do have questions, but it's like they're not the ones that need answering. The ones that really need answering are tied up, and I can't access them because they're a spinning hot mass of feelings and emotions that are so tightly knotted together they're almost impenetrable. Inside my head I can see them, and I can feel them, I can even hear them, but I can't get close to them. They occupy a part of my brain I don't go near, and probably never will, even though I know they contain all the real questions. The memories I'm reliving of my childhood are kind of linked to it, but that's all they are, linked. They're not part of it. That knotted mass, I don't really know what's in there. Maybe part of reliving the memories is to see if I can get access, but I don't know if that would be healthy. Let swirling masses lie, and all that.

But now's not the time for all of that.

I've got the sun on my face and in the barn behind me a little lamb is snuggled into his mum. This is a good day. I should stick with animals, not humans. I'm better with animals.

I once had a pig, a first-time mum who gave birth to a litter of eight piglets, and over the course of a week intentionally killed everyone one of her babies. Was that PND?

The sheep behind me, did she have PND?

Do chickens get it? I had a duck who hatched five ducklings and pushed one out of the nest so it got cold and died. PND?

Even Senorita. A few years ago I made a lovely maternity unit for her – I mean, five-star luxury would make any pregnant woman want to lie down and start contractions – and yet she decided she wanted to give birth up in the woods under a bush. As soon as she finished giving birth, she stood up and ran away from them. Actually, that might just be Senorita and nothing to do with PND at all – she can be like that.

Getting up off the ground I brushed the dried mud off my bum and made my way over to Senorita's pen, leaning on the fence and saying, 'I was just thinking about you.'

The straw was deep and smelled fresh and clean. Senorita was lying over to one side feeding her young. When a sow lies on her side to feed her babies, her teats stick out in two layers, the upper level and the lower level. When the piglets are really tiny, the only way they can reach the upper teats is for half of them to stand on the backs of the others who are feeding on the bottom level. They slip and slide and fall off and climb back up again, it's comical to watch.

All the while Senorita makes the 'come and feed,' noise; a kind of *mm, mm, mm, mm, mm*. She does it for the first few times while they are feeding and from then on uses that sound as the dinner bell when she wants them to come and eat: *'Come and get it while it's hot, come on you horrible lot!'* and will flop over onto her side as they come dashing from all corners of the pen. Obviously in the wild that trick is dead handy.

Senorita knows me well enough that I can climb in and go sit beside her head, pulling her hairy ears and stroking her Cabbage Patch Doll cheeks without fear that she'll do a Ziggy on me.

'How does it feel when they feed? Does it hurt? Is it nice? Can you feel your boobs emptying - does that feel weird? Do you feel an overwhelming sense of love for them and feel like you'd do anything to keep them safe, or would you really rather they buggered off and left you alone to drink gin?'

I had a pig once, Kylie, who every night would sit like a dog in front of me and open her mouth until I poured in a glass of red wine. I got into the habit of carrying a little around with me in an old half-litre water bottle, and she got into the habit of boozing. When she got pregnant, I told her it had to stop. She was not happy.

I wonder if my mum breastfed me? The thought made me laugh. No way, absolutely no way would she have done that.

Looking down at Senorita I continued, 'Does it make you feel close to them?' If it did they clearly didn't feel similarly moved, and were more concerned with going hell for leather at draining her as quickly as possible. One of them, a little black and white podge I'd come to think of as Chunk, had already emptied one teat and moved onto his second.

'I can imagine having a baby and holding it close to my chest, skin on skin, and how that must feel pretty special, but I can't imagine what it must feel like to literally feed something from your own body. It's kind of mind-blowing when you think about it.'

In agreement Senorita closed the breakfast buffet bar by rolling onto her front, groaned and closed her eyes.

'Is it tiring? I guess it must be. So that litter you had up in the woods, the one you ran away from, why was that one different? Why do you love these, but you didn't love them? If you had PND for one lot, wouldn't it make sense that you had it for all of them? Or is PND something that comes and goes, like a cold? Or did you simply learn to control it?'

While the piglets formed a nap-time clump a few feet away, Senorita drifted off into a sleep of her own, and I know that because she started snoring.

Pigs are terrible snorers.

Getting up I leave her to it, and climb out.

That night I lie in bed, just me and Solly; me under the covers, him on top of them taking up far more than his share of the space. Debbie's still up, in the lounge watching TV. I go to bed early so she can have some time to herself, and I get up early so I can have mine while she lies in. As a system, it seems to work.

The room is dark and smells pleasantly of freshly laundered sheets. I keep thinking about Senorita, and the sheep, all the animals in fact, and wonder if there isn't something they have to teach me that I'm missing. Or maybe I'm making it all too complicated. Simple is often better. But how do I simplify things? Well, I could look at me and mum as animals. Take out all the complicated stuff, the games, the wordplay, and reduce us down to body language – how would that look?

Chapter 18

When I think of mum I think of her doing her makeup, that's the dominant image that pops up in my mind, mum sitting cross-legged on the floor surrounded by pots and tubes, brushes, cotton-wool and boxes of multi-coloured eye makeup all around her. It's like a moat surrounding her. Keep out! You are not wanted here! Private property, trespassers will be screamed at. Or was it more like, this moat is keeping me in and not letting me get close to you even if I wanted to?

With that in mind, I begin to drift off, probably giving Senorita a run for her money in the snoring stakes.

Chapter 19

That night, on my 12th birthday, Mum came in carrying presents and the waiter had to lead her over because she couldn't see above the top of them. My heart swelled so much I thought it would burst. Then He came in after her. And after Him, dad's fiancé walked in.

A cosy birthday dinner with both partners. Not the plan, not the plan at all.

The room went quiet and I was aware everyone had wandered away from the table bar mum.

'You thought it was just going to be you me and your dad, didn't you?' she said.

Not lifting my eyes from the scarcely touched steak Diane in front of me – cooked by the chef for me at the table, which in 1979 was considered classy – I nodded.

Reaching out she picked a chip from my plate and whispered, 'Tough,' before scooching back into her place. Then a little louder, 'I'm not with your dad anymore, and he's not with me. We've both moved on. We both have new partners. I don't expect you to understand now, but you will one day. Come on, open your presents.'

They were in a pile to one side. I glanced at them. The paper that had once been bright and shiny now seemed dull and crude. They felt cruel somehow, mocking, hate-filled. I wanted nothing to do with them. 'I still don't want them,' I said.

She reached out, grabbed the two closest to her and slammed them down on the table in front of me. 'Open them!'

Looking down, I shook my head.

'You horrible child. You ruin everything,' and with that she got up and swished both presents at me. I didn't dare move, and sat absolutely still as they tumbled into my lap and off onto the floor.

I couldn't have lifted my eyes if Elvis Presley himself had taken that moment to stroll up and go, 'U-hu-hu.' I heard her get her stuff together and shout over to Him, 'Come on, we're going.'

As she passed she knelt down and said, 'Like it or not, I do love you,' and kissed me on the cheek.

What? I couldn't think; couldn't grab a single thought as a million of them shot by. It was like looking up at the night sky with shooting stars helter-skelter-skidding this way and that. My heart heaved so heavily I actually choked, and those sodding tears that I just couldn't work out how to stop washed down my face again. That was the second time she'd said it. Was this time just words as well? Or was this time different? Did my mum love me tonight? Is that why she brought me the presents? I don't know.

Dad came over and put his arm around me and pulled me close so I could bury my face. 'Oh son,' he said.

That night, back at dad's, I opened the presents, and although I'd suspected it, realised properly for the first time what it must be like for mum to have me as a son. She wasn't nasty and horrible. No, that was me. The truth is, I'm not a nice person. That's why she can't love me all the time. Just occasionally. Every now and then. Birthdays and maybe special occasions, and then I go and ruin it. What a cunt I am.

Dad was watching me. 'You want me to put it on?' he said, reaching the album that sat on the top of the pile.

I smiled and said, 'Yes please.'

He picked it up and went over to the stereo. The first record that was all mine. It was AC/DC, *If you want blood*. Metal had told me I *had* to get it, that it was the best album ever made. I'd asked mum for it, but didn't think she'd even heard me, let alone would actually buy it. But she had.

As the first track started, dad handed the cover back to me and I sat staring down at the picture on the front of a boy in school uniform with a guitar jammed into his chest and blood soaking his shirt, and tried to concentrate on the lyrics and blot out everything else in the world. That was a lot of blotting. But by the time the second track was halfway through, it had actually worked. With the music on I found I couldn't think of my mum even if I tried. Oh my God! *Oh my God!*

The next day at school I was in early, hoping Metal had picked up on my telepathic messages to get in ASAP. Apparently, he had.

'Smoke? he said, strutting up to me.

Not realising he smoked before school as well as after, I said dumbly, 'Won't the teacher be in his class?'

'That's only for after school so we can look at his grot mag. Before school we use the basement where they store all the spare desks and chairs. Come on.'

He led me down some rickety old wooden steps and shouldered a door so it sprang open.

Looking behind us I said, 'Won't we get caught?'

'Impossible.'

'Probable, I'd have thought.'

He was shaking his head. 'Headmaster has no sense of smell. He caught me down here once last term. I told him I'd been sent to collect a new chair. He couldn't smell the smoke.' He was grinning like this was the best news ever, put a cigarette in the side of his mouth and struck a match.

'I got the album,' I told him as he passed the smoke to me.

'Don't bum it,' he warned, and I dried my lips before taking a drag. Then he said, 'What did you think?'

'Loved it!'

'I knew you would. Best track?'

I shrugged.

Looking curious he said, 'You don't know?'

'No. They all sounded pretty much the same. I liked the anger, and the heavy riff (dad's phrase), and the way it stopped me thinking.'

It was only as I looked up and saw his open mouth I realised I'd said something wrong. I tried to backtrack, but it was too late.

'Stopped you thinking, what are you talking about? Stopped you thinking?' He was mimicking, his voice going up so it sounded a little like me. 'Stopped you thinking what?'

'No, I didn't mean that,' I said, desperate to take the words back. Without thinking I'd just assumed it would be the same for Metal, that everyone would listen to the songs and feel that blissful release of not thinking about their mum. Clearly this wasn't the case for Metal. So was he the odd one out or was I?

I had the horrible feeling I'd crossed some imaginary line that must have something to do with growing up and not being childish. I'd never thought to talk about home, and that came as a massive relief. Thank God for that! That's what kids do, and I am anything but a kid. It actually made me quite proud to think that I'd not done something childish without even thinking about it. That's the clearest sign ever that I'm grown up.

'What did I tell you, don't bum it!' Metal said, reaching out and swiping the cigarette out of my mouth.

'Fuck you,' I said, grinning.

'Yeah, whatever,' he said, more worried about his smoke and wiping the butt on his cuff.

It was the weekend before the presents made their way to mum's house. I'd been there since the day following my birthday. I wanted to ask her what she meant when she said, 'like it or not, I do love you.' Did she? And why wouldn't I like it? The only time I got close to talking about it was one morning before school when I decided to take the lead and said, 'Mum, I love you.'

She put her makeup mirror down and said, 'Do you? You've got a funny way of showing it.'

Her eyes stared at me and I couldn't hold her gaze, so I looked down and said, 'Sorry.'

Through my peripheral vision I watched her pick the mirror back up and continue. After a while she said, 'Michelle and her girls are coming over on Saturday. I want you to be nice, okay? No sulking.'

I agreed I would. Michelle was mum's friend, and her girls were Cindy and Sarah-Louise. Cindy was my age, twelve, whereas Sarah-Louise was much younger. I didn't have a lot of time for girls but I liked Cindy and S-L. On and off we'd pretty much grown up together while our mums drank coffee and talked and talked and talked and talked.

When Saturday came around I was sitting on the sofa watching cartoons when there was a knock at the door.

'Open the door! Now!' Mum barked at me. I bounced up and ran. It was them.

'Hi Simon,' Cindy said. She had long black hair with a red ribbon in it above a happy smiling face with a little pixie nose and freckles. She was wearing a dress that matched the ribbon in her hair. She looked nice, for a girl.

While mum and her friend got busy in the kitchen I took the girls into the lounge, and mindful of being nice asked them what programmes they liked to watch.

'We'd rather go out and play,' Cindy said. 'Our mum said it would be okay if your mum did too.'

This was new. I went and asked, and she said as long as I looked after them.

So that's what we did. I took them over the local park and showed them the best parts. First the secret camp in the bushes that the adults didn't know about, then the best tree to climb followed by the tree with the branch that stuck out and was best for sitting. As we walked we talked about our favourite television programmes, and music and school. A lot about school.

Whenever I spoke, Cindy seemed to slow down and really look at me. Not a glance, but a really deep look, like she was interested in what I said. It was weird. Uncomfortable. But also kind of nice, and made something right down inside of me glow warm.

'Do you want to smoke?' I said, as we made our way out of the wooded area and back onto the grass. 'There's always cigarettes hidden in the camp from the older boys. It's really cool. I do it all the time.' I didn't, I'd never done it before in the woods, not at the camp. I knew the cigarettes were there, but I'd never touched them.

Both girls shook their heads and I tried not to look relieved. Then Cindy did something that astonished me. She reached out and took my hand in hers. And held it there. I could feel her soft warm skin. It felt wonderful.

'Can we go back to the branch so we can sit down?' She said.

We walked hand in hand with Sarah-Louise on the other side of her. I felt like a superhero, like nothing on earth could hurt me. I had never felt anything like it before, so much so that the feeling filled me up. I felt taller and more adult than I had ever done before. It was an amazing feeling.

At the tree Sarah-Louise climbed up and took her position on the branch. We didn't follow. Instead Cindy put her arms around me, and kissed me.

The feeling was too much. In that microsecond I felt everything I'd ever felt in my life all in one go, all the emotions and feelings and sensations. Everything. I felt every panicky feeling that one day I might die; I felt every sense of hate and sense of disgust that I'd ever felt when thinking about myself; I felt every illness from throwing up to passing out; I felt every tear shed in anguish and quite a few in humiliation; I felt every ounce of late-night confusion laying in the dark on my bed; I felt all the anger and hatred and frustration in the lead up to masturbating, and the revulsion of afterwards; I felt all the fear I'd ever felt that I'd live my whole life somewhere without lights; and I felt all the hurt from all the times the teacher read out my spelling test scores in class. But the big one, the one that dwarfed all others was I felt every feeling I'd ever felt, not when I looked at my mum, but when my mum looked at me.

Anyone who thinks time is a constant has never been kissed like that. Those two seconds lasted twenty years, maybe more. When she finally broke away I was amazed to see she hadn't aged and become a mature woman, and I guessed I hadn't aged either, at least not outwardly.

'You didn't mind?' she said, looking down between us. I assured her I didn't.

'I'm going to tell mum you two snogged,' Sarah-Louise shouted in a sing-song voice.

'Don't worry,' Cindy said, 'She won't.'

'Will too!'

We hung out in the park all afternoon, and while there was no more kissing we did take every opportunity to touch one another's hand even if it was a fleeting by accident/on purpose bump.

I thought about her every second of every day after that. Even when I tried not to think about her the mental effort it took made me think of her all the more. I still functioned, still caught the train to school and attended class, smoked cigarettes with Metal and came home of an evening, but it was like… you know when you're pottering around the home and you've got the TV on in the background? Well, she was my TV. The world turned, life progressed and all the while she was there with me, quietly keeping me company.

Soon afterwards the invitation was reciprocated, and we were invited over to theirs. I picked out jeans and my very best t-shirt, had a bath the night before and lay awake all night worrying if she'd still like me. That worry intensified on the journey over and hit a peak as mum reached out and pressed the doorbell. As she did, the worry I'd felt lurched into full-on fear, but if I thought that was bad, it was nothing to what was to come.

She actually opened the door and when she saw me she smiled. Behind her Sarah-Louise sang, 'Your boyfriend's here!'

Mum either didn't hear or ignored her, and went into the kitchen. Back in the hallway we stood for the longest time, not looking at each other but feeling the other's presence. When I did glance up I saw Cindy looked as scared as I felt.

Sarah-Louise said, 'Come on, let's all go for a walk.'

I hadn't taken my coat off and stood waiting while they put theirs on. Then we walked down the garden path and onto the pavement. We weren't twenty steps away when Cindy stole her hand into mine. I felt like I'd just eaten the warmest pudding on the coldest day, and a heat came out of me so intense I almost had to take off my coat.

We walked on hand in hand with Sarah-Louise nattering away ten to the dozen beside us. When we reached the corner, we carried on around as permission had not been granted to cross any roads.

As soon as we were out of sight of the house, we all relaxed and Cindy snuggled into me putting her arm around my waist. It was something I'd longed for, but also feared. I didn't know what to do back. Last time I'd just stood there dumbly, but I couldn't get away with that again.

Feeling awkward and stupid and elated and clumsy, I put my arm around her shoulders and felt her sink a little deeper into me. And as she did, as we walked, it was like each step we trod eliminated another bad feeling: there goes stupid; there goes awkward; there goes clumsy; until only elated remained. I felt happy. This is what it feels like. This, right here. This is happy. Well I never.

Then something else came in, something bigger and stronger that smashed all the happy aside. It was fear. In the space of one footstep I went from feeling like I could fly, to feeling like I was about to die. I have never, *never*, felt so scared in all my life, not even the night my mum was beaten up. And so sudden! I couldn't work it out. How could I have gone from feeling that good with this girl who clearly wanted to be with me, and I wanted to be with her, *desperately wanted to be with her*, to feeling this bad?

She snuggled tighter and my insides responded with the command to flee. Run, you fucker!

'Simon? Simon, where are you going?'

I was off. I didn't look back. I didn't shout why I'd taken off, I just ran. At the end of the road I disobeyed parental instructions and bolted between the cars to the other side.

'Simon! No! Simon, where are you going?'

I had no idea, I just had this uncontrollable need to put as much distance between us as possible, as fast as possible. I ran and ran and ran and ran until I couldn't run anymore, where I shambled to a halt, my legs wobbly and my belly full of butterflies. I was panting hard and it hurt, but I didn't feel scared anymore, and that was good, that was very good. I felt like I'd outrun being scared. I was too quick, way too quick for it, and now I was far enough away that it would never catch me up.

Where was I anyway? Looking up I gathered I was on a main road simply by the number of cars swishing past me. On both sides were big houses with red roofs and big bay windows, with nice clean cars in neat little driveways beside well kept gardens. Ahead was a small parade of shops. Behind, nothing but the grey of houses. I didn't recognise any of it. I was lost, lost, lost.

A 12-year-old's ability to recover from hard physical exertion is something the later me would come to admire. But when you're young and in the moment, you just live it. Heaving myself upright, I tested my shaky legs for strength, found they worked perfectly and started walking. The big houses became smaller, then set in terrace runs with cars not parked in driveways, but on the street out front. Still I walked on and on, and as I did I began to wonder what Cindy must have thought, and why I ran away when what I really wanted was to be with her? Didn't I love having our arms around one another? Then why did I feel so scared? I couldn't make any sense of it because it was all so foggy inside my head.

At a junction I recognised the road running off to the left and followed it. I wasn't sure it would lead to home, but it was familiar.

In my mind I returned to Cindy and Sarah-Louise and what they would say to our mums. I knew mine would go ballistic. Running off was the worst thing I could do, but I wasn't in control, she'd have to understand that. Anyone who felt that scared would have done the same, even her.

Suddenly I knew where I was. Home was a couple of miles on. Quickening my pace, I marched forward. I knew no one would be in, that mum would still be in Michelle's kitchen drinking coffee and talking until she was ready to leave, but it would be good to be home, and I'd sit on the doorstep until she got back and she'd be pleased to see me.

When I turned the final corner and could see our home, I realised I'd got it wrong. The car was in the drive. She was home.

My quick pace slowed, then slowed even more when I saw her walk to the end of the driveway and look up and down the road. When she saw me, she screamed my name and I broke into a run, those annoying tears running down my cheeks again.

'Where the hell have you been?' she demanded as soon as I was close enough to hear her.

That slowed me.

'Get here, now!'

I didn't dare not, though I'd love to have run off again.

Grabbing my front and shaking me she shouted, 'Where have you been?'

We were out the front and I felt as though everyone was staring at me.

'You could have been killed,' she said, shaking me again. Glancing up I saw the red hot anger in her eyes. 'Answer me, where have you been?'

Trying with all my might not to cry like a girl and anger her even further, I said, 'Walking.'

'Walking?' She threw me towards the house. 'Get inside, now!'

Cuffing the tears to one side I spun around and said, 'You should be pleased to see me!'

Balking, she said, 'I should *what?*'

Sobbing out of anger and frustration and just the whole sense of injustice because *it wasn't my fault*, I shouted back, 'You should be pleased to see me. You should be pleased that I didn't get killed. You're supposed to be my mum, you're supposed to be pleased to see me!'

The sound came first, a really loud, dull echo followed by the fierce burst of pain across the side of my face. Without knowing how I'd got there I was on the floor looking up at her. Her eyes were no longer angry, but full of hatred, and in that second I knew my eyes mirrored hers and I knew she knew it too. Well good. I'm glad. I sat up, held my face out and waited for the next blow. I wouldn't block it, I'd let her do it. Go on. *Go on, do it!*

In a calm, measured voice, she said, 'Get up to your room and don't you dare come out until tomorrow.'

Chapter 20

I'd got into the habit of sleeping in my clothes when I was at mum's, and lay on the bed listening to the sounds of the house. My tummy rumbled and my first thought was to tell mum, as that always made her happy. But maybe not tonight, as clearly sending me to bed without any tea after she'd slapped me for running off was a punishment and not meant to please her.

I missed Cindy and how it felt when we touched. It was so confusing how I liked it so much but couldn't stand it at the same time. It was too intense. If only there was a way to dial down the truckload of feelings that slammed over me when we were together.

I wondered if this was how mum felt about dad? If it was, no wonder they split up. Nobody could live with that.

And on from that, is that how she feels about me? Has she learnt to rein it in and that's what she's doing? It's possible, isn't it? For a second there was a spark of warm light some place deep inside of me, but then I thought of the hate in her eyes and knew that whatever she did feel for me, it wasn't that, and the light went out. In the dark of the room I reached up and touched my face. It felt sore. I don't mind that she hit me, kind of liked it because it's such an adult thing to do, I just hated her for not being pleased to see me. That's her job, that's what a mum is supposed to do, and she didn't. I didn't think I could ever forgive her for that.

Chapter 20

In the morning, I waited until she had gone downstairs and started her makeup before creeping out of my room. She was sitting where she always sat, her pots and potions spread out around her. When she heard me come in, she gave me a look so loaded with disappointment I felt my entire insides sag.

'I'm sorry,' I said. I hadn't planned on apologising, it just came out. I wasn't even sure what I was apologising for, after all it hadn't been my fault, she must know that.

Eventually she gave a short, sharp, guarded nod. That was my cue. Taking my spot on the carpet I sat without speaking.

'Why did you do it?' she asked.

I didn't know what to say.

'Answer me,' she demanded, her voice stern. But before I could panic that I didn't know, she continued, 'You *never* walk off! You *never* leave the girls, do you understand me? Michelle only let them go out because I told her you could be trusted. But I was wrong, wasn't I? I thought you were maturing into a really nice lad, someone I could rely on, someone I could trust, but how wrong I was. You're selfish, stop crying!'

'I can't help it. I'm so sorry, please don't, mum.'

'So what, did you just decide,' she flitted her hands up like a puppet whose strings had just been pulled, and said in a high voice, 'I think I'm going to go home. I don't give a *fuck!* about anybody else, all I care about is me and I'm going to walk home.' Then she did a little sitting down flouncy dance while humming a dum-te-dum-te-dum-te-dum tune that I guessed was supposed to be me walking off.

'Please don't,' I begged. 'It wasn't like that.'

'Then what was it like?'

'It wasn't my fault.'

'Why not?'

Sobbing I admitted, 'I don't know.'

'You don't know why you let everyone down and proved you can't be trusted. Well that's very mature, isn't it?'

'I'm so sorry.'

'Are you? Good, because we're going back next weekend and you're going to apologise to Michelle and the girls.'

Oh my God, I hadn't thought about seeing them again. I couldn't see Cindy. I would explode, literally, explode. The panic I felt was so big it blocked my throat and stopped all words escaping.

Misreading the look as acceptance, she went back to her makeup.

'As usual you ruin everything,' she continued. 'Your aunt *was* going to come and see you last night, but I had to tell her what you'd done and ask her not to. Such a shame, she was really looking forward to it.'

Oh no. My other mother, I loved her and she loved me. Seeing her most weekends was what I lived for.

'She has some news for you that she really wanted to tell you herself. She was so upset when I told her she couldn't because of what you'd done. *Don't cry, don't you dare cry!* Stop being so sensitive.'

I couldn't help it – in fact, I wasn't sure there was anything I could control anymore.

'She wants to take you on holiday to Egypt.'

That stopped the world. So my other mother wanted to take me away, oh my God!

'Both of us?' I asked, sniffing.

'No, just you. And…' the moment hung while she worked on her eyes. Eventually, after what felt like a thousand years, she continued, '…it's a test, to see if it works between you.' She shrugged, not lifting her eyes from the mirror. 'If it works, she might want you to live with her after all. Now go and get ready for school, we'll talk more tonight.'

We didn't. Oh, we talked about the holiday and what clothes I'd need, the inoculations at the doctor's, spending money that I had to save up from occasional pocket money, all that good stuff, but she never again spoke about it being a test run for me living with her and I didn't know how to bring the subject up. Although I couldn't help thinking about it all the time. I think it was the word 'test' that freaked me the most. The morning spelling tests at school were still a disaster. I tried to act all cocky and this was one in the eye for the system when I handed over my blank sheet, but inside I hated it. More than anything I wanted to fit in, and my inability to spell was just another example of being different. The thought of a holiday-long test scared the pants off me. Truth is, I wanted her to want me. I wanted her to spend the time with me and report back that she found me a delight and wanted more than anything to take me on to live with her. I wanted her to beg mum, who of course would be jealous and refuse to let me go. Or, at the very worst, let me go. Either way I'd be with someone who wanted me. As long as I didn't mess up the test, it would all be better.

In between stressing about the holiday-test, I had other things to worry about. Namely, Cindy. I was having a hard time not thinking about her. I really liked her, but far more than that, she liked me. At least, she had. What she thought of me now after I'd run away from her I could only guess, and the guesses were seldom good. I hated myself for what I did even though it wasn't my fault. Not only that, but I'd let mum down too and proved myself to be a cunt.

The school week dragged on the length of a long, boring millennium. Saturday morning mum said, 'Be ready by eleven. We're going to Michelle's and you're going to apologise to her and the girls for running off.'

My thoughts of Cindy were becoming more complicated, not less. Whenever I thought about her I felt warm and happy inside, but whenever I tried to think about the two of us together I felt panicky and afraid. Why?

In my head I was caught between the fear of seeing her again and the fear of upsetting mum by coming up with a reason I couldn't go. In the end fear of Cindy won. I was too scared, far too scared to go. I went into the bathroom planning on plunging my fingers down my throat but the second I went in there realised I wouldn't need to.

'Are you being sick?' Mum shouted from outside the door.

Sound effects confirmed indeed I was, and the trip was put off. I stayed in bed all weekend and didn't get up until Monday morning. The following weeks were survivable. Life chugged on. I went to school where I continued my silent rebellion, refusing to do the tests they set, refusing to do the homework, or read the books, learn the maths, study the geography or listen to descriptions of the industrial revolution, and nobody noticed. And that was fine.

When school broke up for the summer and all the other students piled out the gates, Metal and I snuck into the TD room for a smoke. As he sparked up I rummaged through the teacher's desk for the girly magazine, but it wasn't there.

'Must have taken it with him. Be a long eight weeks for him without it,' Metal said grinning, taking a drag and blowing a succession of perfect smoke rings before handing me the fag.

Taking it I asked, 'Can I have a cigarette to take home?'

'Mm, 'course! Long eight weeks without a smoke for you too, aye?' With that he took a stick from the packet and handed it over. 'Wait…' he then tore and end off the match box, the bit with the strike on it, and included two matches – 'In case one goes out,' he said.

I had no intention of smoking it, and every intention of mum finding it. I'd been thinking a lot about her saying how she felt I had been mature before I ran away from Cindy, and had been trying to work out how I could regain that status. Planting a cigarette for her to find was risky. I knew she'd go nuts, but at the same time she would have to acknowledge that I was doing adult things, and therefore, by definition, I must be growing up. She hated me already so I didn't have that much to lose. Just the thought that she'd be thinking about me, even if those thoughts were hate-filled, made me feel… important to her?

'Thanks,' I said.

'So, what's young Simon doing over the summer holidays?'

I told him about the holiday to Egypt.

'Nice!' he said.

Nice didn't even begin to cover it.

'How do you feel?' my aunt said the morning of the holiday. She was wearing brown leather trousers and matching waistcoat over a cream blouse with trendy platform shoes, her blond hair immaculate from the cut and style it received every week in Harrods. The boot of her Rolls Royce Silver Shadow was open and I could see packets and packets and packets of Piccadilly Number One cigarettes spilled all around her cases. Adding my bag, she slammed the lid of the boot shut. Auntie was the success of the family, a millionaire back in the days when that meant something, she was a director of a company along with the Colonel, importing and exporting glass bottles from offices in Gayfare Street in central London. This holiday was part work and part pleasure.

'So excited!' I said, just loud enough so mum could hear.

She'd never had any children of her own, instead lavishing all her love on her two golden retrievers, Kim and Becky. Most weekends she'd come and see us, and when she did she was warm and hugged me and brought presents and spent time with me, and I loved her to bits.

Egypt, oh my! We saw the pyramids and the Sphinx, went to the Valley of Kings where I held the key of life and even cruised down the Nile. We saw buses with people hanging on the outside and even sitting on the roof and laughed at the constant bib, bib, bib of cars. I was on my best behaviour. At dinner I'd pour my aunt her wine. When she got up to go to the loo, I stood too and escorted her, waited and brought her back to the table. When the band played, I asked her to dance. When she reached for her cigarettes I reached for her lighter to light it for her. She was warm and kind and friendly. There were moments when I could have asked her if she was interested in having me, but I didn't because I was scared she might say no, and what would I do then? All I could do was try and be good, and hope at the end of it she might want me. When we flew home and mum was waiting for us in arrivals, I ignored her and stayed by my aunt's side.

Afterwards I fantasised about how it might go down when she inevitably called mum to say she wanted me. I imagined mum's face and the realisation of what she was about to lose. I would of course play it cool. For a while I'd be undecided as to where I wanted to live, and I'd watch as they both tried to seduce me into wanting to be with them. And of course I'd secretly enjoy watching mum feel bad for getting it so wrong and hating me when what she really did was love me.

Mum couldn't afford to take time off work to look after me, so through the long summer holidays she got up and went to work and I stayed at home. Throughout this time, food was the dominating factor.

'There's bread on the side,' she'd call on her way out, slamming the door behind her.

During term-time she'd make breakfast for us both, but on school holidays she said I had the whole day to eat while she was at work, and would leave me to it. The instant her car pulled off the drive I was in the kitchen. Toast and marmite, the food of Gods. Rummaging in the pack, I brought out two slices of bread and held them up, searching for mould. Bread was always going off in our house and you had to be careful. But mould wasn't necessarily game over. If the outer slices were bad, sometimes the middle ones were okay, as long as you cut off anything with blue fur.

I checked my slices. They were pretty bad. There was a big stretch of mould along one edge that had bled into the bread itself. Deciding on this occasion they were too far gone and tossing them in the bin, I went back into the pack for some middle slices. Luck wasn't with me. They were just as bad. Grabbing the whole pack I threw it away.

The fridge was empty bar a shrivelled tomato, a tub of margarine and half a jar of spicy pickle. Defeated, I went back to watching TV.

An hour later I was back in the kitchen. Maybe there was a can of beans somewhere? I searched. There wasn't. Back to the TV.

Another hour passed and I was back. There *must* be something, somewhere! Nope.

By early afternoon I'd have eaten a second hand pair of socks if they had a good sauce with them.

In the end I pulled the pack of bread out from the bin and salvaged what I could by cutting around the mould. The trick is to get as close to the mould as you can so you don't lose too much bread, while not getting any mould. What was left was tiny, so I had to do it to nearly all the slices to make it worthwhile, and even then probably only made up half of one regular slice, but at least it was something. Another time I found a can of new potatoes right at the back of a cupboard. Raw they were crunchy and disgusting, so I hit on the idea of frying them in loads and loads of margarine. Wowzers, they were amazing – Masterchef, eat your heart out! One day all I could find was a packet of crumble mix. We had a cooking apple tree in the garden so I went out, picked a couple of apples and made an apple crumble. But these were the exceptions. Mostly, no matter how resourceful, desperate or prepared to put anything in my mouth, there wasn't anything to eat. Those times, I'd put my coat on, double, triple and quadruple check I had the front door key on me, and go out searching the streets for money so I could buy sweets.

Maybe pockets were weaker back then, but there seemed to be a lot of dropped change you could find if you looked. Half-pences were the most common on account of them being the smallest coins. At the local sweetshop you could buy five tiny sweets, like little gobstoppers, for half a pence. Another time I found fifty pence and gorged on two Mars bars *and* a packet of crisps, and, once, a five-pound note. I didn't tell mum about the rest, but I did tell her about the five-pound note. I knew it was a lot of money and I was too scared to spend it, so I still had it in my pocket.

'Let me see,' she said.

I showed her. Without saying another word, she took it.

'I hate you!' I screamed.

Cool as ice cream she said, 'Good.'

Later that night she came into my room and sat on my bed. I turned to face the wall, determined I was never going to speak to her for the rest of my life.

'I know you hate me, but it's not easy being a mum on my own,' she said. 'It costs a lot of money to keep this roof over our

Chapter 20

heads and pay all the bills. One day you're going to be able to go out to work and contribute, but until then, it's down to me to pay for everything. Look at me. Simon, look at me!'

Reluctantly I rolled over.

'When you're home here having a lovely time, I'm out at work earning the money to pay for the heating so you can keep warm, and the food…'

'There's never anything to eat.'

'Well you don't look like you're starving to death to me.'

'My tummy hurts, it's so empty.'

'Don't exaggerate!'

'It does. And it rumbles all the time.'

'That's good. That's how it should be. That's healthy. You should be hungry all the time, stop you getting fat.' With that she reached out and cupped my face in the hand so it was under my chin with her fingers digging into my cheeks, and squeezed. In a low, hissing whisper she said, 'Don't you *ever!* begrudge giving me money again, you ungrateful, horrible child. Do you understand me?'

I couldn't speak, couldn't nod, so did something in-between.

She stood up and threw the five-pound note on the bed.

Bouncing away from it like she'd tossed down a lighted match, I yelled, 'I don't want it!'

'Take it.'

'But I don't want it! Please mum, please. You have it.'

'No.' And she walked out.

'You're supposed to love me!' I yelled. 'Not hate me.'

Her face reappeared at the door. 'I don't hate you. I don't like you, but I don't hate you.'

Less sure, I said, 'You don't want me.'

She started grinning. It wasn't a happy smile. 'No, and neither does anyone else.'

'Auntie does,' but even as I said it, I knew by her look that there had been developments.

Raising her eyebrows she said, 'No she doesn't.'

'But…'

'No buts. No buts, Simon. She doesn't want you either, but unlike her I don't have any choice in the matter,' and she was gone.

I couldn't believe it. What had I done wrong? Hadn't we got on well? Hadn't I been the perfect boy? That was the best test I'd ever sat. I thought I had it in the bag.

It's because I'm a cunt. You can't hide that. Of course she doesn't want me. *Of course she doesn't want me.*

Laying on the bed I tried as hard as I could not to cry. But trying doesn't get you anywhere. They came, the tears, they came. The best I could hope for was not to make any noise.

It took a week of staying awake and listening in to her late night telephone conversations before I began to put a picture together of what had happened, and then backed it up during one of our morning chats by asking, 'Has aunty left uncle and is she now living with someone else?'

Looking surprised, she put the mirror down and turned to face me. 'Why, what have you heard?'

Careful not to make eye contact, I shrugged.

'Tell me what you heard,' she repeated, a little angrier now.

'Just what you said on the phone.'

A three beat silence, followed by, 'You've been listening in on my private conversations?'

'I didn't mean to.'

'Oh you didn't mean to!' she said, throwing her arms in the air, one still clutching the mirror. 'Oh, that's alright then! You didn't mean to. And I bet it wasn't your fault?'

'It wasn't.'

'Of course it wasn't! It's never your fault, is it?'

'I'm sorry.'

'No you're not.' Hands back down, mirror where it was, cold eyes locked on mine.

'I am…' I stammered.

'You're not. You're not sorry because it's not your fault. That's what you're thinking, isn't it?' She reached out and squeezed my kneecap until a pain like an electric current shot up my leg.

Tears. Fuck tears. I hate them!

'Stop crying *now*!'

'I can't,' I sobbed, wishing with all my heart that I could control my stupid eyes.

'Just like it wasn't your fault running away from the girls. You don't like girls, do you Simon? Wouldn't that be just perfect. Or is it only Cindy you don't like?'

Just the mention of her name gave me the same kind of exaggerated reaction a cartoon character has to a whack around the head, kind of a *boing*. It would have been impossible for her not to have noticed, but she didn't say anything. I could feel her staring at me, feel her smile, but she didn't say a word. For the longest time she just sat there looking at me. I couldn't stand it; I felt like she was peering straight into my brain and reading all my thoughts. It was horrible – I'd never felt so vulnerable and exposed.

In the end she just carried on with her makeup, and when she did speak it was back to the subject of my aunt, my other mother.

'You're right, your aunt has left your uncle. That's why she can't take you. I'm sorry.' She looked genuinely upset for me. I think she knew what it meant, and I realised that underneath it all she did want the best for me. I felt flattered. Nice even. Upset that my aunt didn't want me, but I liked it when mum cared.

For two whole weeks nothing dramatic happened, and then I burnt the house to the ground.

Chapter 21

It's a boy!

Wait… and another!

Oh my… she's not finished… and… a girl!

Triplets!

Birth. The most beautiful, amazing, incredible moment on the farm. Messy, mucky, emotional, scary and thrilling, and that's just how it feels for me. This time Mum is a goat called Amber, who'd thoughtfully decided to give birth around lunchtime, which is nice of her. Most of the animals prefer the middle of the night under torchlight, preferably when it's freezing cold and raining.

'You are amazing,' I told her, the last of the tiny little kids squirting out and hitting the floor beside the other two. Perfect, perfect little tiny goats, all damp and bleary-eyed and hungry. They must have been looking forward to getting out and tucking into a hearty meal of mother's milk, and demonstrated this by crying out (in goat, obviously, but I'm pretty good at translating), 'Get me food, *now*!'

We were in an open-fronted field shelter that I'd redeveloped into the goat quarters. If you were a human, you'd see a large airy room the size of a double garage with five huge rounds of tree stumps sticking out of a straw base, and over to one side an old defunked chest freezer with the lid screwed down and a rubber mat on the top, a hayrick bulging with sweet-smelling hay and a heat lamp with a red bulb shining warm in one corner. If you were a goat, however, you'd see things to climb, stand on, sleep on, eat, and warmth for your babies. In short, a five-star goaty maternity unit.

We were all present, except the dad Billy the Whiffy, who would like to have been there but couldn't on account of the fact that he was in handy portion-size bags in the freezer (not the one Amber slept on – that would be weird). His demise was a unanimous decision taken because he really, really, really stank, and the whole urinating in his own face had started to upset everyone. So collectively we decided he'd be much better off used in tasty curries.

'They look so frail,' I said, peering down at the puddle of new life and afterbirth, fighting the urge to pick the goat kids up, wrap them in warm fluffy towels and cuddle them warm and smother them with love.

Amber, on the other hand saw, something different, and, ever the practical mother, moved in to eat the afterbirth.

Now I know this can be a thing, and many mothers and even fathers swear by it. All those nutrients and goodness – but personally, watching someone chewing on slimy, bloody sludge that a minute ago was inside her makes me feel icky.

'It's up to you, but I've got a bucket of food if you'd prefer?' I placed the bucket next to her. Thank goodness she did. While she was busy I removed the sludgy birth sac. 'Just so you know, I'm not pinching this to have it later with some fava beans and a nice Chianti.'

Then I stood back. The golden rule is only intervene if you absolutely have to. Otherwise, leave Mum and babies well alone. Let them get on with it. For now.

With my back against the wall I sank down onto my heels the way I had with the ewe and lamb. Déjà vu? God I hope not.

While Amber's head was firmly embedded in the bucket scoffing the nuts, the first born, a tan boy with a streak of white down his nose, got up onto wobbly feet, bleating, 'I'm going for it, everyone!' took unsteady steps towards her back end and latched onto a teat first time. Houston, we have contact.

Mum didn't flinch.

One down, two to go.

Do goats get PND? Reject their babies? It must happen from time to time, stands to reason. I sent a silent prayer to an I-don't-know-if-you-really-exist-but-just-in-case God: 'Not now, please, have a heart, not this time.'

Outside the weather was warm, with just a slight breeze ruffling the treetops in the distance. The new-to-the-world kids probably didn't even need the heat lamp in the corner, but it made me feel better that it was there.

Minutes ticked by. Then the second boy, snowy white from head to hoof, wobbled up to a stand, fell over, got back up again and made his way over. Holding my breath, I watched Amber stop eating, pull her head out of the bucket and look around just as he latched on.

In a classic case of 'Leave my boobs alone!' she took swift steps to her left, leaving the two boys sucking in air. Reacting the way we all would if you opened your mouth expecting dinner only to have it whipped away, the boys went into full tantrum mode.

Forcing myself not to panic, I stayed where I was, my heart-beat going thin and wispy in my chest. Any more rejections around here and I'd have to start looking at myself – oh God, please tell me this bloody thing isn't contagious.

But Mother Nature's a canny thing. She knows a trick or two. Sure, some slip through the net, but she's got a handle on most life.

Amber looked up from the bucket once more, looked right at the boys, and bleated. It felt like that was the first moment she really acknowledged what she'd done. It was certainly the first time she spoke to them. In that millisecond, I thought, what are you thinking? *Are* you even thinking, or are you working on instinct? You know these are your babies, right? That you've given birth to them? How does that make you feel? Do you feel love? Does your heart feel like it's going to burst open? Do you have overwhelming urges to protect and mother them? Why did you move away from them just now? Are you nervous? Scared? Do you have flashes of the future and all the things you're going to be doing together? Are you worried about getting your body shape back and wondering how soon you can get down the gym so you can be a yummy mummy, and when exactly did they say you could start drinking wine again?

Okay, so maybe goats don't worry about their figure or wine, but the rest of it is valid. Isn't it?

The boys took her bleat for, 'Oops, sorry, don't know what came over me there. Come on, come and get your milk,' and wobbled back to the bar.

I watched as Amber stood firm for them. I watched, and so did the little girl. The last one to be born, she was still on the floor, and she was tiny, a tan-coloured dot of a thing no bigger than a leggy hamster. To survive she needed to share some of the colostrum the boys were scoffing.

Don't interfere unless you have to. Well, if I didn't, she wouldn't make it to tonight. Female goats only have two teats, which is a bit of a problem when you have three kids. So picking up the little girl, I shoved the bigger boy, whose belly was clearly swollen, over to one side, and plugged her in.

Amber didn't bat an eyelid.

Gently rubbing the girl's chin to encourage her to swallow, she took a mouthful, then a second, and began gulping greedily.

'Steady,' I laughed. That was all three feeding. Sometimes relief is the best feeling in the world.

When she'd finished, I phoned Debbie.

She answered on the first ring. 'Hi, are they okay?'

In order to make ends meet she'd had to get a part-time job as a sous chef in a local country pub that specialised in homemade farmer-size meals. She enjoyed the work and the other chefs and the people were lovely, but she missed out on a lot of the farming shenanigans. I texted her a picture.

'Oh, they're *so* cute! How's Amber? How is she with her babies?'

In-ter-est-ing. Clearly we're all on red alert for PND. 'She's fine. They've all had a feed and had some colostrum.'

'Good!' she said. I could hear the relief in her voice and it made me smile.

'So how are we going to do this?' All important matters, and for that read hatches, matches and dispatches, are discussed.

'Hang on, a check's just come in…' she moved the phone away but I could hear her shouting, 'Two Exmoor burgers, one fish and chips and one steak and ale pie with new pots and salad.' Then, to me, 'Sorry about that. Look, I've got to be quick. Leave the kids with Amber for now, but tonight bring the kids into the house with us – we'll put towels in the log basket and keep them in there, and we'll light the fire to keep them warm. They're going to need feeding every two hours so strip Amber out as much as you can into a jug and we'll bottle-feed them through the night. I should be home just after nine.'

'Shouldn't I leave them with Mum?'

'Three kids, two teats, you do the maths. If you leave them with mum, one of them will die. The weakest, probably, whichever one that is.'

Looking down at the little girl, I said, 'Okay.'

'It will only be for a night or two, then they should be strong enough to fend for themselves. I'm sorry, I've got to go. Love you.'

Solomon was delighted I brought friends into the house, and bounded around me as I settled the newborn kids into the log basket. When Debbie got back from work she cooed and cooed over the kids, and we took turns bottle-feeding them through the night, which is why, at midnight, I found myself pacing up and down the lounge, a succession of tiny goaty faces peering up at me over the top of a baby's bottle. To stay awake I decided to phone someone. I could either phone a late-night talk radio show, or Ziggy.

'What's happened? Who's died?' Ziggy said, answering after a few rings.

'It's me.'

'Yeah, I know it's you. What's – you haven't heard from my dad, have you?'

'What? No. Nothing like that.'

'Good. For a minute there I thought… doesn't matter.' He yawned, which made me do the same. 'What's up?'

I told him about the kids and the night-time milking.

'And you decided to phone me. Gee thanks.'

'Don't be an arse, I knew you were awake. It's only midnight, you're always awake at midnight. It's just mornings you don't do.'

'Yeah, well…'

The trick with feeding a goat kid is to hold them carefully by the shoulder so the rest of their body hangs down, which makes it easier for them to take the milk, because their tummies are only little and if you scoop them up there's nowhere for the milk to go. It doesn't look very elegant, but it works.

We'd decided to feed them in reverse order from how they were born. In other words, smallest first. The little girl.

Ziggy said, 'I remember doing the night feeds with mine. Have you tried adding some gin to the milk? Works a treat.'

'Don't tell me, your mother did it with you and you turned out fine.'

'Exactly!'

'When was the last time you looked in a mirror and saw a sober face staring back?'

'Ooooh, she's all grumpy when she's not getting her eight hours isn't she?'

The words were the same we always used to tease and prod one another, but there was a tension behind them that you couldn't quite put your finger on but placed the conversation just this side of uncomfortable.

In my arms, the little girl was full. You could tell by the milk spilling out from the sides of her mouth.

'Hang on, I've got to swap goats.'

'Now that's a sentence not said very often.'

Putting the little girl down, I picked up the middle boy and put the plastic teat into his mouth.

With him gulping greedily, I said, 'You still there?'

'Mm.'

'He's drinking like you at last orders.'

'Good lad. How was the birth, no dramas?'

'There was a moment. The first one she was fine with, but she seemed to go a bit funny with the second, and then ignore the last. But then she was okay. First light I'm going to take them back to spend the day with mum and just keep an eye on them.'

'How's the lamb?'

'Bonded with mum.'

'Seriously? I wasn't expecting you to say that.'

'I know.'

Silence. The only noise coming from the kid slurp, slurp, slurping.

Finally Ziggy said, 'Where are you at with dredging up the past?'

The answer came instantly. I didn't even need to think about it. 'About to burn the house down.'

'Well, that's something to look forward to.'

The little boy was slowing, some milk beginning to seep out from the corners of his mouth.

I know it happened, but I can't remember the details. I can remember the fireman, and I can remember the gut-wrenching feeling of helplessness, standing there in the lounge as everything caught light around me. But they're just snapshots of feelings without any narrative to hold them together. Pictures tossed in the air for me to catch a glimpse of before they tumble back out of sight.

Ziggy asked, 'How does it work – are you seeing it all through your eyes as if it was happening for real, or are you looking down on it watching it like it was a film with you in the starring role?'

The goat had finished. I took the bottle out of his mouth and put it on the side. Luckily with goats you don't have to burp them, and they tend not to throw up. But I wasn't thinking about that. I was thinking about Ziggy's question.

'I don't know,' I said, suddenly aware that I couldn't remember. No matter how much I tried I couldn't work out how the memories were coming to me. The closest I could get was, 'Maybe both?'

A second passed before he started laughing. 'Jesus, this has got very serious for a midnight phone call. Do you want me to tell a dick joke?'

'Hang on, let me swap goats again. Last one.'

The last boy was a monster compared with the other two, and latched on like he was going to devour milk, bottle and my fingers.

'How's the family?' I said.

'That was quick. Yeah, all good. Money's tight, which means we're rowing more than normal, but at least the making-up sex is good. She's in bed. Went up couple of hours ago. Kids are fine. Usual crap, different day.'

'Coming down again anytime soon?' You could plainly hear the hope in my voice.

He didn't answer straight away, and when he did he said, 'I'm not sure.'

'Yeah, of course. Well, I'll expect a drunken crash through the door when I get one then.' I tried to put a smile in my voice, but I'm not sure it worked.

'That it? Goat's fed? Am I dismissed?'

'Bugger off.'

'Yeah, bugger off yourself. Night.'

Nodding, 'Night.'

Frankly, it's a good thing the biggest boy was kept until last, as not only did he drink far quicker than the others, he took much more than his portion and would have continued had I not called a halt and put him back.

I don't know how to rectify me and Ziggy, get it back the way it was before I upset him for not taking the conversation he had with his dad seriously. It's not like it's a huge falling out that we can talk about and get over, it's more subtle; and the subtle ones are the killers. Give me a massive fight over a subtle shift any day.

Not wanting to disturb Debbie after her busy day, I stretched out on the sofa, closed my eyes and yawned.

Chapter 22

'What the hell is this?' Mum yelled. She was holding the cigarette and two matches Metal had given me on the last day of school. I couldn't even remember where I'd hidden them and had completely forgotten they existed.

'Great, so now my twelve-year-old son is smoking. Oh, that's... just... *wonderful*. I can't trust you for one second, can I? Get up to your room, *get up to your room*!'

Upstairs I sat on the bed and thought, well, let's see where this goes. When I took them from Metal it had been my intention for her to find them, a plan I now considered was probably quite rubbish. But so what. I put my hands up to my face to wipe away the tears and found to my delight that there weren't any. Hey, now that's progress!

Downstairs I could hear frantic phone calls, but because it wasn't the quiet of night, and was instead daytime with all the associated noises, I couldn't make out what was being said.

When she came up she didn't knock on the door but yanked it open. 'Downstairs, now!'

I went down and sat on the sofa. She came in, turned off the television and sat at the other end.

'Mum, I'm sorry,' I said.

'Shut it! I don't want to hear another word from you.'

We sat in silence for ages and ages and ages until a car turned onto our drive and stopped. Sounds of the driver's door opening and closing. Then she got up and walked out, warning me, 'Don't you dare move!'

It was Him. I knew it would be. He hadn't disappeared from the scene and was still around two or three nights a week. Sometimes it was good, and sometimes I'd hear them fighting late at night in her room, and in the morning He'd be gone and she'd be plastering on the makeup.

Last night was a good night and we'd been laughing and joking together. I expected that to continue and said, 'Hey.' But a single glance at his face and I realised I'd misjudged everything.

He took out a gold-coloured packet of Benson and Hedges and threw them with all his might at the seat next to me, where they hit the cushion and shot off across the room.

Flinching, I scrunched up into a ball. I could feel Him towering over me, hear His breathing in short, stabbing breaths. And that wasn't the only sound. I heard the front door open and close and mum's footsteps as she made her way down the drive. Then the car started up, reversed out, and drove away.

She'd left me. Left me with Him.

'Sit up,' He demanded. 'You're old enough to smoke, you're old enough to take the punishment.'

No longer able to hear His breathing over my own, I scrunched tighter into a ball.

'I said sit up. I'm not going to hit you.'

He wasn't over me anymore. I could hear Him over to the side. Peeking a look, I could see Him retrieving the smokes before sitting down. Then He lit one.

'How long you been smoking?' He asked. 'By the way, your mother wants me to make you chain-smoke an entire pack to make you sick. Then she's got some crazy idea about taking you to the hospital and walking you through the cancer ward. You've really rustled up a shit storm.'

Uncoiling slightly, I said, 'I know.'

'So how long's it been going on?'

'It wasn't mine. Someone gave it to me at school.'

Taking a puff, he said, 'They gave it to you?'

'Yes.'

'You've never smoked before, and someone handed you cigarette to take home?'

'Yes.'

'Oh come on, that's not true is it?'

'It is true, I swear.'

He didn't answer for ages, just puffed and puffed until He finally said, 'You're a liar. You want to tell me the truth now?'

Sitting up I said, 'That is the truth. I promise.'

The shift was instant, like an on/off switch. One minute He was all relaxed and sitting back, the next instant He was on me, His forehead pushing against mine, His face red, His breath laboured and smoke filled. But it was His eyes. So close they were almost out of focus. They looked... alive; happy, dancing, the blue brighter than I'd ever seen. When He spoke He spoke through a smiling sneer. 'You're a liar, and a coward. You think you're a man but you're just a boy. A scared little boy. A child. You want to be a man? Then act like one.' He moved away so He could wave His arms around. 'Take a look at yourself, Simon-Big-Man. You're so desperate for everyone to think you're all grown up and be the man of the house and take care of your mother that you can't see what a pathetic little boy everyone else sees when they look at you. You want to know what your mother calls you? Boy. I didn't even know your name for the first month, just Boy. Where's the Boy? What's the Boy doing now?'

Every word was a stab in my gut. I felt like one of those voodoo dolls with all the needles sticking out of it while the person it was meant to represent writhed around on the floor actually feeling the pain – but rather than needles, He was using words. And it hurt so much because they were all true. More than anything, I hated the thought they could see all my secret hopes and fears.

'Now,' using me to push against in order to stand up, He walked back to his seat, sat, and continued, 'Shall we cut the bullshit and start again?'

I was empty. Even the pain had gone. There was literally nothing inside me, just emptiness.

'Sit up.'

I did as I was told.

'How long have you been smoking?'

'Just sometimes after school I'd have a couple of puffs on a friend's cigarette.'

Nodding, he said, 'Good. When did it start?'

'I don't know. I can't remember.' Before He could challenge me I added, 'Last term, I think.'

'Okay. Your mother's going to want to know why you brought the cigarette home.'

Should I tell Him the truth, that I wanted her to find it? I felt so stupid, and so ashamed, and so cold – I couldn't stop shivering. Thoughts were all directed inwards and went something like: you're an idiot, but worse than that, you're an obvious idiot. You're a glass person and everyone can see inside you, and that's *bad*. That's *really* bad. The urge to run away came and went, but it was just a familiar reaction, my body going through the motions of what it thought I wanted to feel and wasn't backed up by any real force, and besides, you had to care to run. Instead I grabbed a cushion and gripped it tight to my chest and tried to control the shivering.

'Well?'

'I don't know.'

A flicker of that alive, happy, dancing look in his eyes, like a horror movie trying to show the devil in human form, only way more subtle and a gazillion times more terrifying. So I told Him. I told Him the truth.

He laughed, shook his head, got up and walked out of the room. I didn't feel anything at first, just the cold emptiness, but as the bits and bobs of myself slowly found their way back inside me and took position, the sense of emptiness receded. But the feeling that took over was of utter revulsion towards my stupid self.

A while later mum came back and they spoke in the kitchen, and when they came in mum said to me, 'Don't ever do that to me again, do you understand?'

I told her I did.

'And if you ever smoke again, even a puff, I swear to God I will kill you myself.'

'I won't, I promise.'

We ate, and daytime moved into evening. They opened wine, and at some point He said, 'Come on, let's you and me go and play football in the garden.'

'I can't,' I said. Did He really want me to go out and play with Him after all that had gone on?

'Come on mate,' He said, grabbing my shoulder.

Mum added, 'Go on, go out and play.'

'I don't like football,' I said, doubling down.

'Ooh, you're so surly. Yes you do, you love football,' she said. 'Now go out and play.'

'I don't. I don't like it anymore.' I'd already told them, don't they listen?

Football meant everything to Him and He looked like I'd just vomited over his holy book. Which of course was why I did it.

'Why don't you get us some more wine,' she asked Him, and as soon as He left the room turned to me and said, 'You are *so* stupid. He was trying to be nice and you did that! You stupid, stupid child. I can't stand the sight of you, get up to bed, *now!*'

I didn't need to be asked twice, couldn't wait to get out of there. Taking the stairs two at a time, I bolted up, and once in my room slammed the door shut behind me, wishing it had a lock on it.

Fully clothed, I lay on the bed. Sounds of the evening moved on into sounds of the night. After they had turned all the lights out and gone to bed I could hear the familiar tempo of them arguing, the rise and fall of voices, the clump, clump, clump of his fists, her screams, then crying, then both of them crying, then long periods of silence punctuated by short bursts of conversation. Then nothing.

Only when I was sure they were asleep did I get undressed and slip into bed. A couple of streets away a dog left out howled and barked at the night, and I finally went to sleep.

In the morning, as usual, He was gone. Mum had got up early, and by the time I went down had plastered so much foundation on her face you couldn't see any bruising, if in fact there was any.

'Sit down,' she said when I entered. Knowing this was a prelude to 'I have something to tell you, some information to impart,' my stomach looped-the-loop. But it was okay. Despite my fears, this morning's lesson wasn't about me at all, but about her and Him.

'Despite everything, He likes you,' she told me. 'Do you like Him?'

'He hurts you.'

'No He doesn't! And that's got nothing to do with you.'

I was all out of fight, so nodded.

'Good. Now I don't really care if you two get along or not, but it would be easier if you did, obviously. It's not like I need Him, and I certainly don't love Him' – at that she harrumphed a little laugh – 'but He is good company and He helps out. Just try and be nice and don't be so grumpy. Remember, laugh and the whole world laughs with you, cry and you cry alone.'

'I don't feel like laughing.'

'Then pretend. Make it up,' She did a mock laugh to prove her point, 'Ha-ha-ha-ha.'

It was a pretty good impersonation actually, and even though I knew it was a lie I still felt my spirits lift.

'You now,' She pointed at me. 'Come on Simon, laugh!'

It was so bizarre that I did, and it wasn't even put on.

'Good,' she called.

It ran its course pretty quickly, but if you'd taken a mood temperature in the room you'd have definitely seen a rise.

While she nipped out to the kitchen to make us both a coffee, my face contorted into a grimace. I'm not sure when this had started, but it had become a horrible habit I had no control over. I could feel myself doing it more and more, to the point that when I felt it coming on I'd have to run to the bathroom or find somewhere quick to hide my face so no one could see, or if all else failed, as it sometimes did if it came on fast, put my head in my hands. But in the lounge, with mum in the kitchen, I was safe and didn't fight it. Pulling back my lips and twisting my face, I felt like a chimpanzee pulling an ugly, or one of those old men with no teeth you see gurning on television. I had absolutely no control over it. It just happened. It used to happen once or twice a week but had increased to a few times a day. It didn't hurt and didn't bother me much as long as I could hide it and nobody else knew.

By the time she came back in I was normal again.

'Here,' she said, handing me one of the mugs.

I took it and she sat back down on her knees and reached for some makeup.

'Does it hurt when He hits you?' I asked. No response, not even a blink that I'd spoken. Continuing with her work, she put one pot down and reached for another, then leant into the mirror.

'Mum?'

Again nothing. Finally she said, 'I want you to like Him. When He asks you to play football, you are to play football. Do you understand me?'

'But I don't like football.'

'Yes you do. Don't lie to me.'

'I'm not, I don't like it any more.'

Spinning round to face me she yelled, *'Don't lie to me!'*

Staring into my coffee, I could feel my face begin to tingle and my nose start flaring, and instantly knew it was a prelude to a face contortion. I tried to fight it but I couldn't. It was going to happen, and it was going to happen now. God I've got to get out of here. I started to move but she put a hand out to hold me down.

'I'm not finished with you,' she said.

'Mum, please, I've got to go,' I begged.

She looked a question at me, and as she did it happened. Just managing to get my hands up in time, my face stretched into an ugly twisted gurning shape. When it was over I dropped my hands. My face was red and I felt disgusted at myself that she had seen it.

'What…? don't do that, you look like a silly kid,' she said.

Breathing out, I nodded.

From the corner of my eye I could see her still looking at me and shaking her head. She looked disappointed, and who could blame her? Then she went back to her makeup.

'Whether you like football or not, if He asks you again, you are to say yes. Do you understand me?'

'But I don't see…'

Slamming the mirror down she said, 'You live in my house, you live by my rules. Jesus, you have no idea what I give up for you. None. I'm Mum and you do as I say, and you *will* do as you're told!'

'Okay.' But even as I said it I knew I wouldn't. Going against football was the only thing I had.

'Thank you. For some reason He does like you, you know.'

Gee, thanks. 'Do you like Him?' I asked.

She didn't answer immediately and I thought it was another case of selective hearing, until she said, 'It's complicated. He's useful, and most of the time I can control Him. He's also quite a catch, lots of the girls would like to go out with Him. And He likes me' – without looking up, she waved a vague hand in my direction – 'and you. He can be really good fun to be around, and he's not that tricky to deal with, well, men aren't, are they?'

Confused, I said, 'What do you mean?'

'I mean he's easy to play the game with – look, can we change the subject, please?'

Sipping coffee, I said, 'We haven't seen auntie for ages. Is she okay?'

'It's a very difficult time for her at the moment, what with applying for the divorce and everything. We probably won't see her for a while now. But yes, she's fine.'

And that was the end of that. She finished her makeup, got ready, and left for work. It was a Saturday, and that meant much better telly than during the week, namely, TISWAS. More than anything in the world I wanted to have a cream pie thrown in my face from the Phantom Flan Flinger – oh the heady dreams of a twelve-year-old! The day was hot and I'd opened the French windows to let in some summer air. When the programme finished and football came on, I mooched outside to sit in the apple tree. I thought about Cindy and wondered if she watched TISWAS, and if she did, whether she dreamt of having a cream pie smothered in her face too? I wondered if we'd get married one day, and that thought made me smile even if there was the minor stumbling block of being too in love with her to be in the same room.

When sitting in the tree got boring, I climbed down and went back inside.

Funny, I'm sure I left the television on. Reaching for the on off button, I realised it was already on. But the screen was blank. That had never happened before. I tried switching the channel. Still nothing. Mum was going to go APE! The TV was a rental and she paid out a fortune for it each week. It was a big old wooden box with a bulbous glass screen that sat on a stand that had wheels on the bottom. It was massive and heavy and when you wanted to change channel you had to get up, walk over and press the buttons. I pressed the buttons again. Still nothing.

Then I heard a fizzing noise from underneath.

Looking down, I saw a drop of something molten fall out the bottom of the television and land on the carpet. Where it hit, it sizzled a hole straight through the carpet to the floorboards.

I jumped up and ran out of the room, convinced the telly was about to blow up.

Once outside, I peered back around the doorway the way armed police might in a siege, nervous about being shot at. My heart was pounding. Another drip fell from under the television and I ducked back out, closing my eyes and holding my breath for the inevitable explosion. What would happen when it did explode? Was I safe with just one wall between us or would it rip through that and me? Should I go outside, run down the road?

Carefully, carefully, I looked back in. The drips were now falling in quick succession with hardly a gap between them. The hole in the carpet where they hit was about the size of a tea plate.

God, what should I do? My breath was laboured, my heart pounding. Behind the comparative safety of the wall, I took two steps one way, turned around and two steps back. I looked again, careful, careful, careful.

Drip, drip, drip drip dripdripdrip.

This can't be happening! What do I do? What do I do?

Mum was going to kill me. Literally kill me.

Then I had an idea. Running as fast as I could, I dashed to the front door where we all kicked off our shoes. There was a stack of them. I needed something big. To one side were His. They were massive compared with mine and mum's. I grabbed one and ran back.

I knew what I had to do. But I was so scared. The television was going to blow up, I knew it was going to blow up, and if I was anywhere near it when it did it would blow me up with it. I was going to die, there was no two ways about it, I was going to die. Or at very least be burnt and maimed beyond recognition. Maybe then mum would love me.

Gritting my teeth, I peered in. The drip was now a thin silvery line that seemed to connect the television with the hole in the carpet. The hole was bigger than it had been and smoking around the edges. I could hear the television making sizzling and popping noises behind the screen.

It was going to blow, it was really going to blow any second.

But I had to try or mum would kill me.

Death either way.

Oh God! Should I do it or not? *What should I do?*

Do it. Just do it. Okay. Shit, shit, shit! Taking two quick breaths, I ducked low, and clutching the shoe, moved slowly into the room.

Chapter 23

I have never been so scared in all my life. Never. My heart was racing, my breath raggedy and I could feel my insides knotted into a painful clump.

The distance from the doorway to the television was about ten feet. Keeping an arm up to shield myself from the inevitable blast, I crept forwards, my weight all on my trailing leg so I could rush back if I needed to.

I made it to within an arm's reach of the smoking television, and held the shoe out, chucking it the last little bit so it landed underneath the drip. But it didn't. It missed.

Shit!

Up close I could smell the bitter stench of burning plastic. And heat. The TV smelled hot.

If it hadn't blown up by now, it was definitely about to go up *any second!*

But I had to try and get the shoe under properly and save the carpet. The hole was now about the size of a dinner plate, but I figured you could put a rug or something over it and it would probably be fine.

Holding my breath, I ducked back in, grabbed the shoe and placed it under so the drip fell inside the shoe rather than onto the carpet. Then I turned and ran.

I'd done it! I spun around in the hallway and looked back in. And this is what I saw.

It started with the shoe. It just burst into flames. Then the television itself. Then the lamp on top. The picture on the wall above was the next thing to go up.

The cabinet next to the television caught slowly, starting on one side, the yellow flames licking along the surface, swallowing everything in their path. On the floor, on the other side of the cabinet, was mum's makeup bags and cases. They were the next to go up.

Running out the back door I went around to the open French windows and, dumbfounded, just stared in. I could not believe what I was seeing. It couldn't be real, it couldn't.

Bang, the sofa caught light, followed by the side tables and lamps.

The image that will haunt me for the rest of my life was one instant when everything in the room was on fire, but it all looked okay, like some special effect had been put in there to make it look like there were flames. Everything was alight, with bright yellow and orange flames dancing and twisting, but other than that it all looked normal. The sofa looked as if you could go and sit on it. Even the lamps looked perfect.

Then, as one, it all imploded. Holes appeared in the sofa. Tables collapsed. Dark ugly colours appeared in circles that quickly spread outwards. Lamps shattered.

'Move out the way,' someone yelled. 'Move out the way!'

It was the neighbour: he was leaning over the fence and reaching forwards, spraying a garden hose through the French windows and into the lounge.

Still I stood. The heat hurt, but I couldn't move. I was stuck watching my home, everything I'd ever known, disintegrate before my eyes. Then the smoke came – funny how much later the smoke started. But once it did, very quickly you couldn't see a thing.

The fire engine roared up out front, lights flashing, siren whirring. Suddenly I was surrounded by firemen in facemasks and oxygen tanks on their backs, who rushed inside to turn the electricity off before their colleagues opened up the water cannons. Within seconds, the fire was out, but they kept on, kept on spraying water until everything was drenched.

I just couldn't believe it. I couldn't believe it. How had this happened? Our home was ruined. Gutted. Black with soot and now running with water. Mum ran around the side of the house. It felt like the entire incident had flashed by in an instant, but in reality it had probably gone on for twenty minutes or more, and at some point one of the neighbours had phoned mum's office and told her what was going on. Ignoring me, she started talking to the fireman, then went inside.

I was in so much trouble.

When she came out, she was crying.

She came over and gave me a hug. 'What happened?' she asked.

I told her about the television. Then she went back in and I saw her talking to a fireman. They were over where the television used to be. He was pointing and gesturing. Then they came out.

Mum came up to me and said, 'Why didn't you take the television outside?'

'I thought it was going to blow up. I was scared. Should I have dragged it out?'

Sighing, she nodded before disappearing back inside.

I felt sick. Following her, in I nipped between the firemen, who were all milling about in the embers of our home. The lounge was decimated, not a single thing salvageable. Beyond the lounge, the hall and kitchen were black with soot; not just a bit black, but thick-coated jet black. The walls, the ceiling, the surfaces, everything. The fridge that was once white was now black. The cream toaster, black. The beige kettle, black. Everything black, black, black. It was hard to imagine anything could be saved.

It was the same story in the hallway, the stairs and the landing. Luckily, the bedroom doors had been closed. I looked in mine. It *stank* of fire, and there was a dusting of soot, but it didn't look too bad. Mum's was the same.

Back downstairs, the firemen were preparing to leave. Mum was simultaneously thanking them and fighting back the tears. She looked odd, standing in the charred remains of the blackened lounge in her work finest: orange skirt, cream blouse with a jazzy scarf and high heels, like a stewardess in a plane crash.

When they'd gone I went over to her. 'I'm so, so sorry,' I said.

She nodded without looking down at me.

'I should have dragged the television out, shouldn't I?'

She nodded again.

'Why did you put a shoe underneath it?'

'To stop it burning the carpet.'

Finally she looked down at me. She looked tired, really tired. With heavy words she said, 'I see.'

Sounds of a car pulling onto the drive. We both looked out the window. It was Him. She walked off to meet Him at the front door. I left them to it and went into the kitchen, where I found a sponge and some washing up liquid, and began wiping.

A while later mum came in and told me to leave it. 'Your dad's on his way over. You need to go and stay with him until I can get this sorted,' she said, taking the sponge out of my hand and throwing it into the sink.

'I'm so sorry, mum,' I said, unable to stop the tears from falling, and knowing once they started there was no way to turn them off.

When dad arrived, I had a few bits of clothing stuffed into a black bag for washing the stink of smoke out of.

'I'm really sorry,' I said for the umpteenth time.

'Just go,' she said, and turning to dad, I did.

Dad talked about everything under the sun, except fire, all the way back to his, and over the next few weeks really tried to make a fuss of me, taking me to snooker and his recording studio, but what I really wanted was to talk to mum. For two months I had no contact with her, I was too scared to phone her and she clearly didn't want to speak with me. I know I messed up, I know the fire was my fault and I'm haunted by the image of the lounge looking perfect but overlaid with flames.

Should I have opened up to dad, told him about the nightmares I had every night of fire, the fear, the hurt that I didn't do the right thing and drag that stupid telly outside, and the deepening self hatred? No, of course I shouldn't. I was trying to be a man. I was thirteen. I've got this. I made a mistake and now I've got to live with it. Simple as.

Beginning of school comes and goes. Despite my promise to mum I still sneak off for after-school cigarettes with Metal, because, well, why the heck not?

'The Undertones, that's who you should be listening to,' Metal said one time. 'I'll make a tape and bring it in for you. Why do you never buy your own smokes?'

Shrugging and saying, 'no money,' I handed his back to him and he took a drag.

'What you doing this weekend?' he asked. He liked to keep up with my social calendar.

'I think I'm going home to my mum's.'

'Really? Has she hidden all the matches?' he said laughing, then, making his hands into a megaphone he shouted, 'Don't let Simon near anything that lights, he'll burn your house down!' And rolled up at his own joke.

I laughed too. What else was I going to do? But it did cross my mind – maybe she wouldn't hide the matches, but would I be allowed to use the television again?

Rather than wait for dad to collect me, that night I made the trek to the station and caught a train to mum's. The walk the other end was horrible. I was terrified. I hadn't seen or spoken to her in eight long weeks. I had no idea what mood she'd be in, although I was sure she wouldn't be happy. I had no idea what the house would look like. I didn't even know if I'd still have my room.

But I did have my front door key. I gripped it as I walked, the steps as slow as I could make them whilst still maintaining forward motion. Finally I turned the corner and saw the drive. Her car was on it.

Walking up to the front door, I put my school bag down and, not wanting to use the key, knocked politely.

It was an age before she answered.

'Don't tell me you lost your key?' she said, opening the door. I showed it to her.

'Then why didn't you use it? It's never stopped you before.'

I didn't know what to say and followed her inside. The hallway was light and bright and smelled of paint and new carpet.

'Shoes!' she said and I kicked them off.

The lounge looked amazing, like something out of a home magazine, all fresh and bright and brand new. It looked so different! So modern, and big! The walls were magnolia and the carpet beige. The sofa had a touch of formality about it, by contrast with than the dossy one it had replaced, and had a subtle dark red pattern on it. There were pictures on the walls, bright splashes of colour that I had never seen before. In the centre the table had gone and hadn't been replaced, but there was a coffee table. And a television where the old one used to live. Same spot.

Only this one was much, much newer. We both looked at it, then looked at each other.

I started crying and said, 'I'm so sorry, mum.'

Not unkindly, she said, 'Sit down.'

It felt like we were sitting in the lobby of a posh hotel. It didn't feel like home at all. All the stains and scuffs of us living life in this room had gone. There was nothing of us there anymore. Nothing of me. I sat with my hands under my thighs.

'What do you think?' She asked.

I smiled and told her it looked amazing.

'I had to borrow the money,' she said, 'Although we are going to sue the television rental company, tell them I'm a single mum struggling to bring up a boy and if they don't pay up we'll go to the newspapers. After all, it was their television that caused it all.'

'That's good,' I said.

'Yes,' she agreed, and fell back into silence.

That night He came round, and it became abundantly clear who she'd borrowed the money from. His whole attitude had changed. He was no longer friendly, but sneery. When I went out to the kitchen for a drink, He said, 'Shouldn't you ask before you get?'

'Sorry, please can I have a drink?'

Smiling, he said, 'Of course!'

It was all very confusing. Even their relationship seemed to have shifted. Post-fire they rowed every night, the fights and beatings louder and longer than before. One night mum slammed into my bedroom yelling, 'Get up, quick, get up!'

I guess I'd become desensitised to it and gone back to sleeping in pyjama bottoms rather than fully clothed, and when she yelled, I jumped out of bed, my heart thumping in my chest. She dragged me out of my room and into the spare room where the door opened inwards. Once inside, she started barricading the door, panicking and throwing anything she could lay her hands on in front of it.

'Help me, quickly!'

I started throwing things too. Clothes, bags, an ironing board. We tried to move a chest of drawers, but it was too heavy.

Outside we could hear Him walking up the stairs, banging each footstep down as hard and noisily as He could. It sounded like a giant coming up.

Mum was frantic. Terrified. The higher he climbed, the crazier she got chucking things at the door.

Then outside we heard Him say in a calm, level voice, 'Are you hiding?' And saw the door snag on the barricade as He tried to push it open.

'Go away, leave us alone,' Mum yelled. I'd never seen her this scared and my stomach somersaulted.

'Us? Have you got the boy in there with you?' We heard him open the door to my room. 'Oh, you have! You've got the retard in with you!' The words, while not shouted, were loaded with cruelty.

'Leave us alone,' I yelled.

He laughed, 'Or what?'

'*I hate you!*' I screamed at the top of my lungs. We were cowering in the corner opposite the door and I could hear Mum's loud breathing.

Abandoning the quiet, menacing approach he yelled, '*Open this fucking dooooor!*' And started yanking it back and forth, each snatch forcing the barricade a little further into the room, and the door a little wider.

'Quick,' Mum said, dashing forwards and pushing her shoulder against it. She was crying and saying God over and over again. Her eye makeup had run and she had bubbles forming and bursting under her nostrils.

I tried to help her by pushing my shoulder against it as well. But tears and fear make you weak, and I felt like I had no energy. But I tried. We both did. Yet we were no match for Him. With a heave He pushed the door open enough to get an arm around the jamb, and with his hand he found mum's throat.

She screamed. So did I.

On the other side he was now punching and kicking the door, while the hand inside gripped harder at her neck.

'Mum!' I cried, and watched her twist enough to sink her teeth into his arm. This time He screamed, but He didn't let go.

'I'm going to FUCKING WELL KILL YOU!'

That was all the motivation she needed to twist out of His grip, and we both bolted for the other side of the room.

Smashing the door back and forth, He was in. When He saw us cowering, He started laughing. There was no lightness or fun in the laugh.

For ages He stood over us and He mocked us and He taunted us and He threatened us, and Mum alternated between begging Him to go away and mocking Him back. He did every mean trick in the book, telling us in intimate detail why we were so pathetic, but stopped short of actually hurting us, at least physically. When finally He left the room, went downstairs and out of the house, we got up.

'Let's get a coffee,' Mum said, making her way across the room, which looked like a tornado had ripped its way through it.

In the kitchen I could see her hands shaking as she switched the kettle on before reaching for a bottle of brandy, pouring a slug into her mug and downing it in one. Coffees made, we went and sat in the new posh lounge.

'You're not going to see Him again, are you mum?' I said, knowing she would, even if she said she wouldn't.

'Not after that, no. That's it, the end. He's gone.'

True to her word, He was. For a week. Then He was back.

One morning I asked her why she kept seeing Him.

'It's very difficult for a woman on her own,' She said. 'Especially one with a child.'

'I'm not a child, I'm twelve,' I told her, sitting up a little straighter.

She looked up briefly from her makeup. 'You're a child,' she said, and my sitting up sagged. If she noticed she didn't say anything, and continued, 'It's different for men. It is a man's world. They can do what they want. When your dad left me I couldn't even get a bank account in my own name. Even the Building Society refused to let me take over the mortgage without a man on the deeds. Men are shits, every one of them, including you, and I don't need any of you.'

That stung, and I could feel tears prickle in the corners of my eyes.

'I could get along perfectly well on my own, no problem at all! But society doesn't like that, because society is run by men, and "society",' She put her mirror down so she could do the air marks with her fingers, 'likes to make women think that they can't cope on their own, because if they did and they realised they didn't need men, they wouldn't have them around.'

She took a deep breath. 'But unfortunately, the way things are, we have no choice. To get on, you need a man.' Turning to me she said, 'You'll be fine, you'll be able to do whatever you want. But it's not like that for women. So yeah, for now, He's useful. And that's all He is, useful. He makes my life easier, but I'm in control, make no mistake about that!'

Another glance at me. 'You may not like the way I bring you up; you may even hate my guts, and I hope you do, but you *will* grow up respecting women.'

'I don't hate you, mum,' I said, and in that moment, I didn't.

She didn't even think twice, just said, 'Yes you do.' I think she kind of wanted to think I hated her so it would make her feel better about not loving me, but that's just a best guess; truth is I don't know why she used to say it, but she used to say it a lot.

There was silence for the longest time before she carried on by saying, 'When He has a drink He gets nasty, but most of the time I can control Him. I just need to play the game.'

She'd mentioned this before but I had no idea what she was talking about. 'I don't know that that is,' I said.

'It's… It's how women control men. But men can do it too, and a man that can play the game is *dangerous*!' she said, her eyes sparkling and her face lighting up.

Scooting off her knees so she was sitting cross-legged facing me, she said, 'When your teacher comes in today, say to her, just casually, nice and relaxed like it was a fleeting thought that just occurred to you but was no big deal, say, "You look different. What have you done? Seriously, what's different about you this morning? You look really good." And then turn around and walk away and don't ever mention it again.'

I couldn't *ever* see me saying that to Mrs Parkside, *especially* not in class where everyone could hear me. But out of curiosity said, 'Wouldn't that upset her, telling her she was different?'

'No! She'd love it. Women are complicated. We want to be praised, but praising us makes us feel patronised and annoyed. We want to be told we look nice, but if you do we'll hate you for it and wouldn't bother looking twice at you. If a man walks up to me and tells me he likes me, I wouldn't give him the time of day. Paaaahhh,' she waved a dismissive hand at such an imaginary fool, 'yeah, all day long Buster, get out of my face,' and she giggled like a school girl.

'But,' She continued, really getting into it now, 'If he can play the game, then I'm his, even if he's a paper-bag job.'

I must have looked confused.

Laughing she said, 'Someone who's so ugly you have to put a paper bag over their head. In fact, looks don't matter at all. It's all about how you play the game. Treat 'em mean, keep 'em keen. Flick 'em around,' she held up thumb and forefinger and did three quick flicks. 'That's what I do with Him. I doubt He has any idea why He keeps coming back, but I do, because I'm in control. Oh, he thinks He is, and I let him think that because it's convenient, but He's not. I am. Me!'

I thought about all the nights He used her face as a punching bag, but smiled and nodded.

She did a snap smile, one loaded with sarcasm. 'You don't get it, do you? Why would you, you're one of them.'

Hating the thought that I was under the same banner as Him, I said, 'No I'm not!'

'Yes you are. You're a man, you're all the same. BUT, if you play the game you could have any woman you wanted. Any of them. Think about that.'

I was. I was thinking about Cindy. 'Do all girls know about the game?' I asked, wondering if I saw Cindy again how I'd go about telling her she looked different.

'All of them. And if you don't play the game with them, they'll play it with you and have you eating out of their hands like a puppy dog, and you won't even know what hit you.'

It just seemed so complicated and made me never want a girlfriend, even Cindy, and we were going to get married one day. Would she still marry me if I didn't want to play the game?

'What if I don't want to play games?'

'Then someone will come along who will and take your girlfriend away from you, and you'll spend all your whole life wondering why girls won't stay with you and keep running off with your best friend.'

Metal. The git, I knew it.

For weeks I tried to figure out what she was talking about, but every time I tried it just made me sad. I wanted a girlfriend so badly; I couldn't wait to have someone to love me and spend all our time together and never see anyone else for the rest of our lives, including mum.

But layer on top of that the whole Cindy thing, and the fact that she clearly liked me and just as clearly I loved her, but yet she made me so scared I had to run away. Why? It made no sense? How would we even get married if every time I looked at her I had to leg it?

'We are brought together in sight of God and this holy congregation to witness the marriage of… Wait, where is he going?'

Unless, of course, the missing part that would make it all fit together was playing the game, which kind of made sense but made me even sadder.

One day at school, me, Metal and a couple of the girls were sitting on the fire escape smoking, when one of the girls said, 'She's got something she wants to ask you.'

My heart took off like a bolting horse. 'What?' I said, not exactly chill-dog cool, but you know, a close approximation.

The second girl slapped the first and said, 'No I haven't!'

'Yes you have. She wants to ask you out,' she screamed, getting up and dancing out of another slap's reach.

'No I don't!'

'Yes you do,' she laughed, 'You said you liked him and wanted to ask him out.'

Blushing, she stammered, 'No I didn't!'

Laughing even harder, she said, 'Yes you did! Go on, ask him out.'

I didn't know what to do. The thought of playing the game terrified me. I didn't know how to do it, didn't want to do it, but at the same time knowing if I didn't do it, and do it right, we'd be boyfriend and girlfriend and she'd run off with my best friend. *Shit!*

I was up on my feet. It was the same feeling that overwhelmed me when I was with Cindy, that need to flee for my life. So I did. I gave into it, I couldn't not. I ran. When I was a few feet away and still bolting, I turned and shouted, 'No, I'm sorry, I can't. I'm sorry. And you look different.'

She looked so hurt, even her friend had stopped laughing. A few weeks later Metal started dating her.

'She thinks you're an idiot now,' he told me after they'd been seeing one another for a while.

'Good.'

'Good?'

'Yeah, good.'

'She's right, you are weird.'

'Can I ask you a question? Do you know about the game?'

'Football?'

No. Wrong time. Wrong place. Wrong *person*. 'Doesn't matter,' I said and changed the subject.

As soon as I could, I asked Mum, 'Does everyone know about the game?'

She thought about it before saying, 'No. Not everyone. If they did it wouldn't work.'

'What do you mean?'

'I mean, there has to be some that do and some that don't. That way, the ones that do flick the ones that don't around. It's all about power.'

'What about love?'

'What about it?'

'Doesn't that make a difference?'

'Rarely, if ever. Play the game and you'll get what you want, love just complicates it.'

Love complicates it? 'Who do you love, Mum? Do you love dad?'

Snorting she said, 'No. Not any more. I did once, but not now.'

'Do you love Him?'

'Mmm, in a way. Kind of.'

'But you don't love anyone else?'

'No.'

'No one?'

Exasperated she said, 'No Simon, I don't. Sometimes I like you, but I don't love you. Don't you understand the difference?' I was beginning to. She'd told me she loved me twice, both when He was around and both times because I think from her point of view it was the appropriate thing to say at the time. They were just words, plucked out and used when people were around and the situation called for them. Even later in life when she'd mellowed some, and I was grown up and married and moved to Exmoor, when we spoke on the phone and at the end of the conversation she said, 'love you,' it would be because someone was there in the room with her. Every time, without fail. In a way, I guess it was another version of her playing the game, but this time with me: same rules, different pieces. We both knew what she was doing and it always made me angry. But I guess age teaches you not to give in, and I'd say back to her, 'no you don't,' and she'd laugh. But when I was younger, I didn't know you had a choice not to react with every scrap of emotion inside you.

Not caring, I screamed, 'You're supposed to love me! I'm your son, you're supposed to love me! I hate you, *I fucking hate you*!'

She leapt across, fists smashing into my face and head, her legs and feet kicking my body. I rolled into a ball, screaming and crying.

'Don't you talk to me like that! Don't you EVER talk and swear at me like that!'

Punches rained down, and when they proved ineffectual because of my tight-tucked foetal position, she swapped to forcing her hands in the gaps between my tucked in arms and legs until she found flesh and started squeezing and pinching.

'Look at me,' she screamed, *'Look at me!'*

Slowly uncurling, I opened my eyes and looked at her.

'Never, ever speak to me like that ever again, do you understand me?'

I nodded.

Using the flat of her hand and what felt like all her strength, she slapped my face hard. 'Now get out of my sight.'

Chapter 24

'What are you doing in there? I was getting worried,' Debbie said.

'Never hurry a man in the bathroom. You never know what he's doing,' I said as I walked out, grinning. Actually I'd been shaving, which is always a lottery, as I have to do it with my eyes closed so I can't see my reflection because the feelings of revulsion and hatred when I do are too intense, and it's not until I dry my face and look into the towel that I know if I've nicked myself or not. Some days are good, while on others I can look like I've popped down to the local slaughterhouse to wash my face. Today, luckily, is a good day.

'Mmmm.' She sidled up to me, and on cue so did Solomon.

'Puppy sandwich?' she said, looking down.

'I'm sure we shouldn't be encouraging him, you know.'

Fussing and kissing his head, she said, 'I know, but he's so handsome mummy can't help herself, can she?'

'You look different,' I said. 'What have you done? You look great.' I don't know what made me say it – curiosity maybe? I certainly hadn't planned on it, it just came out.

'Erm, oh!' She looked pleased and started wiggling her hips, lifting her hand to her hair. 'I did my eyes. Just a little. And some lipstick.'

'I'm sorry, I shouldn't have said that,' I said.

'Why ever not? It's lovely.'

She pushed the dog out of the way so she could kiss me properly, and that made me feel even worse.

Outside, I started making my way towards the lambing shed. I'd decided that as long as the ewe was feeding her baby and being sensible towards him, they could go back out into the field today with the others.

Now, I could just walk from here to there. Home to barn. And I should, that's what adults do. But if I do it that way, where's the element of me in that equation? If anything goes wrong with the ewe and lamb, I need to be able to say, 'That's what I did wrong. That's why it's my fault.' I need to have a way of blaming myself. A route back to, 'It's because you're a cunt.' So I tell myself I'm not going to touch any dock leaves or stinging nettles the entire way, not tread on them, brush them as I walk past or disturb them in any way – it's an agricultural version of not stepping on the cracks in the pavement. If I do, the ewe will have rejected the lamb all over again. If I don't, if I manage to reach the barn without touching anything, everything will be good and the ewe will still be with her baby.

The sun is already high and it looks like it's going to be another nice day. The part of the farm around the house is kept trimmed and tidy, but other parts, areas you can't so readily see, are left alone to grow naturally. It's good for insects and butterflies and wildlife. Dodging left around a particularly healthy looking crop of dark green stingers, I narrowly miss brushing one with my sleeve – at least, I think I miss it.

I'm not as bad as I used to be. Not long ago things like spotting a single magpie would send me into a dread-filled depression. One for sorrow, two for joy. But like many superstitions, it began to feel too random. Where's the accountability in spotting a bird? Walking under a ladder isn't too bad I suppose – at least with that you're making a decision to wander beneath it so you can always look back and say, 'Yeah, I messed up.' But birds, no. It's too arbitrary. The more specific you are, the more correct the outcome. I walk from here to there without touching this and the outcome will be X. Get it wrong and fault will be yours to own and keep for ever and ever and ever.

At the barn, I reach out and pull back the door. Inside the sheep looks up at me, and so does the lamb. They're cuddled up and blink as daylight floods in. Of course I feel relieved, but I also feel stupid. I'm not dumb, I know there is no way there can possibly be a connection between touching plants and a sheep bonding with a lamb. It's idiotic and childish and pathetic. But at the same time I also know that if I'd found the ewe had rejected her lamb again, I'd be ripping myself to pieces right now. That's how superstitions work: if they can't get you one way, they get you another.

Purposely leaving the door open behind me, I stood to one side and said to mum and baby, 'Done! You are now officially bonded. Please consider yourselves repaired. The management would like to thank you for...'

But the management didn't get a chance to thank them for anything. *Vroom!* they both bombed past me kicking up their heels, mum first, lamb second. Out the door and off into the field, where I'd left the gates open so they could find their way to the others.

'Charming, not even a tip. I'm on minimum wage here, you know,' I shouted.

Beginning the clear-up process, I thought, so they're mended. Mum and baby. Bonded. Is that really how PND works? Seems very easy to fix though, doesn't it? Force the two of them together and a bond forms.

Actually it doesn't seem right at all, does it?

PND. The where and when are the PN: postnatal, but it's all about the D: Depression. You don't fix depression by enforcement, do you? 'Hey, I feel really depressed when I'm with my baby.' No problem! If you and your baby would like to step into this tiny room we won't let you out until you've bonded, should take two days. 'Does it work?' Well, it does in sheep.

At least it did with mine.

Now I feel bad for what I've done. Looking at it now, it was a shitty thing to do, securing a sheep in a tiny room so she can't get away and crowbarring the lamb into her affections.

But it worked, didn't it?

Depends how you look at it. Depends what you mean by worked. But yes, they bonded. If that's your goal.

I wish I could speak to someone who knew more about PND. I'm kind of angry nobody came back to me.

Sweeping up the straw beds and shovelling them into a wheelbarrow, I set about cleaning the water buckets and feed troughs.

If that's representative of PND, I don't think it's what my mum had. Mind you, it's probably not fair to compare a sheep and my mum. Although if they both suffered with PND, there would be common threads, wouldn't there?

I don't know. I just know I've only got the animals to work things through with. I've got to use them because I've got nowhere else to go or turn to.

The buckets now clean, I turned them upside down to drain, and switched back to the wheelbarrow that I pushed and emptied on the muck-heap. Then I went to check on the sheep and lamb.

They weren't hard to find.

All the sheep had gathered at the top of the top field. It was early afternoon and most of them were dozing or having a post-dinner top-up of grass. All except two. The mum and another ewe, who were beating the crap out of one another.

Really? The first thing you do when you come out is pick a fight? Maybe she is a lot more like my mum then I'd given her credit for.

When sheep fight, it's like a vicious dance involving spinning, head butting, teeth grinding, staring, parry, forward march, back and side steps. Imagine the Paso Doble between two people who hate one another.

'Will you two behave yourselves?' I said, standing between them like a referee in a boxing match. Turning to the ewe, I said, 'You ought to be ashamed of yourself. You've got your baby over there watching you scrap like a fishwife. What's the deal, I thought you'd be pleased to be out?'

She didn't look that pleased. She didn't look that pleased at all, but locking eyes with her, I was surprised at how sad I suddenly felt, and how much I missed her not in the barn anymore.

Isn't that just the stupidest?

'Go and be with your baby,' I said, and walked away without looking back. I have no doubt they carried on fighting, but inside I felt like all my fight was gone.

Last night was the first night the goat kids had spent with their mum and not in the house with us. They were getting bigger and stronger by the day, and mum was very good at trying to share her milk with each of them. All I had to do was top up their feed by giving them a bottle four times a day. I'd already done two feeds, and now they were due an afternoon bottle each.

That done, I did a walk around to make sure everyone was okay and didn't need anything.

I'm just a glorified waiter. An agricultural trolley-dolly. Reaching and looking down at Senorita, I said, 'We have a selection of duty-free perfumes and stylish wrist watches on special offer, please see one of the cabin crew for more details.'

She oinked back at me.

'Yeah,' I said, leaning on the fence, 'well, you shouldn't dismiss the perfume out of hoof. Might make a pleasant change to eau de pig. Just saying.'

She oinked again.

'I've often thought, if the farm did go belly up I'd be pretty good serving tables in a restaurant, don't you think? Attentive and big portions.'

While she lounged in the middle of the straw listening to my rubbish, the piglets around her play fought, biting and tugging on one another's tails, running in mad circles and barging into one another.

Why is it that all my animals fight?

The walk around became evening rounds and I fed and watered and bedded everyone down, and found myself back at the barn wishing the ewe and lamb were still in there.

Back in the house Debbie said, 'All done?'

'Just got the poultry to shut in when it gets dark and the final feed for the goats. Other than that, yeah, all done. I need to change,' I said, heading towards the bedroom.

'Are you okay? How's the lamb and ewe?'

'In the field. Mum's fighting with the others, so she's happy. I've really got to change.'

'Of course. Here,' she handed me a glass of wine that I took with me and set on the nightstand while I stripped off. Then I sat heavily on the bed, picked up the glass and downed it in one.

I hadn't eaten and the liquid felt warming and filling.

I don't remember my mum ever being drunk, but she did drink a lot. Wine, brandy, even whisky. I don't drink spirits, but I've followed her down the wine route. Some nights I try not to drink, but I can't always help myself. It's not so much that it dulls feelings as it's a comforter. Wine makes me feel comforted.

Wine, Debbie and food. My three essentials. I guess there are probably addiction issues to each, but that's not anything I can face. Besides, being addicted to your wife can't be a bad thing, can it? The other two, yeah, sometimes I worry – who am I kidding, I worry about all three. But I'm not a drunk and I'm not that overweight, though I guess in the Debbie department even I have to admit I might be a bit needy, constantly looking for her attention and approval and signs that she loves me. Mainly the problem comes if I haven't got more wine and food than I can possibly consume in one day, or have Debbie around. My chest tightens and I can't think straight. I've even had to get an inhaler to help with the panic. How pathetic is that? *Have you got asthma, mate?* No, I'm just not sure I've got enough wine, grub or wife to get through the night.

Pulling on jeans and a clean t-shirt, I make my way back out to the kitchen.

'Hey,' Debbie said, pecking me on the lips. 'You don't seem yourself.' She's cooking and the smell is gorgeous.

'I'm okay. I need to make some bread.'

Filling my glass, 'We've got loads. Take the night off. Relax.'

Swallowing half and holding glass out for more, I said, 'No, I need to make some.'

Her brow is furrowed. 'You want to talk about it?'

'No.' Yes, but I don't know what to say. I don't know why I feel like this, I just feel... angry. Frustrated. She hasn't poured any more wine, so I drink the second half of the glass and reach for the bottle in her hand so I can do it myself.

'I wish you'd talk to me,' she said, reaching out and touching my arm. 'You look like you're in pain.'

Shaking my head,' No, I just want to make some bread, that's all.'

We buy flour in twenty-kilo sacks, and while Debbie turned and got on with dinner, I took a scoop and added it to a bowl with yeast, salt and water, cleaned and dried the work surface and began kneading.

To cover the silence she started chatting, trying to be normal, and I guess, bring me out of my shell.

'I spoke to my mum today,' she said. 'They've messed up her drugs again, she's back in the hospital in the morning.'

Knead. Sip. Fill glass.

Sometimes making bread stops me needing to drink. Sometimes, but not always. Not tonight.

By the time the dough was made and left to one side to rise, the bottle was empty and I was opening another. I couldn't help myself.

'You should be careful,' Debbie said, watching me.

'I know. I am.'

'What happened today? Is it the lamb? Is that why you're upset?'

'I don't know. I don't know if I am upset. I just feel fed up.'

'Is the ewe still okay with the lamb?'

Irritated she wasn't letting it drop, I said, 'Yes, they're fine. Really.'

'Sorry. I just thought…'

'I can't do this,' I said, snagged the bottle and walked past her into the lounge.

Following me in she said, 'I'm really confused. I haven't seen you drink like this in ages. Has something happened I don't know about?'

Not bothering to answer, I poured another glass. I hate it when people say alcohol dulls the senses, because it doesn't with me. I wish it would! If it did that it would be so much easier. Rather, alcohol's like an amplifier, makes the hurt warm and inviting and nice. It makes the hurt appealing. Makes me want to dive into it. Embrace it. Surround myself and fill myself up with it. I wish the hurt was bigger. I wish it was massive, the size of Mount Everest, and I was buried right at the middle underneath it.

'Simon?'

'Leave me alone, please.' The sips were no longer sips, they were gulps. Stupid small glasses. Constantly refilling.

'But I'm worried about you. I hate it when you clam up and shut me out.'

'I just want to be on my own.' My words were beginning to slur.

'That's the last thing you need. What's brought this on?' She came and sat down next to me.

Shrugging, I said, 'Please, just leave me alone.'

Looking down at her hands, she said, 'Dinner's ready.'

'I don't want any.'

She nodded.

'Please,' I begged, 'I just want to be alone.' I wanted to feel wretched, I wanted to feel hurt, I wanted to feel pain. I love it. It's how I should feel. Strip away all the layers of nicety right down to the core and there's this warm embracing, swirling mass of hate waiting to fill me up. But I can't do it with her here. Not fully. Not completely immerse myself.

It's so hard to describe exactly why I'd spiralled down so far and so fast. I think I felt that this had all been for a reason, set up, if you like: that the ewe rejecting her lamb had happened so I could face some of my own issues surrounding my mum and how I felt about myself, and then it all got taken away. And I'm not just back at square one, I've dipped so far into the dark side of myself I'm at square minus-a-hundred, while the lamb and ewe are cuddled up in a field somewhere playing happy families.

All this darkness, all this self-hatred, all this unhappiness has been let out of its box and with no focus to keep it occupied any longer, it's now having a party inside my brain. Debbie's not seen me like this before. This is new to her. New to us. I don't get aggressive when I drink, or at any other time. She's not worried I'll turn violent. She's worried I'll turn insular and bathe in the negativity, which is exactly what I want to do.

'Something's happened and I don't think you should be on your own,' she insisted.

I've had enough experience with the dark side of life to know where to find it in myself. The trick is not to use too much, like seasoning, too much and you'll spoil it. Just enough. Twisting my face towards her, I made myself look like Him the way He would when He looked at mum or me. Sarcastic smile, cruel eyes, twitch of the lips, and very quietly, just above a whisper, said, 'Why don't you fuck off.'

Chapter 25

'We're getting engaged,' mum said. We were sitting in the lounge, just the two of us. Me in my school shirt and trousers, her in a grey pencil skirt and matching jacket with huge, 'I'm a business woman, don't mess with me' shoulder pads. Her blonde hair was teased and lacquered to give it plenty of shaggy volume, and she looked beautiful, really beautiful. But then she always did. 'Be happy for me.'

A lot has changed. For one thing, I'm older, 15 maybe. The house has changed too. Not long after the fire, mum and Him pooled resources and bought a big house in a posh village.

I knew the engagement thing was coming. There'd been 'we probably will one day' conversations. But still it hit me hard; why would she want to make a commitment to someone who punched her?

'Engaged to be engaged, or engaged to be married?' I said.

She thought about it for a moment, staring at the television in the corner without seeing it.

'It's a commitment,' she said, fanning her face with her hand.

'But why?'

She tutted. 'Because I want to. Don't ruin this. Say congratulations and leave it at that.'

'Congratulations.'

'Thank you. Oh, and I've just come on, remind me string.' She was always telling me to remind her string. I think it was a reference to her tampax, but I'm not sure.

My room was on the top floor, a huge space with a wooden double bed, an electric guitar that I was awful at, and a stereo with hundreds of the most angry, hateful records I could find. I remember when we first moved into the house I asked if I could put a lock on the bedroom door and they said, Why? No way!

'I'm going upstairs,' I said to Mum, who nodded.

As I got up to leave, she said, 'I sat in your room for an hour.'

That stopped me. 'When?'

'Yesterday.'

'But why?'

'Because I'm Mum. Because I can.'

I don't know if she really did – who would want to sit in their teenage son's bedroom? But even so, why say that? What was she trying to prove, that she was in control? I know she's in control!

'But it's my room, mum.'

'No it's not. We pay all the bills, you don't contribute a thing. If you don't like it, you can always go and live somewhere else.'

What could I say to that? Without a word I turned and walked out.

Upstairs I sat on the bed and tried to imagine her sitting in the same spot, looking around. It felt horrible and vulnerable and I hate feeling like that, and I had this overwhelming sense of unease. I'm also 15. I have secrets I'd die if my mum knew about. From the spot on my bed I inched left, then right, all the while peering at the speaker on the floor over in the corner, trying to work out if she could spot what was hidden behind it. I didn't think she could, and if she had I've no doubt she would have pulled me aside over it.

Getting up, I went to put some music on, flicked through the heavy, angry rock and landed on the album I'd been playing to death, Fleetwood Mac's *Rumours*. I put it on dead quiet so she wouldn't be able to hear and went over to the speaker that was hiding my secrets, and, reaching behind it, dipped into my hidden stash of food and pulled out three Twix bars.

Putting one back for breakfast in the morning, I went and sat on the bed and began devouring the bars. For years I'd been hiding food so I always had something to eat. Just the thought of running out, or worse, her finding it, made my breath tighten and my blood pump faster, like fear, but not the same fear when it all kicked off at night and punches were thrown. A different fear, one that reminded me of summer holidays when I was young in the old house before the fire, with nothing to eat and my tummy hurting. Weird how fear can be so varied.

As the music started, I thought, so they're getting engaged. Mum and Him. A commitment just short of marriage, but enough for now. I still couldn't fathom it – they were both so volatile, like two Molotov cocktails with diamond rings on their fingers.

Each pack of Twix had two fingers. With both done from the first pack, I unwrapped the second.

I hate Him. I hate Him for what he does to mum, and I hate Him for how He makes me feel. I hate His sarcastic sense of humour. I hate His cruel sneer. I hate His love of football, and His love of golf – no! His devotion to golf. Hitting a stupid bloody ball with a stick, oh gee, well done you!

The song finished and another one came on. I munched and tried to concentrate on the words. The answer to everything was in the music because they sang about love, and I desperately needed to figure out what love was, and fast. As soon as I did, as soon as I worked out what it was all about, what it looked like, felt like, tasted like, I could change whatever it was inside me that was unlovable and fix it. As soon as I did that, everything would change. Mum would love me, but most importantly I'd get a girlfriend and move out.

The alternative was not figuring out what love was, not mending myself, and being a cunt all my life. *No!* I wanted to punch the wall, release some of the anger bubbling away inside me. *FUCK!* But punching anything makes me like them, like mum and Him. So I swallowed it. Never violence, that's the rule, no matter how bad it gets, never violence because then I'm the same as them.

Concentrate. Concentrate on the music, that's where the answer is, in the words.

But they make no sense. The way they described it is exactly how I'd describe anger, it's exactly the same. It's overwhelming and scary but nice at the same time, comforting and shameful and it fills you up and sometimes you can barely control it, and other times, when you let it go, it makes you feel sad. Is that why mum and Him fight, because it is the same thing?

Another mouthful.

Mum knows what love is. But she won't tell me.

He knows, but I'd never ask Him.

Once I asked dad what love was and he just laughed and said, I don't know, son.

I have nobody else to turn to. Nowhere else to go. Other than music.

Concentrate. Concentrate on the words.

Taking a final bite I stood up, threw the wrapper on the empty pile and started stripping off all my clothes. Shirt, trousers, underpants and socks. Then stood in front of the full-length mirror.

Was love visible? Was it on your skin like a glow, a sheen? I looked, twisted my hips and shoulders, and looked some more. Or was it a smell, like aftershave? I sniffed my arm, it smelt of nothing; maybe it wasn't something you could smell yourself, only others could smell it on you?

Or maybe I was coming at it the wrong way. Maybe I shouldn't be looking for love, I should be looking for the part inside me marked *un*love – after all, that's what I wanted to find so I could repair it, like an old car, reach in and change the bit that's faulty.

I looked and looked, but deep down I knew it wouldn't be that easy. But I had to try, I had to start somewhere.

My thoughts were broken my Mum yelling up the stairs, 'Simon!'

Oh God! Throwing the underpants to one side, I pulled on trousers, grabbed the shirt and frantically started buttoning.

'Simon!'

No socks. No time. Fingers through hair. Opening the door I look down, 'Yeah?'

She nodded. 'Just checking,' and walked away.

Just checking *what*?

'Oh, Mum?'

She came back into view.

'String.'

She stared at me, turned and walked away.

The engagement party came and we all dressed up and she looked amazing in an ivory three-quarter-length fitted lacy dress with a scoop neckline, real pearls around her neck and hair and makeup professionally done. He wore a designer lounge suit and smiled and shook everyone's hand.

Afterwards they went on a post-engagement holiday, and I house-sat. On the last night I decided to go to my dad's straight from school, as I didn't want to be there when they got back. I'd cleared up, put some fresh bread, milk and butter in the fridge and made sure everything was tidy before locking up tight.

At dad's that night we ate dinner on our laps in front of the TV. When the phone rang, dad answered it. Covering the microphone the way you used to do when you didn't want the person on the other end to hear what you were saying, he whispered, 'It's your mum. She sounds mad. Did you leave the house in a mess?'

'No,' I said, reaching for the receiver. 'Hi mum, did you have a good holiday?'

Her voice had ice all over it. 'What the fuck did you do?'

The blood in my veins thickened to a sludgy gel. 'What do you mean?'

'Did you know we've been burgled?'

'*What?*'

'You heard me.'

I felt my heart actually stop and wished it wouldn't start again. I tried to sound confident and assured, but it just came out in a whisper. 'No. Oh God, no. I had no idea. What did they take?'

The flat had a breakfast bar between the lounge and the kitchen, and Dad went the other side of it. He put the kettle on and leaned back against the work surface, crossing his arms and looking at me with sad eyes.

'Everything. My jewellery. Clocks. Stereo. Television. Been through every drawer, every cupboard, every room... except yours. They didn't even open your door. Funny that, isn't it?'

'*I didn't do it!*' I exclaimed, '*I promise I didn't do it!*'

Silence. A long, long silence. I should never have come to dad's. I should have stayed at the house. It's all my fault and now they'll think I did it. I'm dead. My life is over and I'm glad. I hate it anyway.

'I'll see you tomorrow night,' she said, and the phone clicked off.

Putting the phone down, I reached for a stool and nearly missed. Dad came back into the lounge and put his arms around me. 'Oh, son.' He could hear both sides of the conversation as mum wasn't speaking quietly, and I'm sure he would liked to have talked to me, reassure me, but he couldn't because it was true, it was my fault. So he hugged me and I felt like I wanted to die right there on the spot.

Him being nice was more than I could cope with; the floodgates opened and I sobbed so hard I lost all strength in my legs and couldn't get up even if I wanted to.

School the following day. I felt sick. I thought of running away but didn't know how to. I thought of killing myself and found that thought surprisingly comforting, so much so that just knowing I could do it made me feel better. It felt like a power I had that no one else had any control over, only me. I could end it all any time I wanted. It felt good.

When school finished I caught the train and when it pulled into the station got off and walked the walk home. Both their cars were outside. I didn't like to use my key, so I knocked. Mum answered.

'Mum, I'm so sorry...'

Looking beyond me so she didn't catch my eye, she strode out, crashing straight into me with a shoulder barge like a rugby player going for the line. Sprawling backwards into a privet hedge, I watched her pound down to her car, get in, and drive away.

Glancing back into the doorway, He was filling it. 'Come in,' He said. Dragging myself up and out of the hedge, I reached for my dropped school bag and went inside, Him closing the door behind me.

I sat on the sofa. I'm not sure what I'd expected, I'm not sure I'd allowed myself to wonder what somewhere that had been recently burgled might look like. There were yawning gaps where the TV and stereo once stood – I'd expected that, but I found myself working my eyes around the room trying to spot anything else that could be missing.

All the major components of the lounge were still there, the sofas and chairs and the dark wooden side-tables with antique-style lamps, dining table and chairs, side unit. Wait – something was missing from the unit. It wasn't the things themselves I noticed, but the shape was wrong. It took a while to place, and when I did I looked down between my feet. His crystal decanter, the one he won at a golf competition.

Of all the seats He could take, He sat next to me, lit a cigarette and poured himself a finger of whisky.

'I'm sorry,' I said.

He didn't say anything at first, just smoked and drank. When He did speak, He said, 'Sorry for what?'

'I didn't do it.'

'Why would we think you did?'

The 'we' hurt. I had no way of knowing if mum had stuck up for me or not, but the message her little storm-out sent probably meant no.

He took a drag of the cigarette and blew smoke out. 'I know you didn't. The police said there were at least three of them.'

'Three!'

'Yes. But you know that, don't you.' It wasn't a question.

I looked at Him. The cruel sneer, the one He wore when they argued and fought was all over His face, and His eyes shone out like they were lit from the back.

'No,' I was shaking my head, 'No, I don't know that.'

The explosion was immediate. Raising his arm He threw the glass across the room so it shattered on the opposite wall and screamed, *Don't fucking lie to me!*

I tried to scrunch myself as small as I could get on the seat.

Leaning closer He spoke through gritted, angry teeth. 'Don't you think it's odd they didn't go into your room? They went everywhere else in the house, opened every cupboard, every wardrobe, every drawer, but didn't even step foot in your room? You tell me what I should think?'

'I'm sorry.'

'For what? Were they your mates?'

'No! I haven't even got any mates.'

Reaching between us He took hold of my face, and squeezed, and I thought, Hey, that's Mum's trick! 'Don't fucking lie to me.'

My heart smacked a bass drumbeat in my chest. I wanted to cry, but knew if I did it would only make things worse. 'I'm not lying, I promise.'

Two beats, three beats, then He seemed to calm, and let go. 'Okay, so I'm going to ask you and I need you to be honest, because if I find out you're lying to me your life won't be worth living, do you understand me?'

I nodded, pathetically enthusiastic.

'Did you arrange it?'

'No! Of course not, why would I do that?'

'For the money? To look good in front of your mates?'

'But I haven't got any mates. I don't know how to get them, I don't know where you go to get mates. And even if I did know I wouldn't do it. I don't like me and I don't want to go out and I don't want to be with other people because when I do I see myself through their eyes and I want to kill myself because I'm such a cunt.' The outburst was from the heart, was born in pain and fear of what he was going to do to me and desperation that he believe me, and was possibly the most honest I'd ever been with anyone. But of course, the instant I said it I regretted it. I'd said too much. Shared too much. Been way, way, way too honest. But I was scared and I wanted Him to realise it wasn't me. I wanted to tell Him everything so He knew, so He understood it couldn't be me.

He put his head back and laughed. 'Okay. You didn't have people round while we were away? Not once?'

'Not once,' I confirmed.

'And you don't know who did it?'

'No.'

'Not a clue?'

'No.'

'That's disappointing,' He said, stamping the cigarette butt out in the glass ashtray on the floor beside Him.

'I'm sorry.'

'Yeah, so you keep saying. Any idea why they wouldn't have gone in your room?'

The answer was obvious. 'Because there's nothing in there to steal.'

'Mm, initially that's what I thought too. Only, how did they know there was nothing to steal without going in there first, unless of course they already knew? You see, whatever way you look at it, it comes back to you. And then there's the fact that you decided that night, of all nights, not to stay. Why was that?'

I told Him I didn't know, because that was infinitely better than admitting I didn't want to be there when they got back.

Nodding, He held His hand out for me to shake, which was His way of concluding business. I took it, and said, 'So you believe me?'

That light behind His eyes came on again, shining brighter than ever. 'No Simon, I don't. But at the moment I can't prove otherwise. Go on, fuck off up to your room.'

Opening the bedroom door, I stood for a long while before venturing inside. He was right, nothing looked out of place or different. But even so, it didn't feel right. The house as a whole didn't feel right, and my room felt the same. Did that mean they had been in here and just chose not to disturb anything? I hoped so. Just the same, I set about going through everything top to bottom just to check.

About an hour later I heard a car pull up and mum's high-heeled footsteps on the path outside, followed by the front door opening and slamming closed. I imagined their heated conversation, 'Did he confess? No? Do you believe him? No, neither do I.'

Moving across, I sat on the bed, hoping she would come up, rush in and throw her arms around me and tell me she never thought for one second it was anything to do with me. She didn't, and when it got dark, I went to bed. But I couldn't sleep. I thought it must have been an inside job; maybe the cleaner they employed one day a week. Or one of the decorators. Or one of the handymen they got to pop around and do things while they were out at work. The gardener. The estate agent who came back to revalue the place the week before they went away. The gas man, one of their friends, or just someone who'd overheard a conversation about what we had. It could have been anyone. But they thought it was me, and Mum went out and left Him to interrogate me. I could hear them downstairs, moving around, hoovering and bustling about, I guessed, cleaning and trying to get back a sense of home.

The burglary must have put a strain on things, because it wasn't long before the fights started again. And this time, it wasn't just Him and her that were fighting, but everyone.

Chapter 26

Of course I had to take responsibility for the burglary. While I had nothing to do with the actual act, I did leave the place unattended for a night. That was bad. They'd trusted me to protect and look after the home and I had let them down. And why? Because I'd rather go to my dad's. I'd *rather*. I took *rather* over doing the right thing. What a cunt.

I tried to stay out of their way as much as I could, which was easy, as they were newly engaged and more than happy with their own company. They went out most nights. Often they'd ask me to go with them, and I'd say no.

To get my attention they'd stand at the bottom of my stairs and yell up. 'Simon? Simon!'

I'd opened my bedroom door and peered round.

'We're going out for dinner, why don't you come with us?' Mum would say. Sometimes she could be really quite nice.

'I can't. I need to do some homework. Sorry.'

Shrugging, 'Suit yourself,' she left.

Backing into the room, I closed the door and listened as they started the car and drove off.

Music playing, I sat back on the bed. I hadn't done homework in years, and was not about to start now, even though end-of-school exams began in a couple of months and revising and studying was all anyone talked about. I had more important things to think about. I needed a way out of my life; I needed a

205

way of escaping, but academia was not it. My spelling had not improved since I was 11. If anything, it had gone backwards. Classmates had started rifling through my bag and getting my note pad out when I wasn't around and sniggering over the spelling. I didn't take it personally – it was funny. But it made me realise I was never going to pass any exams. My road lay someplace else. But I couldn't even get started until I worked out what it was about me that was unlovable. Without understand and fixing what was broken inside me, I would go through life as I was, and that was unthinkable.

In my search I'd magpied a whole new music library. I still had all the angry heavy rock, but now it sat along side the likes of ABBA, The Carpenters and Phil Collins – the rock I listened to for pleasure, the other stuff was a way of trying to understand love and how I could use that knowledge to fix myself and stand a chance of becoming a person someone, anyone, might love. But my real discovery was late-night radio agony aunts. You could tune in and listen to other people's problems, and I became addicted. Only once did I hear someone call with a problem similar to mine. It was a girl, and she said, 'My mum doesn't love me,' and the agony aunt asked, 'What makes you think that?' The girl started explaining and the agony aunt defended the mother, stuck up for her, twisted it so it wasn't the mother's fault at all and implied that the girl had it all wrong. I started hollering at the radio, 'What if she's telling the truth? What if her mother *doesn't* love her? What then?' I even thought of calling the station and asking for the girl's number, but what would I say to her? 'I've got a mother like yours, maybe we should start a club?'

One night I heard a car pull up outside. Moving to the window, I looked out. It was them, but it was way earlier than they'd normally get back; they'd only been gone about half an hour. As I watched I saw mum get out of the driver's side, which was odder still. She came around and opened the passenger door. He got out, staggered out, and lurched down the path towards the house.

Bolting down the stairs, I met them at the front door. His shirt was ripped and his face and neck had blood drying all over it.

'Go to bed!' Mum yelled, spotting me rushing towards them.

'But…'

'Go to bed! Now!'

I turned and went back up. Clearly He'd been in a fight, and just as clearly he'd taken a beating. I should have felt glad, happy that He'd got a taste of being overpowered and overwhelmed by someone else's strength and aggression. But I wasn't. I felt bad for Him. I wanted to stand shoulder to shoulder and defend Him, how weird is that? I even went to sleep praying He'd be okay. Then in the middle of the night it all got flipped on its head.

The clock read *02:23*.

Sitting up, I listened. I'd started having phantom wake-ups, pinging awake convinced I'd been woken to the sound of mum screaming. I'd even once sneaked down and listened at their door. But it was just dreams. Plumping the pillow behind me, I lay back, sure this was the same.

Then I heard it. A muffled scream, not loud, nowhere near loud enough to wake me. Yet I had woken. And now I was awake there were more noises. Moving. Some banging. Some sobbing. Talking, but too low to make out the words.

Getting dressed in the dark, I stumbled and nearly fell. If I had, the noise I'd make would clang out like a calling card to Him to come and vent His anger up here, and for a second I wondered if that's what I should do. Draw the fire. Yes! Yes!

But I couldn't do it. I was too scared, scared of what He'd do to me. Scared of what He'd do to her. I hated myself for being such a coward. Hated, hated, hated. I deserved every ounce of contempt and more. Once a cunt, always a cunt.

That word. That horrible, horrible word that described me so beautifully. Cunt. That's what spurred me to finish getting dressed, open my bedroom door, and work my way down the stairs.

Their room was on the middle floor. Bottom of my stairs and turn right. I stood outside, the noises from inside now clearly audible. Another fight. Him taunting her. Her taunting Him. Her singsong voice. His sickening smacks. Her cries. His blames.

I wished He'd died tonight. I wished His attacker had pulled a knife and plunged it into His heart. And to think I was worried about Him – what had got into me? And her. I hated her too. And I loved her, and wished she could find a way to love me back. But most of all I hated her, for everything, but mostly, right now, for this. For all of this. *She's engaged to Him, for Christ's sake!*

But I'm a man, and her son. I should protect her. She should be able to count on me. I hate her and I have to protect her. And I hate Him and I'm scared of Him and I'm scared of her and I'm scared of them both and I'm scared of fucking everything – what's wrong with me? So what's dominant, love or fear? Fear is selfish, but isn't love selfish too? *God, I don't know!*

Walking silently back and forth outside their room, I thought, sod it, if He comes out and kills me, so be it. I don't care, I really don't. Putting my hand on my head, I pulled my hair. Then I let go and raised it at the door, preparing to smash it open, burst in and rush Him. But I couldn't do it. I couldn't do it. I'm a cunt and a cowardy custard. Yes, a cowardy, cowardy cunt-stard.

There was no light in the hallway, save a bar of yellow spilling out from under their door. In the residual light I could see the wooden banister opposite, running along with the top of the stairs. What I needed was a weapon. Something that would make me his equal, no, make me stronger. Quiet now, I moved to the top of the stairs and walked down.

There were no knives in the kitchen, save dinner knives – mum made sure of that for obvious reasons. But that's fine. I had a much better idea.

Next to the front door was a window. Through it a half moon light lit the hallway with an eerie silvery glow. Standing sentinel beside the door was His bag of golf clubs. I could see the last little bit of a dozen or more graphite shafts poking out of the gaping leather mouth with iron heads leisurely lolling at the tops. Even in the scant light I could read the word down the side of the bag, *Ping*.

The irony if I whacked Him over the head and killed Him with one of His own clubs was delicious. They were like His babies, like He'd given birth to them, He loved them that much, and yes, I admit, that irony also appealed.

Reaching out I took hold of an iron, and slid it up and out. 'The quality,' I mimicked His voice inside my head, 'is amazing. Top of the range, they don't get any better, or more expensive than this.'

Grinning, I switched the club around so I had hold of the handle, the heavy iron head hovering a hand's width above the floor in front of me as though I were about to swing at a ball, though instead of a ball I pictured his head. 'Now don't forget to shout four!' His voice inside my head admonished, making me giggle.

Turning, I started back up the stairs. Tonight was where it would all end.

As I reached the top I stopped and listened. The light under the door was still on, but there was no noise from inside. Not a cry, a sigh or a peep. Had He killed her? Was I too late?

Standing with the door in front of me I imagined charging in, swinging and slashing and knocking Him out cold, hopefully never to wake again. Taking a deep breath, then another, I held it, raised the club and…

Noise inside. Footsteps approaching the door. Jesus, this is not how it's supposed to happen. Replacing the breath in my lungs with an even bigger one, I stood, gritted my teeth and prepared to smash it down into Him if the door opened and it was Him standing there.

But all that happened was the light under the door went out, then the footsteps retreated and I heard the sound of someone getting into bed.

Oh.

Lowering the club, I looked down at the dark smudge of carpet under my feet. With all light now gone apart from the slithers of moonlight from windows here and there, that's all I could see, smudges.

Retracing my steps, I went back downstairs. But I was too wound up to simply return the club to the bag, and before I had a chance to think about what I was doing, I put it over my knee and snapped it in two.

The instant I did, all the adrenaline washed out of me, and the powerful killing machine became a frightened little boy once more. Oh my God, why did I do that? Oh my God, Oh my God, Oh my God, He's going to *kill me*, literally *kill me*.

I could feel panic surging and my breath labouring like I was having a heart attack. Slamming the two halves into the bag I ran upstairs, not caring about the noise, just sprinting. In my room I tore my clothes off and jumped into bed.

The following morning I came down as late as I dared before leaving for school. He was gone. The golf bag wasn't, it was still beside the front door. In the lounge Mum looked around at me as I entered.

'So, you're up. Make me a coffee.'

Glad not to be in the same room as her, I swerved off into the kitchen.

'I heard you up last night. What were you doing?' she called.

Pulling down two cups, I spooned instant coffee and sugar. 'Nothing.'

Through the window I could see rain and the grey of morning.

'I don't believe you. What were you doing?'

'Why did He get beaten up?'

Appearing in the doorway, she said, 'I think he's been having an affair. Don't you *dare* say anything to him!'

'But you've only just got engaged.'

'I know.' It was like someone had turned the lights off. Suddenly she looked grey and shadowy and washed out, and she hugged around her the dressing gown she wore over her clothes as she finished off her hair and makeup.

'What happened?'

She shook her head. 'I don't want to talk about it.'

Beside us the kettle boiled. I said, 'I heard you last night.'

Angry, 'heard me what, exactly?'

Taking a step back I said, 'fighting.'

'We weren't fighting, you stupid boy!'

Oh God, had I got it wrong? 'But I heard you.'

'We weren't fighting, got it?'

She hadn't finished her makeup. I could see the big red blotches on her cheeks. Besides, I know what I heard. But what was I going to do, argue? So I said, 'I'm sorry,' and handed her the drink, which she took, turned and walked back into the lounge.

She said he'd been having an affair, blimey, that was a new one. Following her I sat on the sofa. What I wanted to ask was, so is that it? Has He gone for good? The golf bag for one would indicate not, but that might just be that He didn't have enough hands and would pop back to collect the last of His things later, and we'd never see Him again. It would just be me and her. The warmth that thought gave me was heady and delicious.

Not quite sure what to say I said, 'Are you okay?'

The lights came back on. She was over by her makeup, sitting on her knees but not working. Straightening, she looked at me and said, 'Why wouldn't I be?'

I don't know. 'Sorry.'

Sounding exasperated and slapping her hand on her thigh, she said, 'Oh, just go to school, will you?'

I didn't move. It all felt wrong; *I* felt wrong. I should show her that I'm supportive, that I care. But I wasn't sure how to. 'Mum…'

'*Don't!* Get away from me. *Get away from me!*'

Getting up from the sofa, I finished getting ready and went to school.

When I got home that afternoon Mum's car was still outside. So was His. And there was a third with a man I'd never seen before leaning against the bonnet, arms crossed the way men do when they want to appear relaxed although they're anything but.

As I walked past and started up the driveway, head down, he lurched away from the side of the car and said, 'Jesus Christ, who the fuck are you?'

Catching my breath in my throat, I froze.

Sighing, his body going from sharp and angular to soft and rounded, he said, 'You're okay, kid. Look, have you got someplace else you can go tonight?'

Still looking down, I shook my head.

'You need to go for a walk then. Do you understand me?'

I nodded, but didn't move. This was bad. This was really, really bad.

'Go on then. And kid?'

I looked up.

'Make it a long walk.'

'Why are you here?' I said.

Dismissive. 'You don't want to know.'

'Are you going to hurt my mum?'

'What? No!'

'Are you going to hurt Him?'

He didn't answer at first, didn't even look at me, just stared up at the house. 'He's been having an affair with my wife.'

I heard myself say, 'Please don't'.

This time he did look at me, and he smiled. 'Okay. I'm just going to wait here, is that all right?'

'Do you promise?'

He actually laughed. 'Yes, I promise. On condition that you go for a walk.'

What else could I do? Nodding, I turned and walked away. He watched me go, and when he thought I was out of sight, he walked towards the front door.

I had no intention of going anywhere. There's a point in the road where it dips down and goes out of sight. I made it to there and ducked down beside a bush. Counting to ten before poking my head up, I watched him make his way towards the house. Shit, shit, shit. Leaving my school bag where it was beside the bush, I ran back up the hill, my shoes clanging on the pavement. He must have heard me because he stopped and turned, then held up both hands and started back towards his car. As he did so I slowed.

Figuring it was over, I started back towards my school bag. When I reached it I looked up only to see him heading once more towards the house. Heart pounding, I swivelled and bolted back up the hill. This time when he saw me he only held up one hand, but got in his car, reversed and drove away.

Not bothering to go back for the bag, I went up to the house and let myself in. As soon as I was inside it was clear they were at it. The screams, the swearing, the taunting, the wicked cruel devil laughing: the go on thens; the don't push mes; the why nots; the I'm telling yous; the you fucked someone elses.

They had no idea I was back, and by the sound of it they had no idea what had been about to happen with the man outside.

Sitting on the bottom of the stairs, I eyed the golf clubs as I had last night.

From the lounge He was saying, 'I didn't go with anyone else. I'm telling you, you've got it all wrong.'

Her: 'I don't care if you did.'

Him: 'What's that supposed to mean?'

Her: 'It means I don't care if you fucked every woman out there.'

Him: 'But I didn't fuck anyone.'

Her: 'Then what was that about last night?'

Him: 'Again? God, we've been over this, he thought I was someone else.'

Her: 'I don't believe you.'

Him: 'You know what, I don't care what you believe. I'm sick of this.'

Her: 'Good.'

Him: 'You're a cold bitch.'

Her: 'Yep.'

Him: 'So that's it? We're through?'

Her: 'Yep.'

Him: 'If I leave, that's it. Finished.'

Her: 'Good.'

Him: 'I can't believe you, this is really what you want?'

Her voice, strong and confident and assured: 'Yes, this is really what I want.'

Storming out of the lounge, he stopped dead when he saw me. For a moment I thought he was going to take it out on me, and I looked away, but he just brushed past on His way upstairs to pack. I was still in the same spot when He came back down, and had to move to let Him by. With the front door open, bags in hand, he stopped halfway in, halfway out as though He were going to give some sort of parting shot, but thought better of it and left, slamming the door behind Him.

Getting up, I went into the lounge. She was on the sofa crying, her mascara streaking down her face. She looked so sad, so alone and broken. I started towards her, and as I did she barked, 'Get away from me!'

I did. I went upstairs, brushing past the bag of golf clubs on route, and thinking, He'll be back. And He was, in under a week.

'Simon? Is that you?' mum called from the lounge. That was odd. It was Saturday afternoon. I'd been up all the previous night writing down song lyrics to see if on the page they had a different impact. Maybe it was the bad spelling or the awful handwriting, but by five this morning I didn't feel any further forward, gave up and fell asleep. Normally that would annoy the heck out of mum, but she sounded almost upbeat.

Looking in, I said, 'Sorry mum, I must have slept in.'

She was smiling. 'Come in here,' she said.

What the hell?

'Sit down. You want a coffee? I'll go and make us a coffee,' and she did.

I didn't dare move. Or breathe. Or think.

When she came in she handed me a steaming mug, and said, 'He went out and played golf this morning. Had a big competition. Did you snap His golf club?'

I should feel terrified, but she was grinning ear to ear. Then, in her jeans and sweat top with her hair bunched in a scrunchy on her head, she started play-acting she was Him on the course, looking into the pretend distance and scratching her chin. 'Mm,' she said, 'I know what club I need,' and reached out to select one from an invisible bag. When she pulled it out she looked at it with her eyebrows knitted, then bent over really, really low to address the pretend ball with a club half the size it should be. Holding the pose for at least twenty seconds, she looked sideways at me and burst out laughing.

'When did you do it?' she said, straightening up. 'Why did you do it? Was it the night we had a fight, the night I heard you up?'

'I'm sorry,' was all I could think of saying.

'Why? Don't be. Did you do it because of me? I didn't think you cared.'

'What? You're my mum, of course I care. What did He say? Was He angry? Is He still out or is He back?'

'He laughed, He thought it was hysterical. He's in the shower.'

He thought it was hysterical? She was clearly tickled by it too. What was going on?

Before I had any chance to process, I heard Him jog down the stairs. When He walked in He looked at me with a genuine smile and said, 'You little bastard,' and held His hand out for me to shake.

World, what are you doing to me?

Standing up, I took His hand and looked into His eyes and He actually nodded like He was saying, good one. Then He stepped back and bent over just as she had, play-acting playing golf with half-size clubs, and taking pretend swings,

216

yelling, '*Two!* It won't go far enough for a *four!*' Then cracking up. They were both cracking up. Of everything I'd expected, this was not it.

That night He said, 'You want to go out for a beer? We'll leave your mother here and you and I go out for one before dinner?'

I looked across at Mum, her eyes saying, do this one thing for me and say yes, please.

Turning back to Him I said, 'Great.'

It was weird. But good, even if I didn't understand what the heck was going on. I felt my shoulders lift, my back straighten, my head move up so I looked forwards rather than down on the ground. I even started cracking jokes, *and* they laughed. At school the following week I felt invincible. In short, I decided, this is what it felt like to be a man. Finally, after all those hopes and dreams of growing up and becoming an adult, I'd done it. For the entire week I hadn't listened to a single stupid record, I hadn't listened to idiotic agony aunts and the whiners that phoned in on the radio, I hadn't played the God-damn guitar because who wants to listen to that? And I hadn't written any childish, embarrassing thoughts or song lyrics about love, because – good God, how has it taken me so long to work this out? – who needs love when you can be liked? Love is a thing that happens irrespective of what you do, and you're either loveable or you're not, but you *can* make yourself likeable. It's obvious, even the most unlovable person can still be liked, isn't that what she'd said? Isn't that what she'd been trying to teach me? *That's why* she was so insistent I understood the difference between love and like. She wasn't being nasty, she was trying to help me. It was all starting to make sense.

Friday night He'd said He was going to take me out again for another drink. He said some of His mates were also going. He's alright, you know. I think I'd got Him wrong.

Friday came and I left school and ran home from the train station, had a bath, got changed, and waited in the lounge for them to come home.

'Fit?' He said, walking through the door.

'You bet,' I grinned.

With Mum bustling in behind Him, He said, 'Give me a minute to change,' and bounded up the stairs.

'Help me,' Mum said, and I grabbed half of the bags she was carrying and together we took them into the kitchen. Talking, I told her about school, and something someone had said that had made me laugh.

'Simon, I don't care.'

'Yeah, but this'll make you laugh,' I pressed.

'Just shut up.'

That made me step back, feeling a surge of the person I used to be a week ago, all weak and pathetic, and not liking it one bit.

'I've had a bad day, and He doesn't help. I asked Him not to go out tonight, but He said He promised you. You know He's using you, right?'

I leant back against the wall but didn't say anything.

Turning, she looked directly at me and held that look for two, maybe three long seconds, then pulled back her fist and smashed it into the side of my face.

What the hell?

Next thing she's punching and slapping and kicking and kneeing me, and when I lifted my hands to push her off she got hold of one put it into her mouth and sank her teeth into the fingers. Still the punches and slaps came raining in, hitting my nose, my eye, my forehead, cheeks, jaw and throat.

When she withdrew, unclamping my fingers in her mouth so my hand fell to my side, she was exhausted, and leant back against the worktop a foot away from me.

I couldn't speak. I couldn't move. My fingers throbbed. My face felt flushed and sore and my eyes streamed with tears. Why? Why did she do that?

Looking across at me she said, 'I saw something in your eyes and got in first.'

Chapter 27

The call clicked over to answerphone. 'Yeah, this is Ziggy. If you're an ex-wife, please press one. An ex-girlfriend, press two. A child who suspects I might be your long-lost father, press three. If you're from AA, NA or GA and are worried because I've missed a meeting, press four. For all other calls, leave a message.'

'It's me,' I said. 'This is about the fifth message I've left you. I'm starting to get paranoid. Call me back, okay?'

I was sitting in the woods on the bum of the General, who had in turn found himself a very comfortable spot to lie down. We were in a clearing under the shade of a big old ash tree. It cannot be overemphasised just how deliciously sumptuous the back end of a fully-grown male pig is to sit on, especially if you're horrendously hungover.

'He's not going to get back to me, is he. I think I've really messed up.'

My face felt too heavy for my skull, as though all the wine I'd consumed last night had pooled beneath the skin, making it a struggle to look up. When I did, the world wobbled as though the ash trees were made from jelly and someone had just given them a shove. 'Ooohh, that's not good.'

It was the morning after the night before. The night I'd told Debbie to fuck off. That bit I remember. I also remember the hurt look on her face, because it wasn't just the words I used, although they were bad enough, but the way I'd summoned my inner *Him* to give them a little gravitas.

Summoning my inner Him. Jesus.

She'd had every right to get up and storm out. Scream something at me, something vicious and cruel. But she didn't. Instead she told me she recognised I was in pain and wasn't going to leave me on my own. So she sat with me, then helped me to bed. But this morning she refused to talk to me, refused to acknowledge me.

'Wouldn't give me the time of day,' I said aloud. The best listeners are the ones who don't try and answer, or make sense of what you're saying, or try and find a solution. The best listeners just listen. Which is what the General does. Both my hands were holding my face up, but I took a chance and let go with one so I could pat his huge side.

'I had to corner her in the kitchen so I could apologise, and you know what she said General? She told me to fuck off back. That's kind of funny, isn't it? So if you're keeping score on the number of friends and wives still talking to me, that's thirty love, advantage everyone else and we're raising the net, ner-ner, n-ner-ner, game set and match, your serve. New balls please!' I'm not a huge tennis fan.

I feel awful. 'It wouldn't be so bad if I knew why I'd done it. I mean, sure, weapons of self-destruction are in my repertoire, but I normally have an inkling why I'm pressing the button. But last night it was all about feeling good. Maybe that's all the motivation I need. Pleasure. Peek inside at all that self-loathing, and it's like an old friend come to stay, a friend who you know is a bad influence and a nasty piece of work, but you can't help liking their company and they make you feel right.'

I used to be self-conscious talking to a pig, but after 13 years you learn to open up quite comfortably. Under me the General kicked out a back leg as he shifted into a more comfortable position and I lifted up slightly until he'd settled.

'Did I tell you the ewe accepted her lamb in the end and they're both out in the field doing fine? It all worked out. How about that?'

Mm, how about that?

'I feel bad for admitting this, General, but I'm kind of annoyed it worked. I mean, I'm glad the lamb and ewe are together and happy, of course I am, that was always the goal and I worked really hard to get there, but I'm also kind of angry that it did. And I know that doesn't make any sense. I think part of it is because it was so easy. Shouldn't PND be more difficult to cure? And if it's not, then maybe that's not what my mum had at all.' Then, 'but I do think it is what she had.'

Hangovers are particularly good for soul-searching because you're already in the pit, all you have to do is open your inner eyes and look around.

'I know everyone's different, and what might affect one person for two weeks could affect someone else for two years. But if PND is what Mum had, she had it for 40-odd years. Which does seem a touch excessive, even to me. Especially to me,' I said with a shrug. 'So when the ewe cured after only two days, it felt, I don't know, unfair. Don't get me wrong, I wouldn't want it any other way, but still unfair.'

And then there's anger. I don't suffer with it anywhere near the way I used to, somehow the farm sorted that out for me, but I do feel confused about the whole growing up around violence. Where did it all come from? Just for a second isolate the violence, and with that in mind where exactly does PND come into it – is violence a symptom of PND? Mum was clearly a victim, but she was also an aggressor, not just towards me, I'd seen her lash out at Him too and start some of the physical fights. Where exactly does PND stop and Mum start? Was that her frustration coming out? *Was* she even frustrated?

The anger I felt was never directed outwards. I was never a fighter. Instead, the anger was a feeling that pointed inward, and if I let myself dwell on it I'd end up physically wincing like I was been punched repeatedly in the stomach. The trick, of course, was not to dwell in it, but I didn't learn that until I got the farm.

Animals are amazing teachers. Whatever emotion you want to learn about, an animal will give it to you by the trough-load. Sadness: a piglet is born sleeping. Fear: one of the mental pigs rushes you, teeth bared. Elation: acceptance as one of them. Love: a dozing head in your lap. And of course, anger: I know your buttons and *I'm going to push them!*

It doesn't matter what your buttons are, an animal will find them as quick as an intuitive woman, and exploit them over and over and over again. So when the anger swells, what are you going to do, explode? Blow up? React? Scream and shout? Stamp your feet – the animals will laugh at you. Storm off – you'll only have to come back. Punch a tree – now you really will look stupid. And don't think an animal won't judge you, oh, they judge all right! If they think you're a prat, they'll let you know, and a loss of respect from them will plummet you down the hierarchy to a point below the runt. Find yourself there and it's pretty sobering.

Okay, for me, my anger never manifested itself externally, it was always targeted inwards, but just the same, you learn to pull it up sharp. Mostly I learnt that anger is something you can control. Shame it's not all that easy.

I was unlovable. Still am. I've searched for the bit in me to fix, spent all my life searching, but I've never found it. Oh sure, there are swirling masses of self-loathing in there, and I'm pretty sure there's a gnarly black core hidden really far down, but as for a *thing*, a *bit* with 'love' written on it that's broken and needs fixing, no, doesn't exist. It feels like last night the drink allowed me to visit a part of myself I don't normally go to. A part I think of as the real me. The really nasty, nasty centre of myself. Nobody else has ever seen it, except mum of course, because when you're a baby you don't have the capacity to hide it, which, I should think, goes a long way towards why she'd never been able to love me.

And over the years I have learnt to hide it. You don't walk around with that kind of stuff showing, not if you can help it. It's hidden behind masks and fronts, layers and layers and layers of them, until that's what the people around me see and know, and, for some, love. The masks and the fronts. Which is fine. I'm very happy with that.

But the problem is that recently the masks and fronts didn't feel as sturdy as they had, and that was really, really, really terrifying. It started with the ewe and lamb, of course it did, but I don't know if it was them or the subsequent trip into memory-land that caused the most damage. What began as a rescue mission for a sheep and lamb grew into much more. I was convinced they would help me figure out PND and the whole mother relationship thing. I was convinced I had more time with them before they bonded.

I rubbed my head – there were even signs that the hangover might be lifting, mainly in not feeling like I was imminent danger of keeling over dead.

'What has come out of it, General, is that if you accept mum had PND, and you mix that with the fact that there's not a *thing* in me that's unlovable, but rather it's me as a package that's unlovable, it does start to make sense. I think where I've been going wrong is to try and pin it on one or the other, when really, it's both: Mum's PND *and* the fact that the person inside me behind the masks and fronts is unlovable. That would explain a lot, everything maybe: why it went on for so long with mum, and also some of the things mum was trying to teach me. Look at it from that angle, and suddenly it all starts to make sense.'

Maybe I did learn something from the ewe and lamb after all – that it takes two to tango; mum was unable to love me, but I was incapable of being loved anyway. We were both equally at fault.

Carefully getting to my feet, I said, 'As therapists go, General, you're not only the best, but the cheapest.' Smiling down at him, stretched out, both eyes open looking up at me, I said, 'Thanks.'

I needed to find the ewe and lamb. Honestly, sometimes I can't even see what's in front of my eyes.

They were in the same field as yesterday, slightly separated from the others but still in sight of them. The ewe was lying down, presumably taking a break from duffing up the world, with the lamb next to her. All the other lambs had formed a gang. He was the only one with his mum.

Not sure how close they'd let me get without some entice-ment, I'd brought a bucket of sheep nuts, which seemed to do the trick. Spreading them in a line down the centre of the field, all the sheep came at a hot-foot run, including the ewe and lamb.

'How was your first night out? Okay?' They didn't look any worse for wear. In fact they looked pretty good with mum hustling for her share of the food, the lamb never more than a breath away from her. It was really nice to see.

I do still feel confused.

I do still feel anxious, and horribly exposed and vulnerable.

I still don't understand mum.

I still don't understand PND.

I still don't understand violence.

I don't like the fact that I feel like I'm losing control. Those masks and fronts, they're not just there to hide behind, they're also my protection.

I hate it that everything feels so uncertain.

Chapter 28

Dad's flat. Following mum lashing out at me I haven't been home for nearly three weeks and have moved in here, a one-bed flat on the top floor of a small block of 24 flats. Dad spends most of the time at his girlfriend's place, so I pretty much have the place to myself.

School is now on study leave, which amounts to me sitting around all day watching TV, listening to music and getting drunk at night in the local pub with a school friend who also has no interest in studying. I haven't heard from mum since the night she punched me, and she hasn't heard from me. That part of my life, the part where I had a mother, is over, I have decided.

The bright morning light through the curtains hurt my morning head. Last night the pub was packed and we sank enough beer for me not to remember getting home. It has only taken a few days to get our faces known by the bar staff and we no longer feel any worry about getting quizzed over our ages. I guess we must both look older than our 15 years.

With nothing to get up for, I don't, and continue feeling sick in bed. The thoughts that spin around my brain are the same ones that always spin around my brain, and revolve around the same old, same old Love versus Being Liked, and the surprising newcomer to my head-fuck, the 'Something She Saw in my Eyes'. That last one is the biggie. What *did* she see? No matter which way I turn it – haven't I seen too much violence towards her, heard too much, cried too much over it, hated it and her and Him for the fights they have, *ever* to do it myself? Yet she said she had seen something in my eyes, and if anyone knows what to look for, it's her.

Was I capable of hitting her? No! Never! Not even as much as I hated her, I still would never do that. But she had *seen something.* Jesus Christ, God help me, one of us had to be wrong, what if it was me?

For a start, it would explain why I was so unlovable. In fact, it would explain a lot. Sinking deeper into one pillow, I grabbed another and pulled it across my face. I didn't want to be violent. I didn't ever want to be like that. The thought of standing over her and punching her and making her feel the way she felt when He hit her destroyed me to my gnarly black core.

But she *had* seen something so bad she felt she had to react and hit me first.

I must be evil. An evil cunt. That word felt like a warm, comfortable overcoat, all-embracing and correct, and I wallowed in it because it felt right.

Just after midday I got up. Breakfast took an hour. A bath, another hour. Getting dressed, 15 minutes. TV, 45 minutes. When you're on your own with nothing to do but try not to spend time inside your own head, the day really drags.

I put on some Phil Collins, the album he wrote about getting back together with his wife. Yeah, I'd gone back to music because I had no idea where else to look.

Halfway through the second side, lying on my back on the floor and just beginning to feel like I might have survived another hangover, there was a knock on the door.

Jumping up, I went and opened it. Standing in the hallway was a lady, late 30s, blond and pretty with loose cotton trousers and a big fluffy baby blue top.

'Sorry,' she said, pointing behind her to the flight of stone stairs leading down. 'I live downstairs and this place is like an echo chamber, do you think you could turn the music down? Only I work shifts and trying to sleep during the day is a bitch at the best of times, let alone one of your neighbours having a party.'

Opening the door and my arms wide I said, 'God I'm so sorry. Yes, I'll turn the music down,' turned and hurried back inside, shouting over my shoulder, 'No, there's no party. Only me.'

'You're Pete's son, right?'

'Yes,' I said, coming back having shut the music down completely. 'I'm Simon.'

'Nice to meet you, Simon. I don't know your dad well, but he seems like a nice person.'

'He is. Thank you.'

Putting her arms around herself like she was cold, she said, 'Well, thank you. For turning down the music. Good taste by the way. Surprising. Boy on his own listening to that. Not what I expected.'

'Um, school project,' I said, grinning.

Smiling, she nodded and left.

The next day, same time, I put the same album on, reached for the volume control and turned it up. Then I waited. I don't know what I was expecting, but she was nice and she'd said I was surprising and unexpected, and when she said that I felt a glow deep down inside, and truth is, I'd never felt that before and I really wanted to feel it again.

She didn't come up and after a couple of hours I turned off the music and slouched on the sofa watching trash TV. My drinking buddy wasn't around tonight so this evening was a night in. Dinner, a late night affair consisting of two slices of toast and a bowl of cereal, accompanied by four cans of beer and a cigarette smoked leaning out the window, took me through to one in the morning. From one to two-thirty I put on more music and walked back and forth, back and forth for the entire hour and a half.

Of course they were all games to occupy time and stop me thinking. I hated thinking about mum, I hated thinking about me and I hated thinking about my life, but discount those and what else was left?

Just pace. Walk. Back and forth. Concentrate on the footsteps. Listen to the music, to the words. *Listen.* Make sense of it.

Knock, knock! on the front door. Quiet, but unmistakeable.

Dad? Reaching for the lock on the front door I undid it and pulled the door open. The hallway light was on a switch with a timer that every floor could activate. You pressed the button and it gave you time to move up or down the stairs. Only, it hadn't been pressed. The hallway was in darkness. From the residual light in the lounge I could just make out a figure. It was her.

As my eyes started getting used to the gloom, she whispered, 'Are you okay? Sound travels and I can hear you pacing, what are you doing, practising for a marathon?'

'Sorry. Sorry, I can't sleep. I didn't mean to…'

'I guess your dad's not here?'

'No. He's at his girlfriend's.'

'You're on your own?'

I nodded.

'How old are you?'

'15.'

'Look, can I come in for a minute? I'm getting hoarse whispering out here.'

'Of course.' I moved out of the way and she walked past me and into the lounge. This time she wasn't in street clothes, but in an all-in-one red cotton jumpsuit with a black shawl around her shoulders and sandals on her feet.

'I expected a furrow worn in the carpet,' she said, smiling. 'You certainly do a lot of walking.'

'I'm sorry.'

'Will you quit saying sorry already? I was just worried about you.' She sat and looked up at me. 'Have you been drinking? Where's your mum in all of this?'

'Um, only a little bit, and I don't know. At her house I guess.'

Getting up she said, 'You sit, I'll make you a coffee. And before you get any ideas, I'm a nurse and looking after people is what I do, okay?'

'I didn't…'

'Yeah, right. Crank the music up again today did we, same as yesterday? Don't worry, I wasn't in. One of the neighbours told me. You can't swing a cat around here without someone gossiping about it. It's that type of place.' She walked into the kitchen. 'Mind you, if I had been in I'd have been pretty mad, I don't take missing sleep lightly. Sugar?'

'Two, please. Thank you.'

Nodding, she said, 'So, want to talk about it?'

'Talk about what?'

'Why you're pacing up and down like a convict in a cell at three in the morning.'

'Oh.'

'And your choice of music gets stranger and stranger. There are a lot of love songs for a boy of your age. Is it girlfriend trouble?'

'No, I don't have a girlfriend.'

'Mm, okay. Milk?'

'Yes please.'

'So what is it?'

Never, ever, had anyone sat and listened to me. All the problems, all the worries, all the confusion and hurt and pain came spilling out. I talked and talked and talked like I had never talked before. I told her everything, about mum, about Him, and about me and about how I had to figure out what love was so I could fix whatever was wrong inside me, and the only two places I knew where to look for answers were late night radio agony aunts and music.

'You're kidding, right?' she laughed.

'No.'

'Okay. So, for the record, I don't think there's anything wrong with you at all – your mum, on the other hand, I'm not so sure about. You're not unlovable and I don't think there's anything inside you that needs fixing. But if you really want to know what love is, you're looking in all the wrong places. You need to experience it. That's the only way. You need to get yourself a girlfriend.'

Feeling ashamed, I told her about my first encounter with a girl and running away. She laughed hysterically. We were on the sofa, her shawl long since abandoned to the floor, and we were lounging back.

'Are you married?' I asked.

'Not any more. Six years into a life together and turns out he wants to shag anything in a short skirt. After the third, *"I'm sorry baby, she meant nothing, she came onto me and before I knew what I'd done it was all over and I feel terrible. Simply terrible. Can you forgive me?"* I moved out.'

'Boyfriend?'

Sigh. 'There are a couple of guys I thought I was interested in. It's very difficult second time around when you're a woman. All the good ones are gone or they have so much baggage there's no space left in their lives for anyone other than them. Oh, they think there is, they put out all the right signs, but when it comes down to it space in their lives is at a premium, and I'm too old for that junk.'

I didn't care that it felt like she just wanted to talk and it didn't matter to her if I was a teenager, a baby or a pensioner – I was a body next to her willing to listen. 'How old are you?'

'I'm not sure you should ask a lady that. How old do you think – actually no, don't answer that,' she said, both hands up and working her hair. '36. Yeah.'

What possessed me, I don't know. Had I thought about it, had it been a conscious action, I would never have done it. But it wasn't. It was purely instinctual, purely of the moment. Reaching over, I moved my face towards hers and kissed her. As our lips touched, I realised what I'd done and froze. Both our eyes were open, centimetres apart. She looked confused, then her eyes smiled, closed, and she kissed me back.

That kiss went down in history as the most beautiful thing that had ever happened to me. It was soft, and passionate and oh-my-God loving. OH MY GOD *LOVING*.

'Mm, hey,' she pulled away just a little. 'Are you crying?' Reaching up, she put a gentle thumb into the corners of each eye and wiped away the tears. 'What's wrong? Have you kissed a woman before, without, you know, running away?'

Her voice was so soft, and so nice and so caring that the tears fell harder and harder. They weren't sobs, and at least my nose wasn't running, it was like the taps had been turned on. I couldn't speak. All I could do was shake my head no.

I moved to close the gap between us and once more our lips were together. But this time she wasn't into it as much. I could feel her hesitancy. Without moving away, she said, 'Tell me what you're thinking?'

'That all the songs make sense.'

Pulling away completely she laughed. 'Yeah, okay. God, you nearly had me there.'

A sudden sting of hurt shot through me and I physically winced.

Catching me, her face turned into a question, then she said, 'oh.'

I don't know how but the next second we were kissing again. Just to feel another person so close was so amazing and I didn't want to run away, I never, never, never wanted to run away.

We didn't make love that night, but we did the following one. She took control and led me though. She was kind, and soft, and so, so very beautiful. She told me not to look so serious, or be so rough. She told me to slow down, smile, kiss, take my time. She asked, was this my first experience, and I said yes. And she said good, that made her happy.

Afterwards she let me cuddle her and kiss her and gently touch her body all over with the tips of my fingers, from the soles of her ticklish feet, to the features on her beautiful face.

'How do you feel?' she asked.

'Like all the pain has suddenly been taken away. Like weights on me have been removed. There was this time when I thought I'd worked it out and that to be liked was much better than love, but that was so wrong – God, did I have that wrong!'

Taking a deep breath, she said, 'I shouldn't be here. I'm too old for you. You need someone your own age.'

'Please don't say that. I love you.' And I did, with all my teenage heart. Looking back as an adult I can clearly remember the intensity of how I felt and how much space inside me that feeling took up, and it felt amazing. But for her, I don't know why she did what she did. Maybe she felt sorry for me. Maybe she realised how broken I was and wanted to try and mend me? Help me? Show me what love can be like? Or maybe she was just turned on at the thought of going to bed with a young virgin. Who knows. But I didn't care then and I don't care now. There's a little bit of me that still loves her to this day.

'Oh dear. You're so cute.' Kissing me tenderly, she said, 'you don't love me, you don't even know me. You look so earnest, so intense. It's so sweet. I hope you don't change.'

'Why would I change?'

Smiling, but not unkindly, she said, 'Because you're a man.'

Her shift pattern at work meant she couldn't come back for three days, then we spent two glorious nights together. On the third night before her work was due to start again, she knocked at the door and I bounded up to let her in. Only, it wasn't her. It was mum.

Chapter 29

'Surprised to see me?' Mum said.

Shocked would be a better word. Sure, my breath caught in my throat and I felt the weights and the pain heap back over me, but I also felt different. Inside. The changes I'd gone through were seismic. I didn't even recognise myself anymore. Love does that.

Pushing past me, Mum slammed the front door closed and stomped into the lounge where she took the centre spot, standing, arms crossed.

Not brave enough to follow her all the way in, I hung back.

'Get in here,' she called.

Oh well, there's nothing she can do to me now. I'm not the same person I was. She would see that. She would be able to tell. She couldn't hurt me anymore. Not after everything that had happened. Her power, her spell, her control over me was gone. So I went in, and sat down.

'What do you think you've been doing?'

I couldn't help smiling at that.

'I'll wipe that smile off your face, you stupid boy! So you've been fucking some bird.'

Oh my God, she knows?

Eyebrows dancing up, nodding, a sneer-smile perfected in the bowls of hell all over her face, she said, 'Yes, I know.'

Like Pinocchio with his strings cut, every bit of me sagged.

'This is your father's flat, not yours. He'd asked the neighbours to keep an eye on you,' her eyes flying up, *'and didn't she just!* Out of concern one of them phoned your father and told him what was going on, her sneaking in and out of here at all hours, and your dad called me.' Thanks for that, dad.

I felt sick, and tired, and scared. I wanted mum to go. I wanted to be with my love – more than anything in the whole wide world, I wanted to be with her.

'I know you,' Mum said, leaning towards me. 'You're my son. I know everything about you. I know what you're thinking. I know what you're doing. And being with her is wrong. She's my age! So I've put an end to it. It had to be done.'

'You can't. We love each other.'

'What? No you don't. You have no idea what love is, you stupid boy, and she certainly wouldn't love you, you're just a kid, for Christ's sake!'

Summoning all my spirit, I said, 'You're wrong. We want to be together.'

'Want a bet?' That sneer, that smile, back.

Slow realisation crept up my spine. 'What have you done, mum?'

'I've been to see her, and I told you, I've put an end to it.'

'You what? When?'

'Just now. You're a child. You're 15. You're supposed to be studying for your exams. But clearly you can't be trusted, so I'm taking you home.'

I was already shaking my head. 'No. I'm not going back with you. I need to speak to her. I need to see her.'

'Too late. She's gone to work.'

'But it's not her shift tonight.'

'Looks like it is now.'

'You can't do this to me!'

Hand on hip striking a pose. 'Watch me.'

In the end mum let me stay in the flat – I guess she figured she'd defused the bomb, and short of dragging me out screaming and shouting by my hair, something she wasn't averse to although probably not in the middle of the night with all the neighbours asleep, what was she going to do?

I waited all night for her to come home from her shift, but if she did, I missed her. Turns out she was renting the flat, and one day soon after, she moved out. I never saw her again.

Because everything reminded me of her, especially pacing the lounge, I took to walking the streets. A lot of the old hurt and pain was back, but not all of it. I missed her terribly, but I also felt let down, like she'd abandoned me. I wonder what Mum had said to her? I can only imagine, and knowing what Mum's like and what she's capable of, I don't blame her for leaving. After all, hadn't she said men with baggage are a nightmare, and my baggage was my mother knocking on her door for a cosy little chat in the middle of the night – figure that one! But it also makes me angry. Really angry. I'm angry at Mum for interfering, and at the same time I'm angry at her for listening to Mum and leaving me. I miss her and I'm angry at her. I hate Mum and I'm worried about her; her makeup was thick. Love, worry, hate, loss, frustration, anger, injustice. I'm so confused.

The walk had taken me to the high street. It had taken about an hour and rained some on the journey, so when I got there the pavements were slick and shiny and reflected the lights from the shops. It was after two in the morning and there was nobody around other than the odd car speeding by. I slowed and window-shopped and thought my thoughts and tried not to get upset in public, even if there was nobody around but me to see it.

I couldn't fully put into words the feelings inside, but it had something to do with feeling empty, and detached, and unseen, like I didn't belong anywhere or to anyone. The only thing that kept me going was the thought that I had been loved. I had been kissed and cuddled – and, by the way, I can report from my now first-hand experience that cuddling after making love is perfectly acceptable and not considered childish, phew on that one! – by someone who wanted to be with me, and share herself with me, and didn't think I was unlovable.

When it began raining once more, I started home.

School exams came and went, and no surprise, I failed them all. About to turn 16 and living alone in my dad's flat, I left school and got a job on a building site carrying brand-new bathrooms and kitchens up umpteen flights of stairs all day. It was hard, backbreaking work, but it paid £80 cash on a Friday afternoon. With beer about a pound a pint, and 20 cigarettes roughly the same, that was enough to last me the whole weekend.

'Come on!' My drinking buddy yelled from the other room. It was Saturday night, best night of the week. 'We're missing valuable drinking time and I'm looking particularly hot for the girls tonight.'

'Yeah, nearly ready,' I shouted back. The mirror in the corner of the bedroom was covered over so I didn't have to see myself, but I did look down at my clothed body and with the palms of my hands smoothed my shirt and jeans. I didn't think I was bad looking, but in truth I hadn't seen myself in years so I wasn't entirely sure. Gone were the days of standing naked in front of a mirror trying to work out if whatever was wrong with me was visible; these days I couldn't stand the sight of myself. I shaved in the bath – luckily that only had to happen once a week – brushed my teeth with my eyes closed and read a magazine at the hairdressers'. Every now and then I'd catch a reflection of myself in a car window or a shop and shudder at the sudden whoomph of hatred I felt.

'Come *on!*' He was getting impatient. My drinking buddy had left school at the same time as me and we'd fallen into the habit of spending Friday and Saturday nights together in the snug of local pubs discussing girls and sinking unhealthy quantities of beer.

Walking into the lounge I said, 'Okay, ready.'

'At last!' he said, getting up off the sofa.

'I just need to…'

'I knew it!' he said, slamming back down again.

Grinning, I said, 'It is only six o'clock. We've got plenty of time.'

'What do you need to do?'

Moving towards the door, I said, 'A little shopping.'

The corner shop was a few streets away. Inside I bought a loaf of bread, half a dozen bananas and a block of cheap butter. Placing the items in a bag and handing over a five-pound note, I felt my body begin to relax. There was only enough food in the flat for one more meal, and I couldn't cope with that. Unless I had more food than I could eat, I couldn't settle; my heart would pound, I'd sweat and feel sick like a junkie overdue for a fix. It was very uncomfortable. The solution was banana sandwiches. Cheap, easy to do, filling, and as long as you kept on top of the stock, plentiful, since a loaf could last me four days. The sense of comfort I got from opening a brand new loaf was indescribable.

Stashing the groceries behind the bins to be collected on my way back, we carried on out.

'Ah, now you've hit a very interesting point there,' my drinking buddy said, shifting several empty pint glasses out of the way so he could point at me across the pub table. 'You see, there's a school of thought that girls like vulnerability, which is codswallop. They say they do, and in the movies they like to make you think they do, but their DNA is hardwired to fall for bastards. It goes back to the caves. A bastard is more likely to go out and kill a dinosaur for her dinner and protect her from a sabre-toothed tiger attack than a Sensitive Sidney. Sure, they'll befriend the Sidney, but he won't get sex. While the bastard is shagging anything in a two-piece loincloth. It's genetics. Two more beers, my round?'

While he staggered up to the bar, I looked around. The pub was packed with the usual weekend crowd: circles of blokes on one side, and circles of girls on the other. Sex and sexuality had been on my mind a lot, to the point of obsession. The shift in going from feeling utterly unlovable to experiencing it physically was enormous, and set up within me a craving to feel it again that was so powerful, so encompassing and dramatic and desperate that I even had to question my sexuality. It was only when I found myself wondering if my bed loved me as much as I loved it, that I realised it wasn't men or women I was in a dilemma over, but just love in general. I'd have fallen for a streetlight if it switched on as I walked past. You want to know what sealed it? The moment I realised I was straight is fixed clearly in my mind. It was watching the 80s singer Blondie on TV. That's how a teenage boy's brain works.

Announcing his return by banging down two freshly filled pints, my drinking buddy sat, and said, 'Bastards!'

Sitting up I said, 'Who?'

'Men. The ones who are successful with the ladies.'

I sat back. These views were new and I vaguely wondered where he'd picked them up. They sounded like something my mum would say, only she'd have twisted it so the woman was the aggressor. Maybe there was a thing here. If both men and women recognised that bastards were successful and got what they wanted, and both decided that's what they were going to be and were playing the game against one another, then that's when heads would butt. And not just heads, but fists and feet and killer-blow words. Does that make my mum a bastard?

What with trying to work out the nuances of sex and love, I had pushed mum's 'I saw something in your eyes', to one side. But it was never very far away. In a way it was my Yang to love's Ying. As much as I needed a girlfriend, I was also terrified mum might be right and I was a woman-hitter. I didn't think I was, couldn't imagine any situation where I would be, but I couldn't get past the 'I saw something in your eyes.'

You see, that raises a massive problem. If I know I have the potential to hit a woman inside me, shouldn't I avoid all relationships so I can't hurt anyone? Obviously, yes. But then what would be the point of carrying on if I could never be with someone who would love me? So I limboed and drank lots of beer because too much thinking about life was making my head hurt.

Drunk to the point that I couldn't walk straight, I said goodnight to my drinking buddy and staggered home. Amazingly, I didn't forget the groceries from behind the bins, grabbed them and weaved my way up the flights of stairs to the top floor, trying not to make too much noise.

Inside the flat the phone was ringing. I could hear it from the hallway. As I went for the key in my pocket, the answerphone kicked in. Whoever it was didn't leave a message, but instead the phone immediately started ringing again. Wobbling rather than darting, I did my best to rush and pick up, but even the grip of fear a midnight phone gives you can't undo a whole night of booze, and, lunging, I missed the phone completely and knocked the answerphone off the side and onto the floor. As I bent down to pick it up I saw the message counter flash *16* new messages.

Seconds later it rang again, and this time I snagged it. 'Hello?'

Before she even spoke I knew who it was, and I knew it was bad. 'Simon, it's mum. Where have you been, I've been calling you all night?'

'What's wrong? Are you okay?'

Pause, then the sounds of her crying. Through the tears she said, 'No. No I'm not. I'm in a, a, um, women's refuge place. The police took me to hospital then brought me here.'

Chapter 30

'*You* were having an affair?'

Mum was sitting on the bed. I'd called a cab, washed my face in cold water for a full five minutes, eaten bread and butter to try and soak up some of the alcohol, changed and when the driver arrived told him to rush.

I had this image of a woman's refuge to be like a commune with a big centre room filled with comfortable chairs and bright cushions and women supporting one another in small intimate huddles. But it was just a room in a ropey B&B.

'Affair's too big a word for it. It was just a bit of fun, and to be honest it got Him back for some of the cheating He'd been doing. Don't look at me like that, please. Don't you dare judge me.' I'm sure that last sentence was meant to come out full of spite, but her spite tank was empty and instead she accompanied it with a smile.

She looked terrible, her hair stripped back into a ponytail, the outside of her lip cut, her eye cut and the entire left-hand side of her face a dark purple and swollen to half its normal size again. Even her grey tracksuit top had splats of blood on it.

'What did the hospital say?'

'They gave me some painkillers and cleaned me up a bit. Can you get me a mirror?'

On the floor was an open sports bag with clothes folded neatly inside. Beside it were her makeup bags, all three of them.

'What are you smiling at?' She said.

'You. Got your essentials.' Unzipping the middle one and reaching in, I pulled out the mirror and handed it across.

She looked at herself and groaned. Sitting on a chair in the corner, I asked what happened.

'Bastard followed me. I told him I was going out with some girlfriends when I was really going to a restaurant. Anyway, he walked in on us. The guy I was meeting is a bit tasty and they went outside for a fight and smashed the hell out of each other. Well I wasn't going to stay around for that, so I got in my car and drove home.' She was still looking in the mirror, twisting this way and that.

'I hoped he'd be knocked into next year and wouldn't come back, because if he did, I knew he'd be mad. When his car pulled up outside I hid in the wardrobe. It didn't take him long to find me, and when he did he just laid into me. I don't know who called the police, or how they got in, but suddenly the bedroom was full of them. They were really nice and took him downstairs and said they were sorry but they couldn't arrest him because it was domestic. But they did take me to hospital and then brought me here.'

'Jesus, mum.'

Looking over the top of the mirror she said, 'I didn't interrupt anything, did I?'

'No.'

'Have you seen her again?'

'You know I haven't.'

Nodding she said, 'Good. Sorry I had to do that, but it was for the best.'

This isn't the time. I know it's not. Don't say anything, not a word. Swallow it. Oh bollocks to that. 'No it wasn't, you were being a bitch.'

She laughed, went 'ouch!' with pain, and her hand flew up to the cut side of her mouth.

Maybe it was the alcohol mixed with a wash of adrenalin, but it made me laugh.

'Don't make me laugh,' she said, waving her hand in front of her face. 'It hurts.' But the laughter was already changing, as though that bubble of emotion led the way for a whole fizz of other emotional bubbles, each getting bigger and bigger and bursting on the surface. Tears were already sliding down her face and seconds later she was hunched over, sobbing.

Getting up, I moved over and put my arm around her, but she shrugged me off, saying, 'Don't touch me!' So I didn't, and sat next to her wringing my hands instead.

Two days later she was back with Him, but it didn't last. Six months after that, He left her for good. He'd found someone else. Someone younger who possessed shorter skirts and a deeper cleavage. How do we know this? Mum had photos. How she got them I have no idea, but she had pictures of them together and I'd often walk in on her staring down at them.

Although they weren't officially married, the separation was as complicated as a divorce. Soon, a 'for sale' board appeared outside the house. I'd kind of moved back in and was spending equal amounts of time with her and at the flat, although changes were afoot on that front too, as dad and his girlfriend were getting married and the flat was going, so God only knew where I'd end up.

One Saturday morning not long after they split, Mum announced, 'I'm meeting the husband of the bird He ran off with for lunch today.' She was in her usual spot at the other end of the lounge surrounded by makeup and a steaming mug of tea. The radio was on, as were all the lights, every single one of them.

'Wait. What? Why? When did this happen?'

'Yesterday. He phoned me,' she said, shrugging one shoulder. 'He wants to know more about what happened, and so do I. So we're going to compare notes. There have been so many lies, we want to get to the truth. And I'm curious what he looks like.'

'Is that a good idea?'

Looking across she said, 'What's it got to do with you?'

Okay, right, so though it felt like we'd been getting on much better, we were right back to that, were we? 'Nothing,' I said. Nothing at all.

She left in skin tight jeans, little pixie boots, low-cut top and bolero jacket, her blonde hair shaggy, her makeup perfect. I watched her walk down the path to her car, a red Porsche convertible, with a sense that this was a really bad idea.

I had to go out. I was 16, I had stuff to do. Important stuff. I didn't return to the house for a couple of days, and when I did she turned to me and said, 'Simon, this is L.B.'

I'd just walked into the lounge to be confronted with a man. Skinny, six foot four with a full head of blonde hair, blue eyes, clean-shaven, with deeply tanned skin, college-boy slacks and jumper, as though he'd just stored his surfboard before heading to his day job in a bank. They were the first impressions. The next set of impressions began with: he looks a decade younger than her.

'L.B.?' He said, offering me his hand with only half attention, the other half on her. 'What's that?'

Coming over, she pinched his chin between finger and thumb and twisted it down so she could kiss him, which was really awkward as L.B. and I were still shaking hands.

'Lover Boy,' she said, letting go and slapping his face hard enough to leave a mark, all without taking her lips from his, which is a very practised manoeuvre.

Squirming, I said, 'Um, yes, excuse me,' resorting to clamping my other hand on his forearm to try and wrench my hand free. Shaking hands is fine, but it's normally a moment between two people, not three, and absolutely definitely should not be undertaken if one of the party is snogging your mother.

Moving away from his lips, mum turned and smacked me hard on the back of the head, saying, 'Grow up,' and sashayed out of the room.

We both watched her go, but for very different reasons.

'Sorry, excuse me,' I said, rushing out. Catching up with her in the kitchen I said, 'Mum, who the hell is that?'

'Tasty or what?' she said, reaching for two glasses that she set down beside a bottle of white wine.

Exasperated and beginning to hyperventilate, I said, 'Mum, who is he?'

'That's him. We met and compared notes on our respective cheating partners and hit it off.'

'So if you two now get together, that means, you've swapped partners? Jesus, Mum! I feel like I'm living in a soap script.'

'Stop being melodramatic. Besides, I won't be seeing him for a week or so and he'll probably have found someone else by then.'

Sensing I was meant to ask, I said, 'Why won't you be seeing him for a week, mum?'

'Because I've booked myself in for a boob job. I've got to be up in London at seven in the morning. See ya!' and walked out carrying the bottle and glasses.

'And you didn't think to tell me?'

Spinning so she could look at me as she backed into the lounge, she said, 'Why would I do that?'

I left them to it. Well, what was I going to do, hang around until they offered me a fiver for the cinema? After work the following day I caught a bus home, not knowing what to expect. She was lying on the sofa in the lounge in leggings and a baggy jumper, under which she had on a sports bra. She looked tired.

Sitting next to her I said, 'Are you okay?'

'Bit sore. Do you want to see them?' and began pulling up her top.

'Mum! No! God…'

'Don't be such a child!' she said, adding a little more softly, 'Make me a tea.'

I stayed that night, and the next, and when it was clear she was fine I went back to the flat for the last couple of nights before it went from our hands into someone else's. Dad was finally getting rid of it.

Pacing the lounge for old times' sake, I thought, so much has happened here it was impossible for the walls not to have absorbed some of the vibe, and smiled at the thought of the next people in the flat sitting on their first night wondering why they felt such a strong need to feel love, and why *everything* felt *so damn confusing*.

When it was all done and I'd packed the few bits I had, I went back to Mum. I expected her to be alone, but she wasn't. His car was outside – no, not L.B's. His!

What the hell was He doing here? They were separated. The house was nearly sold. The last time they were together He put her in hospital. Surely she wouldn't let Him in? Surely she wouldn't have a conversation with Him? Unless He was back here to finish the job and smash her up some more. But why? Maybe we were all doing things for old times' sake.

Outside, I thought, should I call the police? Get a weapon and run in swinging? At 16, I was beginning to fill out, especially working on the building site, but I was still half the bulk of Him. Even putting the size difference aside, the embarrassing truth was that I was petrified of Him. Years of living in an atmosphere of bullying and tormenting and antagonising; all the nights listening to Him punch her; the times when she came into my room to hide from Him; the occasions she got me out of bed and bundled us into the car and drove until morning just so we weren't in the same house as Him; and of course the nights I'd woken up with Mum slamming into my room and screaming in terror that He was going to kill us and dragging me out so we could barricade ourselves into the spare bedroom while He repeatedly stabbed the outside of the door with a bread knife, had taken their toll. Now, standing outside the house with them both inside, together again, I felt sick. Of course, I'd fantasised about confronting Him and laughing as I tore out His eyes, or locking Him in a secret room somewhere where I could torture Him over the course of several months with Him begging me not to hurt Him. But in reality, whenever I was near Him all I wanted to do was run away.

Well, no more. I had to do this, for my own sanity and for that of my mother's. I had to face the bully. I had never told Him how much I hated Him. He must know, but I'd never told Him. Never stood and looked Him in the eyes and said all the things I wanted to say. And I knew I hadn't done that because I was a coward. Because I was scared. That wasn't being a man. That wasn't protecting my mum. In the past I could hide behind being a kid, but when you're 16 that doesn't work anymore.

My stomach churned and my head felt giddy. Breathing deeply, I stood tall, and began walking up the path towards the house. This was it. This was my moment.

Then ahead of me the front door opened and He stepped out.

No! I wanted to get Him inside. What was I supposed to do now, start yelling and screaming at Him out here?

As we got closer I balled my hands into fists.

I slowed my breathing.

Slowed my steps.

Squeezed my fists tighter.

'Simon.' He said as He passed, looking down at me and smiling.

I nodded. Smiled back. And He was gone.

A little voice inside of me sang, *cowardy, cowardy cunt-stard*.

Inside, she was an easy target for all the hatred and loathing I felt for myself but vented at her because I didn't know how to deal with it, so I yelled at her that she shouldn't be seeing Him, and she yelled back that it was none of my business.

The following night L.B. was there.

The night after, it was Him again.

The one after that, they both turned up at the same time, met outside in the street, punched each other a few times in the face, rolled around on the floor a bit, then, bloodied and bruised, got into their respective cars and tore away without either of them going inside to see mum. From the lounge window, looking out, she roared with laughter.

But it was the one after that where it really got interesting, because someone new turned up.

The day had been nice for a change, and mum was feeling stronger and even had a careful bath. She'd gone up two cup sizes, and as the bruising turned from angry purple to healing yellow, she'd spent the day trying on different outfits to see how she looked.

'Simon, how about this one?' she said, walking in dressed in simple leggings and cream blouse cinched at the waist with a jazzy belt, the buttons of the blouse low, the maternal fixed open. She walked on tiptoes, mimicking high-heels.

'Nice.'

'You haven't even looked!' she complained.

Outside a car pulled up. I looked out. The car was nice, but not flashy. From it I watched an older man, late 50s maybe, climb out. He had on a business suit that was definitely not off the peg.

I watched him walk down the path and couldn't help thinking there was something different about him. The slowness of his pace, the way he held himself, his shoulders, his head, and just a general air of ease about him, like he didn't have a care in the world. It was only when I met him face to face and looked into his eyes that I got a sense of the pitch-black darkness about him. But I didn't know that then; that was to come.

'Oh my God,' Mum said, looking over my shoulder. 'Let him in,' and with that she bolted back upstairs.

That's why, that first time, it was me that opened the door to him.

Wondering just how many boyfriends my mother had on the go, I reached for the lock and pulled the door wide open just as he made his final step and stopped.

His eyes met mine and my backbone shivered all by itself. It was very weird.

I expected his voice to be hollow and cold, but it was just normal. Light even. 'Hello.'

'Hi. Mum said to let you in. She's upstairs. You can wait in the lounge if you like.' Stepping back, I made room for him to pass.

Later, when he'd gone, I asked, 'What's his story? I'm guessing he's no primary school teacher.'

She was sitting on the chair fiddling with her sports bra. 'He'd shoot you as quick as look at you. The way he described it to me was, you know when people say about someone that they're very well connected to the underworld, well he's the person in the underworld they know.'

'How'd you know him?'

'Ages ago. We were out one night and there was a fight, and while all the childish men went off to get involved he came over and asked if he could stand next to me to make sure I didn't get caught up in it. And you know something, nobody came near us.'

'Great. Another fighter. Don't you know any boxers you could date too, you know, really make a thing of it?'

'Don't talk to me like that!' She snapped, stopping fiddling and sitting up, her face stony.

Suddenly nervous, I took a step backwards, though not literally. 'Well…'

'Well what? What are you saying?'

'Mum, you have some scary boyfriends.'

'He's not a boyfriend, he's just a friend, so get your facts right. And who I date has nothing to do with you.'

'So you say.'

Beat of silence, during which her face changed from angry to nasty just by adding a sarcastic smile. My cue to leave.

'Going upstairs to play some love songs? If you ever wonder why I have to surround myself with strong men, take a look in the mirror, or are you still covering them up? Maybe I'm hoping some of the manning-up will rub off on you.'

Getting up, I said, 'Why are you so nasty?'

'Oh, I haven't even started yet.'

Making to leave I said, 'I know.'

As I got to the door, she said, her voice all smarmy and sarcastic, 'Simon, love you.'

Punching the door with all my might, I screamed, *'fuck you!'*

Chapter 31

Not long after, I found myself in Lanzarote airport, watching an aeroplane take off towards London without me on it. I watched it hurtle down the runway and up into the midday air with mixed feelings of fear and excitement. When it was out of sight, I turned and walked out of the terminal. I had 15 pounds to my name, no return ticket, a suitcase full of dirty holiday clothes and no idea what to do next.

I hadn't planned on staying. The holiday had been fun, three teenage lads drinking and chatting up girls for two weeks, but even so I hadn't once thought this was how I wanted to live my life. That wasn't the motivation to stay. It was more a case of, I didn't want to go back and live as I had been, not with my mum and not with me; not with either of us the way we were. So when the other two boarded the plane, I didn't.

Finding my way back to the beach, I stored my case in a friendly bar and mooched along the strip, my flip-flops kicking up sand from the hot pavement. It was early afternoon and the sun was high. On the strip the shops didn't close for lunch and their brightly coloured beachwear twinkled in the bright sunlight. Ahead of me, a family pretended to lose their boys when the kids hid giggling behind carousels of sunglasses and hats.

My only fear was food. Not being able to eat. Nothing else bothered me, not finding somewhere to stay and certainly not safety; not caring what happens to you is wonderfully freeing.

'Hey,' a girl said to the family in front of me. She stepped out from a doorway, a folder-type bag proffered in front of her. 'Have you guys played the Lanzarote lucky dip?' She was wearing pink shorts and a Choose Life t-shirt, her hair in a French plait. All the skin on show was dark mahogany.

Half stopping and half peering past her to keep an eye on the boys laughing and ducking in and out of shops, the family tried to sidestep, but Choose Life was wise to that and blocked their path so they'd either have to stop or crash into her.

Feigning interest in postcards, I moved into a shop beside them, so close that the Choose Life assumed we were together and indicated for me to join them.

'Oh, he's not with us,' the lady said, and I smiled and waved an 'I'm just interested in postcards' hand.

Instantly dismissing me from the scenario, she carried on. 'Have you guys just come onto the island?'

'Today,' they confirmed.

She seemed to brighten even further, exclaiming, 'That's wonderful! Well, the Lanzarote Tourist Board employ people like me to help promote tourism on the island with the Lanzarote Lucky Dip. There's no charge, it's free and there are lots of prizes, from bottles of champagne to free tickets to clubs and shows, and the top prize of a holiday. No one's won the holiday weeks, so we know one's due. Fancy a try?' Once again, she held up the folder.

From where I stood, I could see the folder was clear plastic with envelopes inside, each half the size of the postcards in front of me, and on the outside of them were printed the words *Lanzarote Lucky Dip*.

Mr looked at Mrs, who shrugged. But as he raised his hand, she suddenly reached out and grabbed it mid-air, turning to the girl and asking, 'Is this a scam?'

Choose Life shook her head. 'No. It's legit.' Then, turning to me, she said, 'You've heard of the Lanzarote Lucky Dip, haven't you?'

Surprised to be brought into the conversation, I stopped pretending to look at the postcards and looked at her. She gave a *'please'* look.

'Oh yeah,' I said. 'It's definitely a thing over here.'

Still sceptical, Mrs said, 'How do we know you two aren't in on it together?'

'I've never seen her before in my life,' I said. At least that was honest.

'Okay,' she said, letting go of Mr's arm, which continued its trajectory in the direction of the LLD.

'Champagne,' Choose Life confirmed when he'd opened the envelope. 'Not bad. We've got cases of the stuff. It's okay, but to be honest it's not the best. Now your turn madam, see if you can do better than him?'

The fact they'd won a bottle of cheap and nasty bubbly seemed to relax them, and without hesitation Mrs reached across.

'*Holiday*! Oh my God, you won the *holiday*!' Choose Life exclaimed, clearly shocked at the unexpected turn of events. This was fabulous news, and she started bouncing up and down gabbling about a two-week all-inclusive holiday they'd won, and the bonus she got for being the one who gave it away!

If the champagne had relaxed the family, the holiday clammed them back up again. The British just aren't good at random acts of good fortune; tell them it was going to rain every day of their fortnight's stay and they'll happily accept it, but tell them something nice has happened and they go all sceptical.

'No!' Mrs said.

'No!' Mr echoed, both pushing by.

'But you've won the holiday,' Choose Life protested.

'Give it to someone else,' Mrs shouted over her shoulder, and was off in search of her boys.

Dejected, Choose Life stuffed the ripped open envelopes into her pocket and looked up at me and said, 'What?'

'Did they really win a holiday?'

Her face suddenly looked older. 'What do you think?'

'How'd you do it?'

Backtracking. 'Do what? I don't know what you mean.'

'Come on. It's clearly a scam.'

'Goodbye,' she said, and started walking off.

'Hang on,' I called, rushing after her. 'I need a job. My plane home left a couple of hours ago and I wasn't on it. I've got no money and nowhere to stay. Please.'

'What do you want me to do about it?' she said, not breaking stride.

'Please. Help me. I need work.'

'For real?'

'Yes,' I said. 'For real.'

Stopping and eyeing me up and down, she said, 'Charlie's bar. Tonight,' turned and walked away.

Charlie's, okay.

Predictably the bar was packed, and just as predictably Choose Life wasn't there. With nowhere else to go and nothing else to do, I hung out, chatting and laughing with people and gratefully taking their offered drinks. It wasn't until two in the morning that a large group walked in. They were obviously known as all the staff, including the DJ over in the corner who gave them a wave. Scanning the t-shirts, then the faces, I finally spotted her hugging a tall, tanned army-type man. She had changed and was now in floaty skirt and strappy top, but it was unmistakably her.

Excusing myself from a knot I'd fallen in with, I weaved towards the new arrivals.

They were lounging on chairs and a big leather sofa. She was in the middle. 'Hey,' I said, looking down at her and smiling.

Instantly army-type furrowed his brow, looking at me, then her, then me again.

Someone came into the group with a tray filled with glasses of beer. Everyone reached for one.

'Relax,' Choose Life said, thankfully recognising me. 'He was on the strip earlier. Tried to help me with an up. How you doing?'

'Good. Um, sorry, can I talk to you?'

Looking less than impressed, she struggled up, saying to army type, 'I'll be two minutes,' and grabbing two beers from the tray, one of which she thrust into my hands. 'Come on.'

The place was thinning out, most of the clientele drifting off, probably too drunk to remember if they had a good time or not. Heading for a small table a few feet away, she took a seat.

'Two minutes. Go,' she said, lifting the beer and taking a long drink.

Putting mine on the table in front of us and drawing patterns with my finger on the side of the wet glass, I told her what I'd done.

'What are you running away from?' she said.

'Nothing.'

Nodding at the group, she said, 'Every single one of us is here because we're running from something. Or someone.'

'What are you running from?'

She took another drink. 'A life of boredom. Answer the question.'

I thought about it and said truthfully, 'I don't know. It's complicated.'

'Not the police, then?'

'No. Not the police.'

'Good. We've got enough psychos. Girlfriend trouble?'

'Not really.'

Nodding she said, 'Well if you're running away from yourself, you do know you brought you with you, don't you?'

Laughing, I took a drink. 'So what's the scam?'

'No scam. Timeshare. We're OPC's, Outbound People Catchers. We talk to people nicely and invite them to a presentation. For every couple you take up and introduce you get paid. You don't take anyone up, you don't get paid. This is not a charity.'

'The Lanzarote Lucky Dip.'

'That's mine. You have to find your own angle.'

'How did you know she was going to win the holiday?'

Smiling. 'Two pouches. One side's full of champagne, the other full of holidays. You just flick between the two. Man wins the champers, lady gets the holiday. To collect, they have to go to the resort. Works most times.'

'Clever. Do they actually get a holiday?'

Nodding, 'Of course.'

Another sip. Another question. 'Does accommodation come with the job?'

'The company'll find somewhere to put you up for a week, after that you're on your own. But ask around, there's normally a room going spare somewhere. Come on,' she got up, 'I'll introduce you.'

So that was me for six months. I got a room in a shared house and experimented extensively with drink, drugs and sex. It was a wild time. Daytimes were spent as an OPC down on the strip working, and evenings in one bar or another. Simple. But life doesn't let you get away with that kind of lifestyle for long. Sooner or later it all catches up with you. And my catch-up was spectacular.

I'd had a good day, three ups had strolled into the timeshare village with my name credited to them, and, feeling good, I'd stopped off at a watering hole on the way home for a couple of cold beers. The bar was frequented by locals, and I'd expected some of the others to be in there, but as it was, there was nobody else I knew. So I took a seat in a quiet corner and put my feet up.

I'd moved in with a girl I really liked, one of the sales team at the resort. Life was the best it had ever been. The only contact I'd had with mum was a phone call right at the beginning to tell her what I'd done and a postcard I'd sent a month or so later. In either of which I hadn't offered a contact address out here, and she hadn't asked for one. It felt good to be 3,000 miles away from her.

The beer was ice-cold, and the ceiling fans whipping up the air kept it cool. Several holiday makers sat at the bar talking football, while on a table over to my left a couple argued. They were just off the beach and still in swimwear, her with a bright blue sarong wrapped around her, him bare-chested with a straw hat on. Their voices were raised, his accusatory, hers defensive. It was getting animated. And loud.

Someone else in the bar shouted, 'Give it a rest,' which just seemed to escalate things. Suddenly switching his attention away from her, he started screaming and shouting and offering to fight anyone in the bar who could stand. He was clearly drunk and it was very amusing.

'Are you laughing at me?' he said, coming over to where I was sitting.

Without any warning to him, *or me*, I stood up and punched him full in the face. It was automatic, no conscious thought required. Just *bamb!* Rocking back from the blow, I moved in and punched and punched and punched. When I realised what I was doing, I stopped. By then he was on the floor and I was kneeling over him. The bar around me had gone cold and silent. The only voice was hers, screaming at me to stop. His bloodied face lolled to one side and he spat blood, calling me something that sounded like 'saint,' but probably wasn't.

That night I lay in bed staring at the ceiling and feeling vile. All my deepest fears that I'd inherited her violent tendencies had come true. What the hell made me do it? Had I been thinking about mum, was that it? A quick reminder of home and bang, bang, bang, there you go little boy, just like mummy used to make. Or, more likely, was it simply that I was relaxed and let down my guard? Forgot myself? God, that's even worse.

By midnight all the old feelings of self-loathing had piled back in.

At 2 a.m. I got up, turned on the bathroom lights and did something I hadn't done in years. I stared into a mirror. The face that looked back was older than I remembered, and tired, and scared. I thought of mum's words, *I saw something in your eyes.*

After breakfast the following morning, when everyone else had left for work, I dragged the suitcase from under the bed, filled it, caught a cab to the airport and got on a plane home. In the air, I thought, I didn't even tell the girl I was living with that I was leaving. But then, how could I? What would I say? 'I'm sorry but I've got to go because I'm scared I'm like Him, and I'm petrified you'll be next.'

'What made you come home?' Mum asked later that same day, her feet stretched out in front of her. She'd moved while I was away and now lived on her own in a modest house. We were in her new lounge, a small green room that felt too severe to be comfortable. She's also lost weight, which made her new boobs look massive.

That wasn't the only change. L.B. had gone and Mr New On The Scene was a multimillionaire who was involved in some complicated battle with Lloyds of London who were refusing to allow him access to his money, rendering him temporarily skint. Allegedly.

'I'd had enough. You can only live that life for so long,' I said, looking around and noting the *Country Life* magazines fanned out just so on the coffee table in front of us.

We both reached for our mugs of coffee at the same time.

'So you're running away from running away now?'

'Thanks. Appreciate that. Why don't you ask my what it was like? Why don't you ask me what the people were like? Why don't you ask me if I had a girlfriend out there?'

'Okay. Did you?'

I put the coffee back on the table without taking a sip. 'You're not interested.'

'No, not really,' she said, sighing. 'But you clearly want to tell me, so go on, what was she like?'

Shaking my head I said, 'Tell me about this new bloke, the alleged millionaire.'

'Simon, you're going to have to grow up at some point. Get a proper job, a home of your own.'

'I do proper jobs!'

'Why don't you last more than a month with them, then? You've had more jobs than I've had hot dinners. And going abroad isn't the answer.'

'You don't know that.'

'Yes I do. You're back. What a waste of time that was.'

'Why are you so horrible?'

'Why is that horrible? It's the truth. You left school four years ago –'

'Three.'

Sigh. 'Okay, you left school *three* years ago, and all you've done is bum, flitting from one, to one, to one, to one. Tum-te, tum-te, tum-te, tum.' As she spoke, she danced her hand in the air in time with the words, wobbling her head and putting on an airy smile. 'Oh, my name's Simon and I don't care about anyone other than myself, and I'm going to have lots of jobs and live abroad and please myself, and flit, and flit, and flit and do whatever I want.'

Getting up: 'I came here to be friends.'

'I'm not interested in being your friend. I'm your mother.'

I raised my eyebrows.

She jumped up, crossed the distance between us and slammed me against the wall, doing her favourite: upturned hand under my chin, fingers and thumb either side of my jaw digging in. 'I am your mother, like it or loathe it,' she hissed, 'and believe me, there are times when I too loathe it. But you play the cards you're given. Now I want to see you in a good job, with a nice home so I don't have to worry about you any more. That's not an unreasonable hope for a mother, is it? *Is it?*'

I couldn't answer – her fingers were still digging into my jaw. Of course, I could have shoved her off, pushed her away, but she's my mum and a woman and I'm not going to lay a finger on her no matter what. She wants to punch me, stab me, fine, but I'll not retaliate, because if I do, even in self-defence, it makes me no better than Him.

Eventually she pushed herself off me and I let myself out. Actually, the real reason I'd gone to see her was to ask if I could have a room, but that was never going to happen. So I moved in with my dad and his fiancée and tried not to be around too much.

The problem is, of course, mum was right. My CV showed I was unskilled and unlikely to stick around, a moniker that worked equally well to describe my love life as it did my career.

Day one, new employer: *Welcome to the company, good to have you on board! You could have a shining career here, how long do you think you'll stay?*

Me: *Oh, until we know each other well enough that I start seeing myself through your eyes, and then I'll be jogging on.*

Day one, new girlfriend: *I really like you. Do you like me? We could see each other again. If you want to. How long do your relationships normally last?*

Me: *Oh, until we know each other well enough that I start seeing myself through your eyes, and then I'll be jogging on. And just for the record, I'd avoid looking too closely into my eyes if I were you.*

If I could figure out a way of putting a towel over the mirror inside my head the way I do the physical one in my bedroom, life would be so much easier. And I've tried! God knows I've tried! But it doesn't work. You see, what I now realise is the person I hate more than any other isn't actually my mother, or even Him, it's the cunt inside my head. Mum was right. All along, mum was right. She always was.

Determined to make something of my life, I got clean and sober pretty quick, and found myself single and living with my dad and his new wife. I applied for many jobs, but my CV was horrendous and I hardly got an interview. Then a friend told me he knew of a position going as a process server and private investigator focusing on helping victims of domestic violence, which *really* appealed. A phone call later and I was employed. Sometimes life works that way. Knuckling down, I made a deal with myself not to leave the position, no matter what, for two years. And I was good at the job; it turned out I understood domestic violence, who would have guessed?

If a person finds themselves the unfortunate victim of a violent partner, they might well seek protection from the courts, who in turn would employ the company I worked for. Under direction of a High Court Judge and an appointed solicitor, I'd be sent out to chat with the victim and move them somewhere safe if that was what they needed, make sure they're okay, and then go and serve the arsehole with a court order to keep away and stop punching the crap out of them.

I served everyone from well-to-do city types to drug-fuelled crazies. I served people at their homes late at night, in courts, businesses, prisons, bedrooms, bars, brothels, clubs and once in a bath. Surprisingly, not everyone took too kindly to my presence. I got punched, kicked, chased, sworn at, cried on and spat at. But I stuck with it because every woman was my mother and every arsehole was Him.

But my fear was always that violence breeds violence breeds violence. Abused become abusers. Victims become aggressors. If you lived in that world, there was a chance you'd become that world. More than anyone, I had something to fear on that score. So after two years, I got out. I bought a suit, a car and became an estate agent. Then I bought a flat. I hadn't spoken to mum in more than a year.

I was yet to turn 21.

Chapter 32

'Sit!' Debbie commanded. I sat. Solomon the Great Dane didn't. At least one of us was well trained. 'Where have you been?' she continued. 'I've been frantic, you're not answering your phone, you just disappear for the day, *and after last night*!'

'I'm sorry.'

'Forget sorry, Simon, I've been so worried. Where have you been – you've been *hours!?*'

'In the field with the sheep… what are you doing?'

She was fiddling with her mobile. 'Texting Ziggy you're okay. He's going out of his mind blaming himself for not getting back to you – he's been in court for the last two days, by the way. What were you doing in the field?'

Her phone pinged with a return message. 'He says to call you a prick, that he'll phone you later, and that he loves you.'

I wondered what she had told him for him to send that? 'Did he really say that?'

She put the phone to one side. 'Yes. I can't tell you how worried we've all been.'

We were in the kitchen. There were dirty dishes in the sink, half-prepped food on a cutting board and general signs of a day gone up in smoke.

'Were you with the ewe and lamb, is that it?' she asked.

I felt heavy at the prospect of telling her I'd spent the day with my memories. It sounded so lame and navel-gazey.

'Tell me,' she urged. So I did. I spent an hour telling her about my thoughts sitting on the General's bum, and how I was upset that I hadn't had more time to learn from the ewe and lamb. Then how I realised that I'd been looking at my relationship with mum all wrong and trying to pin down if it was me or her, my unlovableness or her PND, when actually it was a combination of both.

'I don't know if I can keep doing this,' she said, looking tired and close to the end of her tether. 'You are not unlovable – how many times? I love you, I love you to bits, so how does that work?'

I didn't tell her she loved the masks and fronts, I'm not a sadist.

Moving on, I told her the memories were screwing me up. Groaning, she actually smacked her forehead on the worktop. But I *had* to see them through to the end. So I'd lain down in the field and let them play out to the finish.

'And?'

I shrugged my shoulders. Looked down. 'There was no big finally, no Hollywood ending. It just petered out. It's like, it answered some questions, but the satellite ones, you know, such as why I am the way I am around food – I'd forgotten how I was always so bloody hungry as a child.'

'Hence making bread all the time,' she agreed. 'I'd already worked that one out.'

'You had?'

'I'm a woman. Carry on.' Do women realise how confusing that phrase is? Is that why they use it? As far as I understand it, 'I'm a woman,' can mean: shut up; don't ask; it's complicated; it's obvious; it would take too long to explain and you probably wouldn't get it anyway; or simply, that's a boring tangent, stick to the main point, which is what I took it for right now.

'Okay,' I said. She knows about the self-loathing, but it's not anything we ever talk about. I'm embarrassed about it. Ashamed. I hate it about myself, which is ironic, I know. So when I spoke the words, I spoke them fast. 'The self-loathing, the guilt, the hatred of violence, the anxiety, it didn't show me anything I didn't already know about those.

'Woo, hang on, not so fast. Back up there a minute.' She stood up and started pacing, which is something she never normally does. Nervous his cuddle was going to go the same way, Solomon snuggled deeper into my side and put a paw on my leg.

Stopping in front of me, she counted off on her fingers, 'self-loathing, guilt, anxiety and hatred of violence. Did I miss any?'

Yes, about a million of them. But I said, 'No, that's it.'

'What about love?'

'What about it?'

'Why didn't you mention it? I thought that's what this was all about, figuring out your relationship with your mum and why she didn't love you. All those other things, the self-loathing, violence, guilt, anxiety, plus all the other things you're not telling me…'

Oh, that's the other thing 'I'm a woman' can mean: you don't have to voice things for me to know them.

'…all leads back to your mum. So, you now believe she did in fact have postnatal depression?'

'Yep. I'll never know for sure, but I think so.'

'Okay, good. How does that make you feel?'

Shrugging. 'Sad. Annoyed it wasn't diagnosed and treated, but then she was never the type of person to open up about anything like that and seek help. She would have seen it as a weakness and probably refused to admit it even to herself. I know she went to a couple of sessions with a psychiatrist in the early days, but I doubt she said much. Sometimes I do wonder how life might have been different if she had been treated. Even with all the drugs and therapy in the world, I can't ever imagine her being a mumsy mum. And she would still have had to deal with me.'

Moving to sit next to me, she said, 'What does that mean?'

'I was unlovable.'

'Okay, so you were born unlovable and she had postnatal depression, is that right?'

'Well, yes. Perfect storm. It's the only thing that makes it all make sense.'

'First, there is no such thing as an unlovable baby, not in the sense you mean. Sure, they can be annoying and frustrating and all that, but there is no such thing as a baby being inherently unlovable. There just isn't. It's something you made up to fit your own narrative because you hadn't considered your mother might have had her own unresolved issues, and for some reason took everything to be your fault, and you've been doing that for so long you now can't untangle yourself from it. Even now, having accepted she had postnatal depression, all you're prepared to do is meet it halfway. It's so ingrained into who you are that I don't know if you'll ever be able to separate yourself from it and that's really sad. Simon, you are not unlovable.'

It's not something you can argue about without it sounding like a line from a particularly dark pantomime, *Oh yes I am unlovable!*

Oh no you're not!

Oh yes I am!

So I grinned and nodded in a, 'good one' way.

Then she threw in an atom bomb. 'I want you to go and see your mum. This week, as soon as possible. I want you to go and see her and talk to her.'

I was already shaking my head. 'No point. She's beyond that, the dementia's too advanced. You can't hold a conversation with her anymore.'

'Doesn't matter, this isn't for her, it's for you. You need to find a way to move on from this, and you're not going to be able to do that without finding a resolution. It was you yourself who said you had to bring it to an end. Well, the memories, the postnatal depression, all of that is only one part of it, and, if you like, only a small part of it. The bigger part, the *far* bigger part, is your relationship with your mother; no 'I remember this,' or 'I think she might have had that.' Just the grass roots of two people, a boy and his mum. That's what you need closure on, can you not see that?'

'I need closure on the relationship with my mother?' I repeated. If I was confused before…

'I know you think this all started because of the ewe and lamb, but I don't believe it did. That was just the catalyst. I think this has been bubbling under the surface for a long, long time and you have an awful lot of unresolved issues surrounding your mum, and the fact that she's no longer responsive because of her dementia has compounded and compounded and compounded them, and turned them into a landmine that the ewe and lamb stepped on.'

Blimey. 'Oh.'

'While we can't fix that, you can still talk to her. And that's what I think you need to do, go and talk to her. Sit beside her bed, hold her hand, kiss her cheek, talk to her and find some closure. If you don't, I'm not sure you'll ever get past this.'

Two days later I drove to Tiverton train station, bought an all-day ticket for the car park and caught the train to London Paddington.

I hadn't been to the nursing home since 2016. Not much had changed. The smell was still the same: fusty clothes, tea and old person's skin. The TV was on, but like before none of the residents were taking any notice.

Not bothering to scan the dining room for mum, as I knew she was now bed-ridden, I looked for nurse Essie instead, but she was nowhere to be seen. Moved on, I guessed, or got out of it altogether – and after the abuse she'd received last time I was here, nobody would blame her for that. Shame, she was really lovely.

Mum's room had changed too. The worse the condition the patient is in, the closer their room to the nurses' station. Mum's was smack bang beside it.

Knocking, I opened the door.

The curtains were open and so was the window. There was a school opposite and you could hear the children shrieking and playing on a break. The room itself was painted a cheery yellow, and there were photographs pinned to the wall beside her bed of mum 30 years ago looking alert and bright and stunning.

In the middle of the bed was my mum.

She was on her back, the beautifully clean covers pulled up to her neck. Her hair was no longer coloured and was instead a shock of white, and short, much shorter than I'd ever known her wear it before. Her skin was crinkly and old, her eyes flat and without even a hint of fire behind them.

'Hello Mum,' I said, and sat on the chair beside her, reaching out for her hand.

She didn't smile. She didn't acknowledge I was there. She couldn't. That part of her was gone, the dementia had seen to that. She was a shell. Anything that had been my mum was long gone. I tried talking to her, but just ended up telling her about the journey down. Anything more than that would have been wrong. After 15 minutes, I kissed her cheek and left.

Outside I phoned Debbie and told her, then walked the streets back to the train station with tears running down my face.

Back home I couldn't get Debbie's fear out of my head, that if I couldn't find a way to bring this to an end I'd never be able to move on. That was when I hit on the idea of her phone. Ziggy's trick he used with his dad. It might not be perfect, but what else did I have?

Her phone was in the back of a drawer in the lounge. I found it, put it on to charge, and when it was full of power went out into the field and found the ewe and lamb. The sheep had settled down and was no longer trying to fight the world, and the lamb was a loner, preferring his own company to that of any of the others, including his mum.

The day was overcast and cool. As I approached, the lamb didn't run away as he always had before, and six feet from him I knelt down. Who knows why he didn't move away, but in my head I felt that this time he was there for me.

Pulling out mum's phone, I held my breath, and turned it on. Then I lifted it to my ear.

'Hello Mum,' I said, 'it's me.'

I think I thought it would feel really weird, but it didn't. Maybe all the time I spent talking to the animals stripped me of any self-consciousness.

'Debbie sends her love.' She didn't, but mum didn't need to know that.

'I've been thinking about you a lot lately, mum. About when I was young – we had some times, didn't we!' I could picture her, not how she is now, but how she was. Sitting at the end of the lounge by the French windows doing her makeup, the radio on in the background, pots and tubes and brushes of makeup and cotton wool pooled all around her. Her moat.

I wanted to tell her about the farm. I wanted to tell her about the animals, how they were my babies, my children. I wanted to tell her about my relationship with Debbie. I wanted to tell her that I was doing okay. I wanted to tell her that I knew she did her best with me. I wanted to tell her so much. But that was all planned. Thought through. What actually came out wasn't any of that. Ziggy's right, you know. In the heat of the moment, you don't know what you're going to say until it comes out.

The image of her in my mind stopped doing her makeup, turned and looked up at me. Then smiled.

I started crying. I couldn't help it.

'I miss you mum. I miss you, but you were bonkers.' That made me laugh, and I did that strange cry/laugh thing you do when you can't work out which emotion to feel, so you feel them all.

'Did you suspect you might have had postnatal depression when you had me? Did you hate me? It's okay if you did. It wasn't your fault. If anything, I was as much to blame. I think something went awry with both of us the moment I popped out. The buttons marked 'love' didn't flick on. From that moment, we were both compensating. Trying to figure out ways to make it work. And we did. Kind of. It might not have been pretty, but we made it through, didn't we? What I'm trying to say is, it doesn't matter anymore. Remember when I was really young and we'd fall out, and after a while you'd hold out your little finger and I'd wrap my little finger around it and we'd shake, which meant, all forgiven, move on? Well, mum, I'm holding out my little finger.' And I was. 'All forgiven, move on. I love you mum.'

Switching the phone off, I dropped it, before flopping onto my back, my head hitting the ground much harder than I intended. While I nursed it, I felt a tugging on my jeans. It was the lamb.

'So?' Debbie said the second I stepped through the door.

I'd taken the long walk back, the one that went beside every animal in the place. You could smell summer waning and giving into fresher air, and there were just the beginnings of a few leaves dropping from the trees. Soon the weather would close in and I'd be worrying about rugs and straw beds and dinners for the animals topped up with boiling water to take the chill off.

The last pig I checked on was Senorita. She was snoozing, her not-quite-so-little ones asleep next to her. I'd have to take her away from them soon, wean them or they'd suck the life out of her, but for now I quite liked the family feel.

In the hallway I kicked off my welly boots. 'The little lamb nudged me. I finished talking to mum and he came over and pulled on my jeans. Can you believe that?'

Hugging me, Debbie said, 'The animals like you.'

'I know.'

She'd closed the door to the lounge, so for once it was just the two of us without Solomon in between. She looked nervous. I smiled, and realised I wasn't putting it on.

'It's done.'

'How do you feel?'

I'd like to say I was looking down on her like some big protector wrapping my Popeye arms around her so she felt safe and secure, but she's considerably taller than me. I thought of getting a few books to stand on, but decided it might break the moment. 'Now, I'm glad you asked me that,' I said, 'because here's the good news: the person you loved is still here' – I threw my arms out wide – 'how lucky are you!'

She groaned.

'You groaned!'

'I know.' Then her face darkened. 'Be honest with me.'

I will. In time. But not now. Truth is, I'm still me. Sad, but true. Don't get me wrong: I understand more about the person I am, and why I do the things I do, but I'm still me. My best-case scenario from all of this was that I'd walk away as someone else, but of course that's preposterous. I'm not that lucky. Oh don't worry, this isn't an 'oh, woe is me' ending, because that's not at all how I see myself. But equally, I don't give myself unwarranted airs and graces. I am what I am, a man shaped by experiences, a bit messed up and a bit battered and bruised by life. But then, aren't we all?

Some of my experiences have been rubbish, such as the postnatal depression I'm sure mum had, the domestic violence, my own self-hatred and the sense of being unlovable, but on the flip side I've also got my wife whom I love very much, my farm and my animals, without which I know for certain I would have gone down a much darker path, and it's highly unlikely I'd be here now.

But I found a way, and it feels like it had to be extreme. I had to go and live off-grid on a farm and have Senorita and the General as my best friends (and Ziggy, but, you know, he can be a dick and in the best friend leaderboard he's way below the pigs). Anything less wouldn't have worked. My therapy is sitting on the bum of a 55-stone porker while he in turn lies in a muddy puddle, telling him my problems. And it works! For the most part. He might be fat and smelly, but he's a very good listener.

Yet even I realise that can only get you so far. The biggest step was writing it all down. As Debbie said, I need to move on, and writing this book is my way of trying to do just that. I don't know if it will work, but it feels good now it's complete. It feels healthy. And hopefully, finally, I can begin to repair.